Praise for *Davey Johnson: My Wild Ride in Baseball and Beyond*

"I played in New York for Davey for six terrific seasons and consider him a valued friend. He has a great story to tell. I remember his Rolaids commercials during his tenure as Mets manager. I guess dealing with our group gave him ulcers—but we loved playing for him!"

— **Keith Hernandez**
Five-time All-Star and 1979 National League Co–Most Valuable Player
11-time National League Gold Glove first baseman
Two-time World Series Champion and New York Mets captain
SNY and WPIX Mets commentator

"I was very close to Davey—he was a good friend. During my 10 years as manager of the Cardinals, it seemed like we were fighting with Davey's Mets every year for the pennant. The Cubs-Cardinals games may have always packed the house, but the biggest games—the biggest rivalry—was always with the Mets."

— **Whitey Herzog**
2010 Baseball Hall of Fame inductee
1982 World Series Champion and Major League Manager of the Year
1985 National League Manager of the Year
Member of both the Cardinals and Royals Halls of Fame

"Davey Johnson is a rare Renaissance man in sports, blessed with intelligence and curiosity extending well beyond the white lines. He was into his own form of analytics long before it became an influential trend, as a terrific player absorbing everything he would put to use as an equally successful manager. When, after the 1986 World Series, I felt compelled to apologize for being so rough on him in the *New York Post*, his response showed how he endured so well: 'Don't worry about it, Lyle. You have a job to do; I know that. No hard feelings.' A graceful guy with a sense of humor and the ability to see the big picture."

— **Lyle Spencer**
Major League Baseball columnist
Author of *Fortitude: The Exemplary Life of Jackie Robinson*

"Davey earned my respect as one of the truly great baseball people I've had the pleasure of playing for. A player's manager and good friend, you have to appreciate all he has accomplished in the game."

— **Mookie Wilson**
1986 Mets World Series hero
Member of the Mets Hall of Fame
Currently Mets team ambassador and roving instructor

"Davey Johnson is one of the reasons they call it the big leagues. All through his career as a player, manager, and ambassador of our game, he's got to be in the top tier."

— **Steve Blass**
1971 World Series hero and All-Star pitcher
Longtime Pittsburgh Pirates broadcaster
Author of *Steve Blass: A Pirate for Life*

"I have always been intrigued by Davey's knowledge of baseball—especially hitting. When we were teammates in '73 with the Braves, Davey, Hank Aaron, and Darrell Evans all hit 40 or more home runs and I chipped in with 21. I hit in front of Davey, and when we were in the on-deck circle, he would tell me what he was looking for and how he wanted to set up the pitcher—which I didn't really understand until later. But the thing I remember most about Davey was when we'd go out, he wasn't ashamed to dance! He was proud of the fact he could dance! He's always been the same. That's the thing I like about Davey—his consistency and his personality."

— **Dusty Baker**
Three-time National League Manager of the Year
Member of the 1981 World Champion Los Angeles Dodgers

"Davey Johnson is one of baseball's great managers and great storytellers—the kind of guy with whom you'd love to drink beer and watch a game. His book is everything a baseball fan could hope for—endlessly interesting, insightful, and fun to read. With or without beer, you'll enjoy every moment in Johnson's company."

— **Jonathan Eig**
New York Times bestselling author of *Ali: A Life*

Davey Johnson

My Wild Ride in Baseball and Beyond

Davey Johnson

with Erik Sherman

TRIUMPH
BOOKS

Library of Congress Cataloging-in-Publication Data

Names: Johnson, Davey, author. | Sherman, Erik.
Title: Davey Johnson: my wild ride in baseball and beyond / Davey Johnson with Erik Sherman.
Description: Chicago, Illinois: Triumph Books, 2018.
Identifiers: LCCN 2017056302 | ISBN 9781629374116 (hardback)
Subjects: LCSH: Johnson, Davey, author. | Baseball players—United States—Biography. | Baseball managers—United States—Biography. | BISAC: SPORTS & RECREATION / Baseball / General. | TRAVEL / United States /Northeast / Middle Atlantic (NJ, NY, PA).
Classification: LCC GV865.J594 A3 2018 | DDC 796.357092 [B]—dc23
LC record available at *https://lccn.loc.gov/2017056302*

This book is available in quantity at special discounts for your group or organization. For further information, contact:

Triumph Books LLC
814 North Franklin Street
Chicago, Illinois 60610
(312) 337-0747
www.triumphbooks.com

Printed in U.S.A.
ISBN: 978-1-62937-411-6
Design by Florence Aliesch
Photos courtesy of the author unless otherwise indicated.

This book is dedicated to my children, Dawn and Davey; my stepchildren, Jeremy and Ellie; my brother, Fred, and sisters, Kris and Patty; my wife, Susan; and all the teams I was fortunate enough to play for and manage, as well as in loving memory of my beloved Andrea and Jake and my parents, Florence and Fred.

Contents

Foreword

IN OCTOBER 1983, ABOUT the only thing that most New York Mets fans thought of when they heard the name Davey Johnson was that he had made the final out of the 1969 World Series. Of course, they probably remembered that he had an outstanding major league playing career with the Baltimore Orioles and a few other teams, and perhaps that he was a successful manager in the Mets' farm system, but for the most part he was a relatively anonymous baseball figure who probably didn't excite the fan base much when it was announced that he had been hired to manage the floundering ballclub.

That all changed with one sentence.

During the press conference to announce the move, Davey's first remark was, "I would like to thank [general manager] Frank Cashen for being smart enough to hire me."

That's not how managers spoke when they were hired, particularly when it was their first big-league job. They usually made boring remarks dripping with humility, speaking generically and exciting no one. We learned on that fall day that Davey Johnson is neither boring nor humble, and for the next six and a half years the New York Mets, and a relatively young broadcaster, were much better for it.

I was that broadcaster, although I didn't work with Davey on an everyday basis until 1987, the year after Johnson managed the Mets to the World Championship; having turned that franchise completely around almost overnight. I had been hired to host an extensive pre- and postgame show on the Mets' flagship radio station, WHN, which included a daily interview with the manager. Although I had been a constant in the Mets clubhouse as a reporter for other New York radio stations and had regularly asked questions of Davey before and after games, he didn't really know much about me. Our on-air partnership was something of a shotgun marriage, and early on there were a couple of times I thought he might use one on me.

Most pregame shows with major league managers are fluff pieces that serve no real purpose. The skipper is rarely challenged by his interviewer, and the show is little more than a promotional house organ for the ballclub. I knew that this would never work in New York, and I needed Davey to be on board with me. The only way the show would have any real value to the listener would be if the manager was asked the same questions on the air as the newspaper beat writers would ask him following a game. Anything else wouldn't be transparent.

Early on, this didn't seem to be a problem. The team played reasonably well, but after we taped a show following a tough loss, Davey became irritated at my line of questioning. He said that he didn't feel that he had to defend his strategic moves on his own radio show, but I stood my ground and he reluctantly acquiesced. However reluctant he might have been, it seemed that a light bulb went off in his head. Because listeners could call into the postgame show and were often critical of Davey's strategy, he came to the realization that he could use our pregame interviews as a platform to explain his strategy as well as to disarm the audience and occasionally send messages to his players or the front office at the same time.

My favorite example of this was early in that 1987 season. Mets reliever Roger McDowell began the season on the disabled list, and when he was ready to rejoin the ballclub, whatever corresponding move Cashen made to get Roger onto the active roster did not sit well with Davey. I started the show by saying, "Davey, you're getting Roger McDowell back tonight; what do you think his immediate impact will be on the team?"

His answer was "Well, Howie, Frank Cashen did a dumb thing today…"

Our interviews were always taped a few hours before game time, so after we finished and I had turned the tape recorder off I told Davey that if he was even the slightest bit uncomfortable with how that sounded, I would be happy to tape it again. I thought he was going to bite my head off. He was emphatic that he wanted that to air exactly the way he said it because he wanted to let Cashen (as well as a sizable listening audience) know that he thought Frank had made a mistake. When Davey said that, I knew we were in business. This would be no ordinary manager's show because this was no ordinary manager.

Gradually, I gained his trust. Midway through our first season, 1987, WHN, which had been a country music station, converted to a 24-hour all-sports format and changed the call letters to WFAN, the country's first all-sports radio station. Now, fans could call the station all day and night, criticizing and second-guessing every manager or coach in New York. Davey would hear it all, and our pregame sessions became must-listens for all Mets fans because Davey held nothing back. He could tell that I was learning how his managerial wheels turned, making me well-enough informed to usually have his back when callers wouldn't understand why he made (or didn't make) a particular move. His increased comfort level with me enabled us to discuss virtually anything on the air, and not only baseball. Occasionally we talked about books he was reading, or his favorite subject—golf—and which of his coaches he took and for how much that morning on the golf course.

My favorite discussions with Davey were off the air, before or after the tape recorder was turned on. He allowed me to pick his brain about absolutely anything and anyone involved with the Mets, and the amount of baseball that I learned from him was immeasurable. Eventually I went from a pre- and postgame host to a play-by-play broadcaster for the Mets on both radio and television, and several years ago I told Davey that I am convinced that if not for our pregame sessions during those three and a half years, I don't think I could have become a big-league broadcaster. He taught me so much and never, ever made me feel out of place or the slightest bit in over my head.

There was, and still is I suspect, a sensitive side to Davey as well; something the public rarely saw. There were a couple of times along the way when the front office had sent signals that his job could be in jeopardy, and at those times there were days when we taped the show that he seemed a bit like a wounded puppy. These were quite memorable because he allowed the fans to see that there was a different kind of person beneath the brusque exterior than they might have imagined. He sometimes confided that he wasn't sure if the fans truly liked or appreciated him. That's why I was so thrilled when, on the final day of the 1988 season, with the Mets on the way to their 100th win of the season, he received a long standing ovation from the huge crowd at Shea Stadium when he came out of the dugout to make a pitching change. That ovation meant the world to him.

Having seen his work from a unique vantage point, it's clearer to me now than ever before that he was the perfect manager for that team in that town at that time. His brashness set the tone and was largely responsible for the persona that made those Mets teams what they were, even though they were largely despised by the rest of the industry. His intelligence often kept him a step ahead of the opposition, and his trust in me, and ultimately his friendship, is something of which I am eternally proud and grateful.

—Howie Rose, Broadcaster, New York Mets
WOR Radio 710 New York
September 2017

Foreword

WHEN DAVEY JOHNSON CAME up to the Orioles at the end of the 1965 season, we all knew he was a math major and a really smart guy. I'm not saying our club didn't have baseball smarts, but Davey was more cerebral than most. For example, in just his first full season with the club in 1966, he studied the batting stance of our slumping veteran superstar, Frank Robinson, and offered him some hitting advice. It obviously helped, as Frank went on to win the Triple Crown that year.

Then, as a young second baseman, Davey once came out to the mound and said to me, "Give them the 'Bob Gibson.'" And I said, "What are you talking about?" Davey explained that he wanted me to use a more athletic windup—like Gibson had. It was moments like that I knew he would one day become a big-league manager. He was just always inquisitive, always engaged, and always in the game.

Davey was also a forerunner with mathematical concepts and statistical analysis—what is known today as sabermetrics—which wasn't always appreciated by management and teammates. Once, he walked into Earl Weaver's office with his *Optimization of the Orioles Lineup* data, which would show Earl our best computer-generated lineup. But Weaver dismissed it, tossing it in the trash.

Obviously, Earl didn't want anybody to think that he wasn't the smartest guy on the field or that he wasn't running the club. That's what Earl was about.

Another time, Davey paid a mound visit to a struggling Dave McNally, who was missing the corners and throwing the ball down the middle. "Hey, Mac, have you ever heard of variable chance deviation?" Davey asked. McNally replied, "What the hell are you talking about?" "Well, it's a mathematical theorem. If you want to analogize it to baseball, if you are trying to throw the ball for the corners, and it's ending up down the middle , throw it for the middle of the plate, and maybe it will end up on the corner." And that's when McNally told him, "Why don't you go back and play second base?"

Davey was just so intelligent that we affectionately nicknamed him *Dumb-Dumb*. And he did kind of march to the beat of his own drum throughout his entire career. But that's what made Davey Davey. That's the whole dynamic of Davey Johnson.

Of course, Davey would go on to become a highly successful manager with several teams. But it wasn't always easy for him—despite winning wherever he went. If you look at his time with the Mets, obviously he had a talented ballclub that competed in a lot of different ways. But they also had a lot of guys who had problems off the field or had, shall we say, *intricate* personalities. Plus, it was New York. And when you start winning, everybody really notices it—including general managers and owners. And then all of a sudden, they might think, *Do we really need him? Ah, we can probably win without him.* Most people want to be the smartest person in the room. And maybe because Davey had the ability to confound some of them like he did, making them feel like they were less smart than he was, it grated on them and caused some problems for him. Maybe that's what makes Davey Johnson so interesting.

When he got the Orioles job in 1996, I was broadcasting half of the team's games. Prior to the season, I asked Davey, "So now what's it going to be?" And he goes, "Cakes [his nickname for me due to my love of pancakes], let me tell you just one thing. My teams usually play up to their expectations."

Now, that told me a couple of things.

One, he was very positive. He knew that they were going to have a winning team. And maybe he got a little bit of that eternal optimism from Weaver. Davey was on the same clubs that I was when Earl would tell us each spring that if everybody did their job we had a good shot to make the playoffs and get into the World Series—which was huge back then. My first World Series check was $11,683.04, which was almost $4,000 more than I was making that year.

And two, Johnson had good clubs and people genuinely enjoyed playing for him.

But there was more to Davey than that. He had "No I's, No R's"—no indecisions, no regrets. Most managers like Davey are the best in the game because they're prepared—they know who's hitting well, they know who's available, and they know what matchups are going to probably get opposing hitters out. So you don't have any regrets because you made a decision. And I always thought Davey felt pretty comfortable with any move he ever made from the dugout.

That sums Davey up pretty well. From the time he came up to the Orioles throughout his playing and managerial career, you knew he was a confident guy who understood what he needed to do to be successful.

—Jim Palmer
1990 Baseball Hall of Fame inductee
Three-time Cy Young Award winner
Eight-time 20-game winner

Preface

ONE RAINY FALL EVENING in 2015, I was at the Bull and Bear Steakhouse in Manhattan with my wife, Susan, and another couple when baseball author Erik Sherman joined us for a glass of wine before dinner. Amidst the mahogany décor at the circular bar, Erik and I discussed the possibility of writing my autobiography.

Truth be told, I didn't have a burning desire to write a book. But I felt that because I had experienced so many bumps in the road throughout a very successful baseball career both as a player and manager, my story could show some people how to deal with adversity and serve as an inspiration to them.

Near the end of our discussion, I put my right arm around Erik and said, "If we're going to do this book, it's going to be spectacular. I've never gone halfway with anything in my life, and I'm not starting now."

Once we agreed to forge ahead, there would be no holding back. And I believe that's what makes this book a compelling read.

I'm a lucky man. For more than 50 years, I was involved in a game that I've loved since I was a very small child—going all the way back to when I was a batboy during spring training for the Washington Senators.

And it's been an incredible ride ever since.

But if you think the process involved in putting this book together was easy for me, you would be wrong.

I've always been the type of person who lives in the moment. I don't live in the past like a lot of other former ballplayers or managers. When something went badly or ended in my life, I just moved on to the next challenge. I could always compartmentalize.

So when I got fired from a managerial job or was traded as a player, I thought, *It's fine. I like working for smart people, and if they were dumb enough to get rid of me, then I didn't want to work for them anyway.*

I would never look back. I never read the newspapers. I never listened to what others were saying about me. *Never.* I just moved on.

So when I was forced to relive and analyze some of the more difficult periods of my life, it angered me. There were a lot of untruths out there that I didn't know about or had chosen to ignore. So aside from the purpose of this book seeking to help others, it evolved into also setting the record straight about a lot of things.

At one point early in this project, I challenged Erik and myself to try to discover the reason why it always seemed I would get fired relatively soon after turning bad teams into winners. By the end, we came up with several theories. First, I was never afraid to speak my mind with authority. Second, because of my commercial real estate interests, I never had to worry about money. Third, there are a lot of general managers and owners out there who resent their manager getting more credit than they receive for having a successful ballclub. And last, because I was an Army brat as a kid, change never fazed me—another year, another base, another experience.

But it's still kind of a shame.

Would I have liked to manage the Mets forever? *Yes.* The Reds? *Certainly.* The Orioles? *Absolutely.*

And in all those cases, right after I was shown the door, their teams went right down the drain.

I mean, I averaged 96 wins over six-plus seasons with the Mets.

How in the hell can you get fired for that?

I don't know of any manager who was as special as I was who kept getting the ax. All I ever did was successfully increase the value of the assets of any ballclub I ever worked for.

But I guess that's why I'm doing this book, too. It's all kind of weird, but also pretty interesting.

I get asked all the time, "Do you miss the game?"

Well, I don't miss the traveling and the hotel rooms—that gets old real quick.

But baseball is still in my blood, and from my comfortable leather couch in my home office, with my dogs Abbey and Murphy by my side, a day hardly goes by during the baseball season when I don't watch a game on television.

Always the manager, I pay particular attention to the lineups before games and the full box scores after them. I see things that the average baseball observer doesn't see. I notice if some highly paid player is still in the lineup when he shouldn't be just to make the general manager look good. And if I see three left-handed hitters in a row at the top of the lineup, I think, *What a gift that is to a left-handed pitcher.*

I hope you enjoy reading about my thrilling and, at times, wild ride through baseball and life in these pages.

As I told Erik time and again while we wrote this book, *I can't make this shit up!*

—Davey Johnson
Winter Park, Florida
Spring 2017

Acknowledgments

DAVEY AND I WOULD LIKE to give special thanks to the following for their time and contributions to this book.

Jeremiah Allen arranged the introduction that ultimately led to Davey and me teaming up to work on his autobiographical project together.

Wally Backman, Jim Palmer, and Mookie Wilson gave valuable insight into Davey's career as both a player and manager.

Alan Cohen, Fred Johnson, Roy Markell, and Don Waful provided unique research and background information on Davey's life—both personal and professional.

The staff at the National Baseball Hall of Fame and Museum—led by Bruce Markusen, manager of digital and outreach learning, and Matt Rothenberg, manager of the Giamatti Research Center—was of immense help in providing documents and files that proved invaluable to the process.

Michelle Bruton is a terrific editor who provided sound guidance, encouragement, and enthusiasm throughout the entire project.

Robert Wilson, a master at giving sage advice, is not just a literary agent, but like another editor.

We would also like to give recognition to various publications that aided us in triggering memories of events throughout Davey's long and illustrious career. They include *Brooks* by Doug Wilson, *Winning in Both Leagues* by Frank Cashen, *Bats* by Davey Johnson and Peter Golenbock, *The Bad Guys Won!* by Jeff Pearlman, *Doc: A Memoir* by Dwight Gooden, *If at First: A Season with the Mets* by Keith Hernandez, *A Pirate for Life* by Steve Blass with Erik Sherman, *Mookie* by Mookie Wilson with Erik Sherman, the *New York Times*, the *Washington Post*, the *New York Post*, the New York *Daily News*, the *San Antonio Light*, the *Birmingham Post-Herald*, *USA Today*, the Albany *Times Union*, the *Baltimore Sun*, *Sports Illustrated*, the *Wall Street Journal*, the *San Antonio Express-News*, the Associated Press, United Press International, the *Los Angeles Times*, the *Sporting News*, the *Atlanta Journal*, the *Baltimore News-American*, *Baseball Quarterly*, the *New Yorker*, the *Philadelphia Inquirer*, the *Miami Herald*, the *Guardian*, *Baseball Research Journal*, New York *Newsday*, the *Washington Times*, the *Cedar Rapids Gazette*, the *Newark Star-Ledger*, the *Cincinnati Post*, and the *Cincinnati Enquirer*.

Websites included BaseballReference.com, NBCSports.com, ESPN.com, Big12sports.com, Amazinavenue.com, Heavy.com, Bleacherreport.com, MLB.com, Reuters.com, DistrictOnDeck.com, Syracuse.com, FaithandFearinFlushing.com, TeamUSA.org, Yahoo! Sports, and FunWhileItLasted.net.

And last, but certainly not least, we would like to thank our wives, Susan Johnson and Habiba Boumlik, as well as my children, Alex and Sabrina, for all their encouragement and the sacrifice of countless hours of family time so the riveting story of Davey's life could be written.

—Erik Sherman

Introduction

"WELL, I GUESS THEY still like me up here," Davey Johnson told me one winter afternoon as we ate lunch at the LaGuardia Airport Marriott hotel lounge.

Davey had flown up to New York from Florida for the day to take part in an autograph signing at a Long Island card show and intimated how impressed he was by the strong showing.

Almost on cue, our bartender, an attractive young brunette, asked Davey if he wouldn't mind having his picture taken with the chef and a couple of waiters who had recognized him. As had been the case a number of times while we worked on this book project together, he was more than happy to oblige his fans.

As he sat back down on his stool to finish his lunch, the bartender, obviously not a baseball fan, approached him.

"Excuse me, sir, forgive me for asking," she said politely. "May I ask what you are famous for?"

With a deadpan expression—yet with a slight twinkle in his eyes—the manager of the last New York Mets team to win a World Series gave the humblest of responses with his slight, signature Texas twang.

"Well, I had a little something to do with that club across the street."

And then, before she could respond, he deflected the attention away from himself.

"This is my friend Erik," he told her. "He's a famous author."

This exchange personified the real Davey Johnson whom I got to know and the general public knows so little about. He's never spent much time thinking about winning personal awards or the possibility of making the Baseball Hall of Fame. He simply went where he was needed the most, with the goal of improving the fortunes of every club he ever played or managed for.

And incredibly, in more than 50 years in baseball, he accomplished that *every* time. Clubs that hired him saw striking improvements soon after he came aboard and, in most cases, declined badly soon after he left.

So when it came to just flat-out winning, Davey had few peers.

Most baseball fans, of course, identify him with adjectives like *swaggering* and *cocky*.

And why not?

He once famously told his 1986 Mets on the first day of spring training that they weren't just going to win the championship, but *dominate*. But that was simply Davey being Davey—saying what he really believed. And like with most things, he turned out to be right.

There isn't an individual in the history of baseball with a more impressively diverse résumé than Davey Johnson. While a small fraction of baseball men have won championships with several different teams, nobody can claim titles around the *globe* like Davey can—winning not just stateside in cities like Baltimore; New York; Cincinnati; and Washington, D.C., but also in faraway lands like Japan and the Netherlands.

And nobody can profess to have lived a more truly Gumpian baseball life than Davey has—seemingly always finding himself at the center of some historic event or period.

He played for championship teams in Baltimore; got the last hit off of Sandy Koufax; introduced sabermetrics to the big leagues; set an all-time single-season home run record for second basemen;

was in the same lineup with Henry Aaron *and* Sadaharu Oh in the games when each surpassed Babe Ruth's home run total; became the first non-Japanese player ever with the storied Tokyo Giants; managed the '86 Mets, as well as for controversial owners such as Marge Schott, Peter Angelos, and Rupert Murdoch; piloted Team USA in the World Cup, WBC, and Olympics; and finished his career by leading the Nationals to their first postseason appearance with baseball's two brightest young stars in Bryce Harper and Stephen Strasburg—bookends to a managerial career that began by guiding two other rising All-Stars, Darryl Strawberry and Dwight Gooden, with the Mets.

As a baseball author, I have interviewed countless players, managers, coaches, broadcasters, and writers. But in my two years of knowing Davey, he has taught me more about how to *think* about baseball than any 20 of them put together.

But his life hardly revolves around baseball.

A Renaissance man in the truest sense of the word, Davey has also been an incredibly successful land investor, pilot, scratch golfer, scuba diving teacher, and mathematician.

In short, he's lived the American dream to the fullest.

Davey is an engaging, brutally honest storyteller who has never shied away from expressing his views.

And that's what makes this memoir an important work in the annals of baseball history.

—Erik Sherman

| one |

January 30, 1943: Lessons from My Father

I ALMOST NEVER MET the man who would turn out to have the greatest influence on my life.

I was a war baby, born in 1943, when my father, Fred Johnson, a tank commander, was overseas during World War II. Communication was different back then, with letters taking up to six months to arrive back home from the battlefields. For all my mother knew, my father may have already been captured by the Germans when she delivered me.

In a common thread of my father being intensely secretive about his time in the war, he never let us know for sure exactly when he became a POW.

The single thing he ever told me about the horrors he faced was how he once had a problem in a prison camp he was held in and, as punishment, had some of his teeth pulled out without Novocain.

But then, just a few winters ago, nearly 30 years after my father's death, a window would miraculously open to give me insight into what my dad endured during the war and the incredible courage and resolve he displayed in fighting for his country.

While I was the manager of the Washington Nationals, I received a call from Jason Smorol, the general manager of our Triple A affiliate Syracuse Chiefs. A hot-stove event to celebrate the Chiefs was taking place at a hotel convention center in nearby Salina, New York, and he invited me to attend.

Jason said the longtime president of the Chiefs, Don Waful, who is now 100 years old, would be there. Don had also been a German POW and was detained at a camp in Szubin, Poland, for allied officers called Oflag 64. His section of the barracks held seven other men.

Incredibly, one of those men was my father.

I mean, what are the odds! I couldn't wait to meet Don. Considering his age, I didn't expect him to say too much, but was eager to hear anything at all he had to say.

As it turned out, Don was sharp as a tack, with great recall.

While we spoke, I almost had tears in my eyes. He described the terrible life of being a prisoner.

Don explained that while no one is firing at you, you've lost your liberty and live every day at the mercy of the enemy. You're trapped and surrounded in a camp by barbed-wire fences with a sharpshooter carrying a machine gun positioned in a tower above you. You sleep on straw mattresses with no wooden slats and eat mostly black bread made of sawdust and dried-up leaves. Only occasionally would you receive decent, edible food by way of the American Red Cross.

And then he talked specifically about my father, saying he would charge a hill that no other tank commander in his unit would dare.

I always knew my dad was a brave man. A heroic man. But he never told us much of anything, instead keeping so much to himself. He would often say things like, "Whatever you accomplish, you don't want to blow it out for everybody to know. You hold it within."

It was advice that I tried to heed throughout my entire life.

But now I was finding out just how brave, just how heroic, my father was from this kind, elderly man.

Don would tell me the story of how my father escaped the clutches of the Nazis not once, but twice.

The story goes that my dad was captured the first time in Africa and transferred over to Italy. Soon after they arrived, my father and other prisoners were tied up with ropes while they were being led to a train. Somehow, my father had put one of his folding knives that the Army gives you up his rear end. So, on the way to the train, my dad took it out, cut the ropes he was attached to, and escaped into the night.

He spent the next six months or so in the Italian hills with the "Resistance" until he was recaptured and sent to Oflag. He and his fellow prisoners, with the help of Russian soldiers, would escape the camp in January of 1945 and safely get to the other side of the Elbe River in Germany.

The Germans would soon surrender to end the war in Europe and my father returned home, meeting his two-year-old son for the first time.

******

I grew up a classic Army brat.

A few years after the war, we left Florida and lived in places as culturally diverse as Germany; Georgia; Wyoming; and San Antonio, Texas. The experience gave me a worldly view on life and made me adaptable to nearly any situation. It shaped who I became in my adult and professional life and made me a stronger person.

Right away, I had to learn resolve and show no fear.

When I was seven years old, we lived over in Germany. It's difficult to describe how tough it was living there in 1950. In one instance, neighborhood kids locked me up in a toilet room on some vacant lot. It was awful, but I managed to get myself out. To show I would not be intimidated, I later got some revenge by throwing apples and acorns at the German kids as they rode by on their bikes.

You learn to survive and become fearless, because that's what you have to do. A year later, we had to leave Germany as the Berlin crisis began to escalate in the early 50s.

As I got a little older, sports played a critical role in my objective to adapt to life wherever I went.

A perfect example was when we moved from Florida to Texas when I was 12. We flew into San Antonio International and the whole family went straight to the Fort Sam Houston Hotel.

The first thing I saw as we drove up was kids practicing baseball on a field. I ran over there and said to the coach, "You need a ball player? I can play."

The coach asked, "Where can you play?"

I said, "*Anywhere* you need me."

He let me swing a few times and take some grounders. Impressed, he said, "Son, go back to your hotel. I got your room number. Don't tell *anybody* anything."

Later on, he called me up and said, "You're on the team!"

I had immediately become a part of the fabric of my new surroundings.

From there I went to Alamo Heights High School and played basketball, baseball, football, golf, and track before continuing on at Texas A&M.

My point is that I was used to going to different places and blending in. I was dragged around like a red-headed stepchild, but I quickly realized a person's talent transfers whether you're playing in Fort Benning, Georgia, Wyoming, or any other place.

So wherever I went, different people, teachers, coaches, and places never fazed me because I was an Army brat. All the things I went through kind of challenged me, but I continued to meet those challenges.

You adjust and survive.

******

One of the early lessons I learned as the son of an Army man was the military hierarchy—to never go above the person ahead of you. My father was the ultimate command for me. And it was this protocol that I adhered to throughout my entire baseball career as both a player and manager.

As a big-league manager over 17 seasons for five teams, I would never go and talk to the owners about stuff concerning the ballclub because my boss was the general manager. It would have been like a stab in my heart if I talked to anybody other than my GM about business. It was just something I could never do.

In retrospect, other guys stayed in organizations a lot longer than I did because they talked to the owner. And maybe my approach could be seen as a fault of mine, I guess, because I got fired a bunch of times. Looking back, I think I would have been better off if I could have offered my opinion to the owner as well as the general manager. But it just wasn't in my heart to do so.

My father was one of the toughest people I ever met. He had been a very skinny kid who survived polio and took a Charles Atlas course to build himself up. By 10 years old, he was doing one-armed push-ups and chin-ups and could walk up stairs on his hands. My dad would become a southern California wrestling champion. No challenge, including severe health issues, was ever too great for him, and he really instilled that in me, to the point where I actually went looking for and welcoming challenges to overcome.

When I would get fired as a manager, it was a new challenge in my life. The same was true with the risks of real estate investing, in which I earned more money than I did in my baseball career. I'm a risk-taker, but only in the things I know about. That's why I have generally stayed clear of the stock market.

The lesson here is that when opportunities come up, it's important to take advantage of them, but to also make smart choices by using good judgment.

One of my father's greatest gifts was creating a do-or-die, never-quit environment for his children because that's what most people have to go through to succeed in life. You had to compete to achieve your goals.

Nothing is ever given to you.

******

One of the most important milestones in my life occurred when I was 17 years old. For years, my father and I arm wrestled, but I could never beat him. But then, one night at an officer's club, we engaged in an arm wrestling contest, squeezing one another's right hand for hours—well past midnight. Neither of us would give up until I finally brought down my dad's arm. The match was so physical that he had to wear a sling for a long time because I slammed his arm down so hard.

The lesson learned was that my father wanted me to earn everything, even something like an arm wrestle.

It was at that time when I knew I was now independent from my father. I had to work so hard, but when I finally beat him, a part of me was now free—I was on my own. I was so proud of that. Don't get me wrong; I had the ultimate respect for my father, but it was *always* important to compete. It was a coming-of-age moment for me and we both knew it.

My brother, Fred, who was two years older than I, had a similar relationship with our father, but I think it was even harder because he was the oldest child. My dad would beat up on Fred even more so than he did with me, and I think that was very difficult on my brother. I learned from what Fred went through and I think being a close observer of their relationship is why I had a little more success with my father. It was one of the first cases where I closely observed others and became astute at understanding human nature.

I really learned a lot from my brother and always looked up to him. He helped me grow up by dragging me everywhere he went. There is usually a sibling rivalry between brothers, but from my experience, I was blessed by the influence he had on me.

In turn, Fred and I tried to protect our two younger sisters from some of our father's more dominant child-rearing methods.

Christine, the third oldest—a beautiful cheerleader—was probably the kid who came out the most well-adjusted among the four of us, taking a lot after our mother, not to mention being the best-looking of us all.

The youngest, Patty, was always the last one to see what was all going on. She was a wonderful girl, but I would say she had a little bit of an inferiority complex and always had deep concerns about saying the wrong thing. She tried to compensate for that by working too hard. In a loving way, my brother and I always had to get on her and tell her not to worry about things so much. But as the youngest, Patty was the one who had the most trouble adjusting and was definitely the one we helped the most.

And it worked.

Today, Patty is well-adjusted; married to a great man, who is a professor; and has a couple of wonderful children.

But what happened to the four of us was typical of the lifestyle of a family with a dominant father from the military. It's a major challenge for everyone.

******

My father was likely always a person who kept things to himself, but his time in the military definitely exacerbated that. He saw and experienced some terrible things in the war and, like so many veterans, kept a lot of pain in his life to himself. You never know what somebody else is going through, and people deal with their individual pain in different ways.

For my dad, it was drinking, which became a routine, to say the least. After we settled into San Antonio, he used to play golf with his crew, then go to this little joint near Fort Sam Houston. He'd go there, eat something, and drink there. He would always drink beer. When he would come home at night he would drink bourbon.

I didn't hold this against him. But it made it hard on the family—particularly my mother. I don't think he was cheating on her during that time, but just dealing in his own way with what he went through in the war and prison camp. He was never mad at any of us, nor did he act like a drunk, beating people up or doing wild things—he was never that way. I always felt that he was just dealing with his own personal demons.

As a father, not surprisingly, he was very strict. He didn't do a lot of praising when we did something well, but he really let you have it when a job was done half-assed. In this way, we were different. He was a great man, but I realized his parenting approach of being so hard on me psyched me out at times.

He was a tough Swede, but deep down he loved his family. He just used some unconventional methods to show how much he cared for our well-being.

For example, when I was a senior in high school, it seemed like everybody was smoking. So to make sure I didn't become a smoker, one night my father put his Lucky Strikes on the table and said, "Let's smoke. You and I will smoke them together."

I started puffing, but I didn't want to inhale.

"No, you've *got* to inhale," he told me.

And these were the days when cigarettes didn't have filters.

So I took about three puffs, inhaled, and immediately had to go run to the bathroom to throw up.

My days of smoking cigarettes ended before they even began.

I decided to be different as a father and a big-league manager. I wanted to stress the positives with my kids and players, not the negatives. It's about understanding human nature. I was really interested in understanding people and their personalities, their wants, and their desires. Because of my father's toughness—how he berated my brother and me, or always tried to arm wrestle and beat me throughout my early life—I wanted to accept people the way they were. Not that I wouldn't challenge them, but I always put much more value on a person's makeup than their talent. I came to appreciate people who wanted to succeed.

When I started managing, I was more interested in a player's personality and what he wanted in his life and how much drive he had.

I would often ask a player, "What are you willing to give up to get to where you want to go?"

Everybody can judge talent, but it's much more difficult and important to judge makeup.

I think I always wanted to be a good person for my father, so I was always trying to create a positive makeup with drive as something to prove to him.

A person's makeup is everything. That's why I took a less naturally talented player like Wally Backman as my starting second baseman with the Mets over Brian Giles. It's why I gave shortstops such as Kelvin Chapman and Ron Gardenhire a chance to start over other players with superior talent. I can probably name a thousand other cases when I did that as a manager. Every position I filled, I wanted to know their makeup.

In doing so, I developed some extremely gritty and competitive teams. It was one of the differences in how I ran my ballclubs compared with others and a key ingredient to my success as a manager.

******

My mother, Florence, served as a perfect counterbalance to my father in many ways. She was for her children 100 percent and was always very encouraging. We all looked up to her. I can't say anything other than she was wonderful.

But that didn't mean she didn't push us, too.

If not for the war cancelling the 1940 Olympics, she would have qualified for the Games as a swimmer. In fact, as a freshman at Florida State College for Women she set a southern record in the 100-yard crawl while competing in a telegraphic swimming meet.

She was a classic swimmer and the best at in town teaching it. Because of her, all four of her children became excellent swimmers. And she taught us survival techniques by making us jump into a lake with our clothes on, because a lot of people panic in that situation. That was a hard thing to teach young kids, but she did it.

Her encouraging ways had a major impact in the way I would develop my ballplayers in the future.

So we were lucky to have parents with such different approaches in raising their children. Both were so gifted, smart, and athletic. They raised some really good children. A seemingly perfect couple.

But eventually, my father's drinking, staying out, and keeping things inside became too much for my mother. He began withdrawing more than ever. He still held an iron grip on us, but he played his golf and had his friends, and all of this contributed to a separation from my mother. They would divorce shortly after I began my professional career.

It was very emotional to see them break up, and it was a hard thing to deal with. Divorce had become a more common thing in the 60s. Prior to that, couples tended to stay in bad marriages, through thick and thin. So, in a way, this was also a sign of the times.

Although my siblings tended to side with my mother in the breakup, I never lost respect for my father. He had been a big influence on me and would remain so. I can't say I learned much from the divorce, except maybe the importance of communication in a marriage.

My dad would marry again, this time to a woman in the Army, moving just a couple of blocks down the road from our house. My mother, however, never remarried, content to take care of us kids.

******

Not long after I began managing the Mets in 1984, I took a flight back from a West Coast trip to visit my ailing father at Fort

Sam Houston. After complaining about some back pain, he had been diagnosed with bone marrow cancer—not an uncommon condition for a heavy smoker like him to develop.

The doctor gave him five years to live, but only if he did chemotherapy.

"Dad, you've got to do the treatment," I told him.

He agreed.

Before leaving, I added, "I'll come back when I can to check up on you."

It would be the last time I would ever see him alive.

"I'm not going to live with this oxygen in my nose," he would tell the doctors after I left. "If I can't survive without it, I don't want it."

So he took the oxygen out and would soon expire. End of story.

My father could have lived another five years. He could have been around to spend more time with his friends and family. He could have lived to see me manage the Mets to a world championship in 1986. But that wouldn't have been typical of my father. He wasn't going to ever depend on anyone or anything to keep him alive. He didn't want the oxygen in his nose, and he wasn't too keen on going through chemotherapy.

You have to be a strong man to make a choice like that. I don't know if I could do the same. He was just too proud to live under those circumstances.

I flew back to Fort Sam Houston to bury him. Despite how hard he was on me, I knew he was always proud of everything I accomplished. He didn't ever have to tell me anything.

In both life and death, perhaps my father's greatest gift was not just teaching me how to live with honor, but showing me how to die with honor, as well.

two

June 2, 1962:
Signing Day

"YOU COST YOURSELF *A lot* of money."

That was the straight, blunt feedback I received from Tom Chandler—my Texas A&M baseball coach and a man who was like a second father to me—after I signed a professional contract with the Baltimore Orioles following my sophomore season.

Chandler was a "bird dog" scout for the Houston Colt .45s and had once told me, "If you ever want to sign, let me know."

Back in those days, for any baseball team to offer you a contract, the player had to come out and say publicly, "I'm ready to sign a professional contract." Then, every team that was interested in that player could offer a contract. Nothing could be done until the player committed.

"The Orioles' scouts were the nicest people to me," I tried to explain to Chandler.

And while the money may have been better with another team or if I had waited another year or two, I wasn't going to let it be a deciding factor. Besides, as it turned out, any money I may have missed out on was more than made up for by winning the World

Series early in my career.

The bottom line was the Orioles *wanted* to sign me. Two of their head scouts, Jim Russo and Dee Phillips, were with me all the time. I had talked to a ton of other scouts, but none of them showed me the respect that the Orioles had.

So one night after a trip to Galveston Beach in my '49 Ford, I arrived home at 11:00 PM to find Russo and Phillips waiting for me. And I got what I wanted. Without an agent, at 2:00 AM on June 2, 1962, I signed a professional contract with the Baltimore Orioles for a $25,000 signing bonus, a $1,500 scholarship per semester to finish college, a $500-per-month salary in Class C ball in the California League, and a progressive bonus should I get promoted to a higher class level.

And hopefully before long, I thought, I would be playing alongside guys I greatly admired, like Brooks Robinson and a young first baseman named Boog Powell.

So when the Orioles showed up at my house and wanted to sign me more than anybody, it was really a no-brainer. I never had any second thoughts about it, despite all the scouts calling me after the fact telling me I had made a big mistake.

Still, I felt bad because Chandler was such a good man to me and he really cared about his players, teaching us life lessons as well as improving our game.

One of those lessons occurred when I was looking at colleges. Tom offered me a four-year baseball scholarship to play for him at Texas A&M.

I quickly accepted.

But later, when we went to dinner, he said, "It's one year."

"But Coach, you offered me a *four*-year deal, not *one* year." I replied.

Chandler looked me right in the eyes and said, "That's what's wrong with the youth today. They all want security and not an opportunity."

I think that's the greatest quote I have ever heard from any man.

It hit me right between the eyes. And that statement stayed with me for the rest of my life.

From that point on, all I ever wanted was an opportunity. More important, I liked the *challenge* it presented. When I got traded or fired, it was always a new opportunity. I wanted to do something good for whomever I was working for, but if it didn't work out, I felt confident there was another opportunity coming. I never looked at the fact I got traded or fired, but rather that it afforded me another chance to make things better, to win, or to do something good. It didn't matter to me how my getting traded or fired was perceived by others. My only goal was to do the best I could in the situation I was in and with the challenges that were put before me.

Looking back, I never really felt bad about any situation I was in because it was always looking forward to the next challenge that fueled me. It was really that simple.

As it turned out, I actually received a scholarship in basketball a month into that first year at A&M that had better perks than the baseball one, anyway. I moved out of the shitty baseball dorm and got to stay in Henderson Hall, which had a swimming pool, a chef, the whole nine yards. I was the starting guard on the freshman basketball team and Chandler was able to use the baseball scholarship he would have used on me to recruit another player. So it was a win-win all around.

There were two basic reasons I decided to turn pro after my second year of college. Each revolved around disappointments in elimination games in both the basketball and baseball seasons. I would consider each tragic, because we could have and should have won both games.

In basketball, I was now the starting point guard on the varsity team. We played rival Texas Tech and they had a little left-handed shooter who averaged 35 points a game. All we had to do was focus on beating him. So in the first half, every time he ran for a shot, I'd beat on him—playing very aggressive, intimidating defense. The first half ended with their star shooter having only six points, me having two fouls, and our team with the lead.

But then I didn't play the entire second half. I thought, *what the hell?*

We lost the game and our coach, Bobby Rogers, said to us, "Oh, hey guys, I'm sorry. Are you coming back next year?"

I spoke up first, saying, "No, I don't think so."

Then the baseball season came around and we were one win away from clinching a berth in the NCAA tournament. We were playing Texas and facing the best pitcher in the league. I hit a home run to put us up two runs and made a couple of sparkling plays at shortstop, and I thought, *we're going to the NCAA!*

But then in their final at-bat, our team unraveled, culminating with our third baseman diving for a ball hit in the hole that he deflected away from me, contributing to a three-run rally and eliminating us from the playoffs.

After the game, I declared, "I'm signing!"

******

From the time I was 10 years old, I knew I wanted to be a major league ballplayer. It wasn't even a question. It was my goal, my obsession.

I lived in Winter Park, not far from Tinker Field in Orlando, a park named after the Chicago Cubs' Hall of Famer Joe Tinker, immortalized by the "Tinker to Evers to Chance" poem by Franklin Pierce Adams. During spring training, Tinker Field served as the home of the Washington Senators.

The Senators had a pitcher named Joe Haynes who lived across the street from me. He had a son who was eight, and I would go over to their house and play catch with him. Even though he was younger, I wanted to hang out with him because I knew his father was a major league pitcher.

One day, Haynes watched us play catch and liked the way I threw, so he took me to Tinker Field to be a batboy for a day. Being in the clubhouse with Haynes, Eddie Yost, Mickey Vernon, and the rest of the Washington Senators was one of the great experiences of my life. I wanted to be like those guys. During the trip home, I even told Haynes, "I want to be just like you."

I was skinny and small for my age, but that didn't matter when it came to baseball. And a big reason that was true was having an older brother like Fred, a gifted pitcher with a slingshot arm who threw very hard. We would go out and play catch all the time.

In fact, in the Pony League, composed of 13- and 14-year-olds, nobody in his age group could catch him, so, with Winter Park being a small town, I kind of got drafted into catching him. You could still see the bones in my chest and I looked more like five years instead of two years younger than everybody else, but I had been doing it for years, so, aside from the catching equipment being huge on me, it was no big deal.

What was a big deal, however, was the rivalry I began in little league with Jackie Billingham, who would go on to become a pretty famous big-league pitcher, most notably with the Cincinnati Reds.

As 12-year-olds, Jackie and I were the best players in our league. Midway through the season, playing for the Giants, I was 9–0 as a pitcher with nine home runs. Two of those home runs were against Jackie, and we were the only team that had success against his team, the Pirates. I would get so pumped up to play games against them.

The Giants were primed to win their first pennant ever.

But as we got ready to start the second half, my father got transferred to San Antonio and—despite an offer from a teammate's parents to stay with them for the balance of the season—I had no choice but to leave in the heat of the Little League season and relinquish my quest to win the Triple Crown.

Jackie's Pirates would end up easily winning the championship and, because his mother was the official scorekeeper, his nine home runs enabled him to win the Triple Crown instead of me because, as she ruled, I was no longer in the league.

For a kid obsessed with baseball, the sting of leaving midseason was just another casualty of being an Army brat. It broke my heart.

But as fate would have it, Jackie and I would face off again in the big leagues. Two kids from Winter Park—what were the odds?

In the majors, I hit .316 with a couple of home runs off of him. So I always good-naturedly needle Jackie when we see each other at local Winter Park events about how I owned him in *both* the little leagues and the big leagues.

It's funny how after all these years knowing Jackie, nothing ever changes.

******

By the time we had moved to San Antonio, I had lived in more places than most people do in a lifetime. But my goal remained the same—to one day become a big-league baseball player.

In the four years I played baseball at Alamo Heights High School, the most interesting experience I had was with a pretty good young player at nearby Jefferson High School named Jerry Grote. He was a catcher and a pitcher and when I pitched against him, he couldn't touch me. But when he pitched against me, I wore him out. He was an intense competitor with such a long memory that, perhaps taking offense to my success against him in high school, he ran over my leg, tearing a ligament, when I was playing first base for the Braves in 1974.

Anyway, we were the only two high school players from San Antonio to be selected to a national team of U.S. All-Stars to play a team of New York All-Stars in the Hearst Sandlot Classic at Yankee Stadium. The annual event was the brainchild of sportswriter Max Kase and was backed financially by media magnate William Randolph Hearst. It was a huge deal because many of the players selected to play in the game either signed professional contracts or were able to secure scholarships for college.

Grote, who would go on to become a two-time All-Star catcher with the Mets, was my roommate at the Hearst Classic. Known for his toughness, he made me sit on his back and shoulders while he did push-ups.

As it turned out, I made more of showcasing my talents during batting practice than I did during the actual game, hitting two long home runs—with one of them landing in the upper deck.

There is no doubt in my mind that my selection, exposure, and performance at the Hearst Classic helped me land a scholarship at Texas A&M.

******

My signing bonus of $25,000 was a lot of money back in 1962.

But I had little trouble deciding on where to spend it all.

The first thing I did was to go out and buy a set of Haig Ultra golf clubs, the No. 1 clubs at the time. My father had them, so I bought a set for myself for $300—including the bag.

Next, I replaced my '49 Ford with a brand-new 1962 green Pontiac LeMans convertible, a simply beautiful car that cost me $7,000.

Then, in my first of many real estate deals, I bought a lakefront lot from my grandfather's estate about 200 feet from Bear Gulley Lake in Florida for another $7,000. It began a trend of buying Florida real estate and making as much as tenfold profits in just a few short years. Real estate investing was in my DNA, as my maternal grandfather had started both the Winter Park Golf Course and Winter Park Land Co., among other projects.

The rest of my bonus went to Uncle Sam.

So there I was, 19 years old with a new set of golf clubs, a new convertible, and a lakefront lot in Florida, ready to fly off to Stockton, California, to start my professional career in Class C ball in the Baltimore Orioles organization.

I was in hog heaven!

| three |
July 1, 1962:
Learning the Orioles Way

"HEY, COACH!" I SHOUTED out toward the mound as I dug in during my first batting practice session at Stockton. "How about throwing me some breaking balls?"

The tall and strapping Harry Dunlop, who served in the military during the Korean War and had the distinction of catching three minor league no-hitters in a two-week period—including one from Ron Necciai in which the pitcher struck out twenty-seven batters—glared back at me and said, "Hey 'Rook,' I'm the *skipper*, not the *coach*!"

That exchange was the first inkling I had that I was now in the pros and not in college anymore.

The Stockton Ports were a talented young team with a bunch of great guys, such as 20-year-old pitcher Darold Knowles and 19-year-old catcher Larry Haney, both of whom would one day join me playing in the major leagues. In fact, our club was so young that Dunlop not only managed the club, but, at 28, was also one of our catchers.

It was truly a great atmosphere both in the clubhouse and on the field. We played in one of the biggest ballparks—Billy Hebert Field—in the California League, with our dressing room way out in left-center field, about 450 feet from home plate.

But best of all, I flourished.

As a 19-year-old, I hit over .300 and led the team in triples and slugging percentage as the shortstop. It was a smooth transition from college ball to my first taste of the pros, and it caught the attention of the entire organization.

Including Earl Weaver.

"I want you on my team," Weaver, the Double A manager at Elmira, told me in Thomasville, Georgia, at spring training the next year.

Nodding with a grin, I told him, "That's fine."

Weaver got to pick and choose the players he wanted and he always chose the best of them. In this sense, he was like an old used car salesman, always able to finagle the organization into giving him what he wanted. As a result, his minor league clubs were always big winners.

So when we came out of spring training, I knew I was getting promoted to Double A ball in the Eastern League to play for the future Hall of Fame manager.

Even way back then, Weaver was an intense competitor both on and off the field.

During that first spring training, one of my first encounters with Earl was on the golf course. I had to give him five shots a side, but I still beat him and it drove him crazy. His competitive spirit was second to none. You could sense it on him.

On the field, I would hit ground balls during practice with him in Elmira. Several times he would bring up how the only reason he didn't make it to the big leagues was because there was a guy ahead of him, Marty Marion, the perennial All-Star St. Louis Cardinals shortstop.

I would think, *Yeah, and the fact that you couldn't hit worth a shit!*

I would never say that to Earl, of course.

But that was Earl. He was a career minor league infielder for parts of 14 seasons and stood barely 5'7", but he just loved to compete. He didn't have a whole lot of talent as a player, but did everything he could with what he had. And it was that part of his makeup that made him a great manager. He positively *demanded* a lot from his young players to get the most out of them. In fact, he was harder on the kids than anybody I've ever seen. He would yell as loud as he could—*Swing! Swing! Swing!*—at his young hitters when they were batting—stuff like that.

There was just such a fire, an intensity about Weaver—especially in tight games. Sometimes he couldn't even watch because he was so into them. In those instances, sitting on the bench, he'd bend over, put his head between his legs, smoke a cigarette, and say, "Tell me what happens. I *can't* watch."

But there was another side of Earl, too. He really got to know his players. We were very close right from the beginning. And in turn, when I began managing, I tried to be close to my players. I learned that from Earl.

From a tactical standpoint, I always felt that Weaver's greatest talent was in how he handled pitching staffs. And later on in Baltimore, of course, pitching was the bedrock of our success.

******

Other than playing for Earl, there were two specific experiences that left a big impression on me while playing at Elmira.

The first was when, coming out of spring training, I met one of my new teammates, a left-handed pitcher named Steve Dalkowski. He must have had between a 105 and 110 mph fastball. One day in the outfield, I asked him if he could throw a ball through the wall. So he picked up a ball, got a running start, and fired one right through the outfield wall! It was unbelievable!

Dalkowski, who never made it out of the minor leagues, would have seasons where he would average nearly two strikeouts per inning. The problem for Steve was that his walks-per-inning ratio was about the same.

The other instance involved my future managerial adversary in the 1986 World Series—John McNamara.

I was having a heck of a year, hitting a bunch of home runs and batting .330 when we had a game in Binghamton, New York, against the Triplets. They had a pitcher named Edgar Millerstrom, who had a really good arm, going that day, with McNamara, the player-manager of the Triplets, catching behind the plate.

The first two pitches Millerstrom threw me were curveballs, and I bailed a little bit.

Then I said to myself, *Don't move, son. If he throws you another one, hammer it!*

The next pitch, McNamara called for a fastball up and in that hit me square in the face, smashing my nose and front teeth.

I went straight to the hospital and the nurse asked, "You're the ballplayer that got hit in the face, right?"

I said, "Yeah."

Incredibly, she asked, "Where did it hit you?"

I said, "You've got to be kidding me. I mean, *look* at me!"

Millerstrom's 90 mph fastball chipped three of my front teeth. I would need to have my nose reset. I've often wondered if McNamara even remembered what he and Millerstrom did to me years later when we faced off in '86. But at least I got my revenge on him during that World Series.

Two days later, I was back in uniform when we traveled to Reading, Pennsylvania, to play the Red Sox. I was on a powerful painkiller called Darvon Compound-65, which has since been discontinued. Reading was throwing a left-handed pitcher named Guido Grilli whom I used to wear out. So in a big spot in the game, with the bases loaded, Weaver walked over to me on the bench and asked if I wanted to pinch hit. I jumped at the chance. I went up there and Grilli threw a couple of 80 mph fastballs right by me to strike me out.

I was devastated. I remember crying in the shower thinking I was washed up, that if I couldn't hit Grilli in that situation—*with the bases loaded!*—my career was over.

But Weaver did a great thing. Once I was off the painkillers and feeling a little bit better, he put me right back in the lineup the very next day despite my looking timid in striking out the previous game. I always thought, *thank God for Weaver*, because by getting me right back in the lineup, he made sure I was never afraid of getting hit again.

Away from the field, getting hit in the face did have a lasting effect on me. For many years, I would walk down a street and see that ball coming right between the eyes. My subconscious would make me literally jump to the side.

But, at least in the batter's box where it counted, I had no fear.

Sadly, the same could not be said for one of my longtime teammates up in Baltimore.

Paul Blair was an exceptional center fielder. He probably played the shallowest of anybody I've ever seen because he could go back on a ball better than anybody I've ever seen. He had tremendous instincts, and playing shallow helped compensate for an average arm. Paul would win eight Gold Gloves for the Orioles.

Early in his career, Blair was also a great hitter. I always thought he was almost as good as I was. And like me, he used to stand very close to the plate.

Well, in a game against the California Angels in 1970, Ken Tatum smoked him with a pitch, hitting him just below the left eye. Unlike me, he didn't come back right away—instead, he had to sit out for three weeks. When Blair came back, he moved a foot off the plate. As a result, he could never hit the outside pitch and was never the same hitter after that. He was just so afraid of getting beaned.

So once I was back in the lineup from my facial injury—confidence restored—I continued a torrid hot streak through the first half of the season. In just 63 games at Elmira, I had as many home runs—13—as Philip Barth, who tied me for the team lead over the entire season. My .326 batting average led the club.

My performance earned me a promotion to Triple A Rochester of the International League to begin the second half of the 1963 season.

One stop away from the Show.

******

I always tried to make the most of the off-season. During my minor league tenure, I used that time to focus on two areas—getting my degree and honing my baseball skills at winter ball.

With my education, I decided to finish college at Trinity University in San Antonio, Texas, for three reasons.

First and foremost, it's a great school. I probably couldn't get in there today because of the high SAT scores they require for admission.

Secondly, because I was only making a little bit of money, I could stay with my mother.

And the last reason was related to a matter of the heart—I was dating a great-looking girl who went there and whose father was the head of the home building department. That field of study was important to me because of my interest in real estate.

After three semesters completed around Winter League ball in places like the Dominican Republic and Puerto Rico, I spoke to a counselor in the home building department.

I said, "Man, I have 120 hours in, but still no degree. I can't take plumbing or electricity."

He reviewed the credits I had and told me, "The closest thing you are to getting a degree in is mathematics."

So I went to see the head of the math department and told him, "This subject is the closest thing I can do to get a degree. I have to take two courses. But the problem is the courses aren't offered after the baseball season, so how am I going to do this?"

He said, "You can take them with me."

Now, this is where things kind of got hairy, but it's a true story. The math head was married and a father of two children. So imagine my surprise when he told me, "If you'll just take your clothes off and let me look at you, I'll give you an A."

Shocked, but without pause, I told him, "I ain't doing that. Be as hard on me as you want, but I'll take these two courses with you. I want to get my degree the *right* way."

I took integral calculus and another tough course with him and him alone. Despite his giving me a hard time, I took them and passed them both. I could have gotten my degree the easy way, but wanted to earn it.

So I had my 160 hours, enough to finally get my B.S. degree in mathematics at the great institution of Trinity University.

Pretty fucked-up story, isn't it?

I don't know what ever happened to that head of the math department and really don't care. But that was my weird, wild path to getting a degree in a subject I found would later help me in my managing career to determine the most potent lineups of the respective teams I piloted. I would come to believe that you can apply mathematical formulas to human performance. And, in the process, it would give my players the optimum chance to shine.

As for Winter Ball, there was added importance in it for me the higher I moved up in the Orioles organization. The quickest way for me to reach the big leagues was going to be if I learned to play second base. That was because standing in my way at shortstop was future Hall of Famer Luis Aparicio with a young defensive stalwart, Mark Belanger, coming up to take his place.

During one Winter League, I played for a Maracaibo, Venezuela, team that Aparicio managed. I played second base and one of the first things he did with me was take me to the left-center-field wall. He then picked up a ball and threw it all the way home on a line— no more than 10 feet high.

I said, "How in the hell did you do that?"

"You have to strengthen your arm by playing catch 15 minutes a day, every day," Aparicio said. "And when you're not playing in a game, throw some batting practice."

I learned a lot from Aparicio. He was a great influence and a good man. By the time the 1964 season at Rochester came around, I was ready to play second base.

******

I hit home runs all the way through high school and college, right up until Triple A. But as I quickly found out, that wasn't the "Orioles Way."

In my first Triple A game, I went 3-for-4 with a triple and a home run against the Syracuse Chiefs. After the game, my manager, Darrell Johnson, best remembered for later managing the Boston Red Sox to the 1975 American League pennant, told me he wanted me to hit more balls the other way to right field—like Brooks Robinson.

Up until that point, I just hit the ball where it was pitched. If it was down and in, I pulled it to left. If it was down and away, I hit it to right.

But Darrell was my manager, so I tried to work on how he wanted me to hit. I used to take extra batting practice and as I was hitting these soft little line drives over the first baseman's head, a lot of people asked me what was wrong with me. The end result was that I became a little bit of a defensive hitter. It was just bad instruction.

Darrell was a .234 lifetime major league hitter with just two home runs, but at the time I believed in him and followed his guidance. Again, it was that chain-of-command mentality that had been instilled in me from birth. I wanted to please him. To move up, I always believed you had to impress the person in front or ahead of you. I always tried to do the right thing—whatever my superiors wanted me to do.

I have to admit that Darrell was right about one thing—he was teaching me exactly the way Brooks hit. Brooks regularly inside-outed fastballs the other way to right field.

So for the next three or four years, I was nothing more than a "Punch and Judy" hitter, to be honest. But then once I was established in the majors for a few years, I decided it wasn't for me.

I thought, *Just go back and hit the ball where it's pitched.*

That's when I started hitting the ball with authority again. Unless I was hurt, it was easy for me to be a .300 hitter with power.

My first year out of Baltimore, I hit 43 home runs with the Atlanta Braves and tied the all-time single-season record for home runs by a second baseman. But I never really looked back at my career and worried about *what could have been* if I had stuck with my original approach to hitting because I always tried to do whatever my manager wanted me to do. Besides, Darrell was a good man. During the '86 World Series, he was one of the Mets' scouts and we invited him to Boston to help our left fielders with the sometimes tricky caroms balls take off the Green Monster by hitting them fungoes. Anything I could do for him at any time of my career, I would have done.

So despite the bad hitting advice, I still had a solid '64 season at Rochester, splitting time between second and shortstop.

The thing I remember most about my time at Rochester was how much more of a veteran ballclub it was compared with Elmira. We had 26-year-old Earl Robinson in left field, who had played in parts of four big-league seasons; Luke Easter at first base, a 48-year-old onetime Negro League player-turned-slugger for the Cleveland Indians who hadn't played big-league ball in a decade; Joe Altobelli, a 31-year-old outfielder who was three years removed from the major leagues; Joe Pignatano, a 34-year-old catcher trying to get one more shot at glory in the Show; and Ozzie Virgil, a 31-year-old infielder who bounced back and forth between the minors and majors throughout a 17-year professional career.

One of my fondest memories was how Easter would take the time to talk with me, giving his opinion on different aspects of the game. He especially liked to say to me, "Hey young buck, *don't* let them beat you with the fastball. Just *don't* let them *ever* beat you with the fastball."

Easter just pounded me with that nugget of advice all the time.

Virgil and Robinson were similarly helpful to kids like Blair, Curt Blefary, and myself.

Being teammates with all these veteran players was a tremendous experience and would make my eventual ascent to the Orioles all the more seamless.

And, fulfilling a lifelong dream, that ascent would come the very next spring.

four

April 13, 1965:
The Debut

MOST BIG-LEAGUERS CAN tell you everything there is to know about their first game in the major leagues. Not only can they recall the team they played, the pitcher they faced, and every detail of their first at-bat, but also more mundane things like whether it was sunny or cloudy; warm or chilly; or if the wind was blowing in, out, or to left or right field.

For the record, I struck out pinch hitting for our starting pitcher Steve Barber on Opening Day, 1965.

But I actually had to look that up.

I remember very little about the day.

For me, being around that star-studded Baltimore Orioles roster—a tremendous mix of veterans and up-and-comers—was an education in becoming a major leaguer and what I remember the most about that time.

There were the guys I had grown up with in the farm system, such as Paul Blair and Curt Blefary, and young stars Boog Powell, Jim Palmer, and Dave McNally, which helped make the transition easier.

But now I was also teammates with some of the all-time greats, such as Brooks Robinson, Luis Aparicio, Robin Roberts, and Harvey Haddix. It made it simple to blend in because of all the talented players around me.

And I took full advantage.

I didn't have the natural talent many of my teammates had, so I needed to learn from them. I studied every player I ever played with. I was a student of the game, never shy about asking questions, seeking advice, and trying to learn as many different aspects of the game as possible.

Some of that knowledge seeking began in spring training, not just with Orioles players, but also with veterans from other clubs.

Since there was a continued urgency on my part to develop at the second-base position, I reached out to Bill Mazeroski of the Pittsburgh Pirates and Bobby Richardson of the New York Yankees—two of the greats at the position. The three of us trained in Florida and I had already played golf with them both, so I was comfortable calling them for help. They knew I was hungry for knowledge and, curiously, like so many ballplayers you play against, were more than willing to work with me to improve my game.

I asked them both the same question—"What do I need to do?"

Both believed the most important thing I needed to work on was my footwork around second base.

I think that's missing from the game today and why they don't allow runners to slide inside or outside the base path, because nobody knows how to teach second basemen to avoid the runner the way Maz and Richardson did with me.

After a month or two, I learned the footwork so well that nobody could take me out at second. I didn't have the quick hands like Maz—nobody did—but I had the footwork down as well as he and Bobby did.

In all my years at second base, while no runner ever took me out with a slide, I was injured once by Gates Brown, who leaped through the air and landed on my left foot as I was making a throw to first on a double play.

But right after it happened, as I lay on the ground, I told Gates, "The next time you come down here I'm going to throw the ball right between his eyes."

Sure enough, the next time Gates came running in to second, he was all the way out on the outfield grass. He knew I was looking for him.

I broke my toe and needed 15 stitches because of Brown. As they were stitching me up in a Detroit hospital, Boog was in the room, providing his support. But he had a hard time watching the procedure. As blood was coming out of my foot, Boog fainted and knocked over all the catgut sutures. I guess he couldn't take a little blood.

Another thing I adopted from Maz was getting a flat glove, because I wanted to be able to make a quick transition to my right throwing hand like he did. I could never emulate the transition as well as Maz, but I tried to get as close as I could.

Both Maz and Bobby also broke down the throwing from second to first on a double play in a three-step process for me. It was always—one, keep your head down on the ball as you look it into the glove; two, take it out of the glove; and three, throw it toward first. They said you actually didn't have to look for first base before throwing it because first base never moves. This last point keeps you from peeking at first before having full control of the ball. The extra fraction of a second this gives you also helps in not getting taken out by a runner.

They ingrained all of this in me.

Keeping my head down on the ball into the glove was especially important when Brooks' quick throws from third used to sail on me. If I didn't keep my eye on the ball the whole way, I couldn't gain proper control of it out of the pocket of my glove.

Of the Orioles who helped me, our third-base coach, Billy Hunter—who, like me, had to make the transition from shortstop to second base when he played back in the '50s—helped the most, working with me daily on my new position.

Aparicio, who was my roommate on the road, and I picked up where we left off in winter ball and always played catch together for 15 minutes before each game. Later, when I became a manager, I always put throwing for 15 minutes each day into my program for all of my players, whether they were pitchers or fielders.

Another benefit I had as a young player rooming with Aparicio pertained to my wardrobe. He used to throw his silk ties in the wastebasket all the time. I would go in and get them because I couldn't afford nice ties back then.

I once asked him, "You don't mind if I take them?"

And he said, apathetically, "No, I'm done with them."

Luis was a real mentor to me in many ways.

******

I would be in the majors almost a month before I got my first start. It's ironic because of all the work I was putting in at second base after being a shortstop all my life, but my first opportunity to play regularly was at third base. That was because Brooks Robinson got injured in early May.

Playing third would be a challenge and a learn-on-the-job kind of experience. It's a lot harder than any other position because it's so reactionary. By contrast, at second base or shortstop, you always have time to field the ball.

I honestly didn't know at first where to position myself at third—I was in no man's land over there. Correct positioning at third was so important and nobody taught me that. In the beginning, I positioned myself one step behind the bag and that's where, I found out the hard way, a lot of balls hit will short-hop you and eat you up.

We were playing the Yankees in Baltimore in one of my first starts at third. Clete Boyer hit a sharp ground ball that bounced up and hit me so hard I think I had American League President Joe Cronin's name tattooed on my face.

I was really getting beat up over there.

Boyer, who was a superb third baseman, became good friends with me that year, and he taught me to position myself out of no man's land by playing either at least two or three steps behind the bag or even with it.

That was great advice and likely helped save me some money on future dental bills.

But for all the help and knowledge I was receiving from veteran players and coaches that I would use on the playing field and as a future manager, I can honestly say that didn't apply to my manager with the Orioles, Hank Bauer. In fact, I would say what I learned from him was how not to manage.

I was struggling at the plate early that first season in the big leagues. Once, while we were on a plane, he came over to me and asked, "Are you a guess hitter?"

"No, I'm not a guess hitter," I replied. "I hit off the fastball. I look for the fastball, but if the pitcher has got a really good breaking ball, I think, in the back of my mind, he might throw me a good breaking ball."

Bauer, an ex-Marine who had a chiseled, square jawline and partial buzz cut, glared at me and slammed his fist into the bulkhead of the plane, breaking his hand.

"That's what I thought!" he exclaimed. "You're a *guess* hitter!"

I thought, *I didn't think looking out for a fastball made me a guess hitter.*

Bauer—a former Yankees great during their dynasty in the '50s—walked away and left me pondering his unique way of communicating with a young player.

I do give him credit for the way he handled the pitching staff the following year, when we would win the World Series. But then, in 1967, it was like he forgot almost everything he knew about guiding them and we were terrible. That's why, when our general manager Harry Dalton asked me who could replace Bauer midway through the 1968 season, I said he had to hire Weaver, a master at handling pitchers. It was a no-brainer for me.

I would actually learn a lot about pitching by sitting next to Robin Roberts and Harvey Haddix. I was intrigued about how they approached their craft.

Roberts was one of the most amazing men I've ever known. He was highly astute yet down-to-earth and gracious, always more than willing to talk with me. At 38 years old in 1965, he got players out as much with his pitching intellect as his talent.

In one game, we were leading the Yankees 1–0 and Robin had a shutout going in the seventh inning. Between innings on the bench, he said to me, "I've been using a little four-seam riser for seven innings to set up my curveball. Now, Davey, I'm going to throw my four-seamer a little bit up in the strike zone and they're all going to pop it up because they're going to try and take me out of the yard."

So he goes out there and the Yankees hitters did exactly what Robin said they would do—pop everything up—and we won 1–0.

A week later, we went to Boston against a great hitting ballclub and he told me the same thing with identical results. The future Hall of Famer just knew how to pitch.

It was the same with Haddix, who may have pitched the greatest game of all time in 1959, throwing 12 perfect innings for the Pittsburgh Pirates before losing the game the following frame 1–0. Harvey, 39 years old and playing his final major league season, was just a little guy and told me, "I just compete. I read the hitters and go after them. Then I expect my defense to help me."

I was just very lucky to play with and learn from them both.

While I was never shy about asking veterans questions, I was also never timid about verbalizing my observations about other players—no matter their stature.

One time in my first season I approached Dave McNally, an outstanding pitcher, and said, "Mac, you're throwing too many breaking balls. You have the best pitch in baseball, the running fastball down and away. If you throw that, nobody will hit you."

Another time the following year, while still officially just a rookie, I noticed that Frank Robinson—in the middle of his 1966 Triple Crown season and one of the greatest players I've ever been around—had his front foot six inches closer to the pitcher than usual. He had likely moved it there because pitchers were throwing him more breaking balls. As a result, he was late getting his bat head out in front and went into a 3-for-18 slump.

"You've always had your front foot close to home plate and this has always been where you stood," I told Frank, showing him where the scratch marks made by his spikes were and where they used to be in the batter's box—usually six inches in back of mine.

"Why don't you just back up to where you were before?"

Frank said he would try it.

Robinson would hit two home runs that night in Chicago, and was 12-for-17 in the ensuing four games from when he moved back in the box—with five home runs in all.

He would tell reporters, "It's really Davey who's responsible for this surge. Moving back those six inches has made a tremendous difference. I see the ball better, don't rush my swing, and am more relaxed."

I'm glad I had the courage to tell him what I saw.

******

I would eventually get sent back down to Rochester and found my stroke, finishing the season at Triple A hitting over .300 despite breaking my hand at one point near the end of the year. I wouldn't get called back up because Adair had a solid year both at the plate and at second base.

I may not have distinguished myself quite yet in the big leagues in that '65 season, but I accumulated a wealth of knowledge and experiences that would serve as a stepping stone to success in future years.

I found you can always learn by paying attention.

five

October 9, 1966:
The First Championship

WHEN I LOOK BACK at a year as wonderfully transformative as 1966, so many things resonate in my mind. I remember very clearly in spring training fighting for the starting second-baseman job and, of course, how the season climaxed in October with our Orioles team sweeping the heavily favored Los Angeles Dodgers in four straight games.

But over the course of a 162-game regular season in which we ran away with the American League pennant by nine games, a lot gets drowned out. So what becomes the most vivid in my memory of that season are the special moments and interactions with the legendary players and characters of the game.

For me, two such instances stick out more than most from that season.

The first was during an exhibition game we played that featured not only one of the greatest pitchers who ever lived, but also one of its biggest personalities—Satchel Paige.

By that time, Satchel, the former Negro League and Cleveland Indians star, was 60 years old—one year removed from becoming the oldest pitcher to ever appear in a major league baseball game when he threw three innings for the Kansas City Athletics against the Boston Red Sox. In my only at-bat against him, I walked, but I could always say I faced a true living legend.

After the game, I went up to him—knowing even then how great he was—and asked, "Hey Satch, what's your best pitch?"

"It's my 'B' pitch," Satchel said.

"What the hell is a 'B' pitch?" I asked, bewildered.

He said, "It be where I want it to be!"

I laughed, of course, and have told that story—one of my all-time favorites—a countless number of times to my pitchers over the years.

The other highlight occurred in Game 2 of the World Series.

Sandy Koufax, who from '63 through '66 may have had the greatest four-year run of any pitcher in the history of the game, was on the mound for the Dodgers. Koufax never pitched against American League teams during spring training, so I didn't know what to expect. But obviously his reputation and stardom preceded him.

Still, I remember thinking, *How tough can this guy be? Jesus, he's not that tall and he throws right over the top.*

The first two pitches I thought were going to hit me, but were right on the inside black of the plate at about 95. I thought, *Maybe this guy is pretty good.*

I popped up the next pitch—a curveball—to second and took a seat on the bench. In my next at-bat against him, it was the same result—this time popping up to the catcher on a sacrifice bunt attempt.

But then, in the sixth inning, I singled hard to right field—the last hit given up by Koufax in his storied Hall of Fame career.

He retired after the season.

The next spring, we were in Vero Beach and I went up to Koufax and said, "Hey Sandy, great to see you, man! How are you doing? By the way, guess who got the last hit off you in your career?"

Koufax looked me right in the eyes and said, "Davey, when that happened, I *knew* I was washed up."

As he walked away, I thought, *That's a damn good point!*

******

There was great confidence in our club entering the '66 season. We had won 94 games the previous year and had added Frank Robinson to the middle of our order after obtaining him in a trade for pitcher Milt Pappas—probably the greatest trade the Orioles ever made. So we certainly felt we had an excellent chance to win the pennant.

Personally, however, my focus was to continue improving at second base, trying to be a good teammate, and producing offensively. And, ultimately, I went into spring training looking to take Jerry Adair's starting second-base job. Adair had held the position for five years and was coming off a solid all-around season in which he actually received some MVP votes. He was also one of the best defensive players of his era—setting major league records in 1964 in both fielding percentage and fewest errors by a second baseman for a season. I looked up to Jerry, but I wasn't going to be happy being his backup—I wanted to play every day. And I wasn't afraid to say that to the press or anyone who asked.

Ever classy, Adair would simply say he liked my competitive spirit.

And his taking the high road to my cockiness didn't surprise me. We had a very close-knit ballclub that was like a family. We had competitions within the team, but it never kept us from respecting one another.

The tide started turning my way during a spring training game at Tinker Field. I was on second base with no out when Booger hit a long fly ball to right-center field. I tagged up to go to third, racing as hard as I could for the bag. Billy Hunter, our third-base coach, started waving his arms to send me home.

I was surprised, quickly thinking, *Why would he send me home with one out?*

But I kept running hard and scored all the way from second on that sacrifice fly.

Remembering the play, Bauer said to me the next day, "You're going to open the season at second base."

As it turned out, Adair and I would split time at the position until about six weeks into the season. At that point, Adair was homerless and had just three RBI in seventeen games. After I had a big game in Minnesota, going 4-for-5 to bring my average up to .260, Bauer, looking for offense at the position, decided to make me the full-time second baseman.

Adair was understandably upset over what he perceived to be a relatively quick demotion after the quality years he had in Baltimore, and he complained to management. He protested enough, apparently, that the Orioles would trade him to the Chicago White Sox in exchange for pitcher Eddie Fisher a couple weeks later.

So for the next seven years, I would be the Orioles' starting second baseman. But more significantly, I would also be a part of perhaps the greatest defensive infield in baseball history.

******

Baltimore had always been a Colts town.

The Orioles had had some good years, but had never won a pennant in the modern baseball era. For as good as we were to that point, attendance was in the middle of the pack in the American League.

The Colts were just immensely popular not only in Baltimore but around the entire country at that time. About the only thing we had in common with them was the fact that we shared the same field—Memorial Stadium. We certainly knew when it was football season by the way the field would get all chopped up.

Even I was a big Colts fan. I followed Johnny Unitas, Earl

Morrall, John Mackey, and Co. relentlessly. Unitas, in particular, was like a god to me and millions of football fans around Baltimore. One of my earliest thrills was meeting him and attending some of the same sports dinners together.

Basketball was big too in Baltimore, with Kevin Loughery, Wes Unseld, Earl Monroe, and the rest of the Bullets. As someone who still loved playing basketball, I had the privilege of working out with them at some of their practices at the Baltimore Civic Center.

The city had such a great sports environment that I certainly never felt special because of all the other talented players in town.

But make no mistake, football was No. 1.

Still, we made believers out of Orioles fans right from the start of the '66 season. We broke out of the gates by winning our first 12 out of 13 games and when we moved into first place on June 7, we never looked back, remaining in the top spot for the final 90 games of the season.

I didn't put up the big power numbers like Booger and Frank did, but I was hitting in the clutch and driving in some big runs. I think I focused more than usual in big spots because I was surrounded by great players and didn't want to embarrass myself. I wanted to be as good as them to make me feel more like a part of the team. It helped that there was no pressure because, as this was my rookie year, I wasn't expected to do too much. But I expected myself to come through.

It really was such a great team in every way. And we had so much fun away from the ballpark—far different from today's game. Sometimes it saddens me to see all the pressure on players now. Of course, they're making a ton of money, but every little detail is picked out on them.

Today, players tend to leave games and go in separate directions. They have their agents, business managers, nutritionists, and personal trainers.

So one of the things I actually did like about Bauer's managing style was not imposing too many rules on us. He treated us like grown men—something I always tried to do with the teams I would later manage.

Bauer had just a few rules.

First, players weren't allowed to drink at the same hotel bar where he was. Second, players had to wear a coat and tie on road trips. And last, he enforced a midnight curfew.

So how exactly did Bauer enforce a curfew?

Once, during the '66 season when we were in New York—always a city we enjoyed going out in—Bauer gave the hotel bellman a baseball and asked him to have every player who came in past midnight autograph it. Bauer fined everybody who signed that ball $100.

Bauer had his shortcomings, as far as I was concerned, in handling the pitching staff and occasionally getting too carried away like he had when punching the bulkhead of a plane after concluding I was a guess hitter, but he was an intense competitor and loved the game of baseball.

When I managed, I took treating my players like grown-ups a step further than Bauer. I always believed that they were at the top of their profession and should behave as such. I never felt the need to be doing curfew checks and teaching them to stay within any rules off the field. I believed my guys were making a living and supporting their families and that they knew how to take care of themselves.

This wasn't college.

I did put out a rule book every spring with what I expected on the field.

Did I enforce it a lot? Only when necessary.

I always felt like the respect I gave a player had to be earned. But I also believed the respect I received from a player had to be earned, as well.

One of the starting points was that after a player leaves the ballpark, he is his own man. If he did things outside of that that affected his performance, that was when I would come in, because

I wanted my players to live up to their potential. But to start out and assume that the player is not going to do the right thing, to me, would be to also assume he couldn't do the right thing on the field.

I felt I had to show them respect. I had guys who were 19, 20 years old making my clubs. Their performance dictated it.

So, in a sense, I give Bauer credit for showing me how not to impose too many rules on a ballclub.

$$******$$

We clinched the pennant in Kansas City in a late-September game against the A's. For the next three hours, we had a wild celebration in the clubhouse. After we drank, doused each other with, and sprayed 72 bottles of champagne, one of our pitchers, Moe Drabowsky, pretended to be our owner, Jerold Hoffberger, and called a liquor store to deliver another 72.

The only thing I remember about that night was almost dying of alcohol poisoning. I wasn't used to drinking all the alcohol that I did and came out of the celebration in worse shape than anybody. I ended up passed out in the shower with the water running on me. A few of the guys pulled me out of there and our trainer Eddie Weidner put ice all over my body to try to bring me back to life. I made it on to the team bus on fumes.

The guys usually picked on me, especially on bus rides, in a brotherly kind of way, but on this occasion one of them actually toasted me.

"I've got to be the luckiest Okie ever to come out of Oklahoma," Eddie Fisher said while hoisting a beer in his hand on our trip to the Kansas City airport. "If it weren't for Davey, I wouldn't be here."

Of course, Eddie was referring to my beating out Adair at second, which allowed the trade for Fisher to happen.

While this was a night of celebration for our team, we were truly always a close group of guys. We could say anything to anybody on the club. Nobody ever got mad or hit anybody. We just shared our deepest feelings with one another, which I found to be the beauty of that team. And it came from the top all the way down. Hoffberger was an unbelievable owner.

It was a rough flight after all the partying, but we arrived in Anaheim in one piece in the early hours of the morning and, to our surprise and appreciation, the hotel had a sign greeting us in front that read, WELCOME CHAMPS!

But all I could think of was sleeping off what would be one hell of a hangover. I figured with two weeks before the start of the World Series, I would be able to take it easy the next day.

But I was wrong.

I would be the only starter to play all nine innings that night.

******

We would have to wait until the final day of the regular season before knowing who our World Series opponent was going to be, as it would take the Dodgers the entire length of the schedule to eliminate a surging San Francisco Giants team.

We arrived in Los Angeles a day after the Dodgers clinched to get ready to play the first two games of the World Series. It hardly mattered that Vegas had us as big underdogs. Nor did the task of facing two of the greatest pitchers ever—Don Drysdale and Sandy Koufax—for the defending world champions strike fear in our hearts. And we found it amusing that a bank flashed a sign on the way to Dodger Stadium that read, *Would you believe the Dodgers in four straight?*

This was because we knew we had a great team. Our younger players knew each other very well, as we had a great deal of success coming up through the minor leagues together. And among our veterans, we had three guys—Frank, Brooks, and Booger—who would finish in the top three in MVP votes that year and all drive in more than 100 runs. Frank, of course, had his Triple Crown season, leading the league in home runs, RBIs, and batting average. We looked at the World Series like we had a job to do—to become world champs.

I was floating on cloud nine.

I was still just 23 years old, and much of what we experienced was a little overwhelming for me.

For one, we were staying at movie star Gene Autry's chic Continental Hotel and Autry himself was at the door to greet us as we arrived. A big fan of his, I was in hog heaven.

Then, before Game 1 at Dodger Stadium, I noticed Ol' Blue Eyes himself, Frank Sinatra, sitting in the front row right above our dugout. Frank and I would later become very good friends, and when he would perform in cities I played or managed in, I would often sit backstage and reminisce with him. We really liked and trusted one another—he was a very nice man. It was obviously an honor to know him like I did. He was a lot bigger star than I was way back then. Those were the days!

As to be expected, I was nervous going into the first pitch of Game 1, but once that was over and done with, I was fine the rest of the way because I was so involved in the games.

In Game 1, Drysdale was pretty tough but we got to him early—the key when going up against great pitchers. Frank broke the ice by lining a two-run homer to deep left field in the first inning. Drysdale, ever trying to intimidate, knocked back Brooks, the next hitter, with a brushback pitch. But then Brooks retaliated by planting one into the left-center-field stands to put us up 3–0.

We scored again the following inning to take a four-run lead and knocked Drysdale out of the game after just two innings.

It should have been smooth sailing from there, but unfortunately for us, our starter, Dave McNally, was having serious control problems, walking five Dodgers in just two-plus innings.

Clinging to a 4–2 lead in the third, Bauer brought in Drabowsky and he was outstanding—striking out 11 over six-plus innings of one-hit ball to preserve a 5–2 victory. I remember the next day reading Jim Murray of the *Los Angeles Times*, who wrote, "It was the first time a Polak came into the World Series with a fastball instead of a rake."

You couldn't get away with writing that today!

Jim Palmer, just 20 years old, outdueled Koufax in Game 2 with a 6–0 win. Both pitched well, but we benefited the most when Dodgers center fielder Willie Davis made three errors in one inning—two by misjudging fly balls and the other with a poor throw—and allowed us to plate three runs in the fifth that gave us a 3–0 lead. I picked up a couple more hits in that game to give me four for the Series and maintain a .500 batting average.

We returned to Baltimore's Friendship Airport in the wee hours of the morning to what must have been around 10,000 adoring fans. For at least those few days during the World Series, we had taken center stage away from the Colts.

After hitting well against Drysdale and Koufax, I was really figuring to wear out Game 3 Dodgers starter Claude Osteen, but he pitched a gem, limiting us to just three hits over seven innings. But our Wally Bunker was even better, tossing a complete game shutout before the largest crowd in Orioles history. Paul Blair's home run in the fifth was all we needed in a 1–0 victory that put us up three games to none.

We closed out the series in Game 4 in a practically identical fashion to the previous game, winning 1–0 behind McNally's complete game shutout and a solo home run—this time courtesy of Frank Robinson.

Our pitching and defense were the story of this World Series. We only used four pitchers, who thoroughly dominated the Dodgers, keeping them to a meager .142 team batting average. And in the field, we didn't commit an error.

The city of Baltimore went into a frenzy, with thousands of fans celebrating in the streets. The *Baltimore Sun* called it "the zaniest celebration that Baltimore had seen since the U.S. defeated Japan in World War II."

Winning the World Series presented a terrific windfall for me. I was only making the rookie minimum of $6,500 that season, so the winner's share of $12,794 felt like all the money in the world. I took that check and invested it in some more real estate. I tried to buy all of Florida. I thought I was the richest man in the state.

So in deference to that bank on the way to Dodger Stadium I would say, "Would you believe the Orioles in four?!"

| six |

Spring Training, 1969: "Dumb Dumb"

I walked into Earl Weaver's office at our Miami Stadium spring training site prior to the '69 season with a four-inch pile of computer printouts under the heading OPTIMIZATION OF THE ORIOLES' LINEUP.

I said, "Earl, look at this shit. This will help you."

Weaver thumbed through the first few pages and, with little reaction, tossed them in the trash can.

I admit that part of the reason I put the report together was to prove to Earl that I should be hitting second in the lineup instead of seventh. But the other part was because Earl and I were friends going back to our days in the minors and played gin and golf together. Despite our occasional professional disagreements, I never outwardly talked about them, showed him up, or embarrassed him, like Jim Palmer seemed to enjoy doing. Any conversations we had were usually one-on-one in his office.

"Earl," I continued, undeterred, "the printouts won't change how the great talents like Frank or Brooks or Boogie will perform, but for the rest of us peons it will show a better place for us to hit in the lineup."

I'm pretty sure Earl looked over my data and studied it later because he eventually became very good at making out the starting lineup. But while I was in his office, the printouts remained in his "circular file."

For a time, Weaver, like many managers of the day, was content to use slips of paper showing the number of hits and at-bats a player had against a certain pitcher. And that's what he used to make out a lineup card.

In his defense, aside from this being the accepted way of managing then, I think this was also his way of giving another guy an opportunity to play. In that sense, it was very good and everybody accepted it.

However, a few years later, when Don Baylor was on the club, we were playing in Milwaukee and he went 3-for-4 with a triple and a home run. But the next day, Baylor wasn't in the lineup. So when I asked Weaver about it, he showed me his little sheet and said, "Well, he was 0-for-3 against this pitcher."

I said to Earl, "This guy's a streak hitter. When he gets hot, he hits *everybody*."

Then, I questioned the small sample size Baylor had against the pitcher.

"The standard deviation chart says you need 500 chances to be able to predict within plus or minus five percent of an event," I told Earl. "It's like flipping a coin. If you flip it three times, it may be heads all three times, but if you flip it 500 times the chances are it's going to be close to 50/50."

Earl didn't understand.

But obviously, based on his body of work and success, his way ultimately worked out pretty well for him.

******

I've always been fascinated with computers. Mathematicians want access to the latest technology, and back in the late '60s, that was the IBM 360—a huge computer. I created the *Optimization of the Orioles' Lineup* report while taking a computer course at Johns Hopkins University in the offseason. The Orioles' owner, Jerold Hoffberger, who also owned the National Brewing Co.—best known for producing Colt .45 malt liquor—allowed me to use his company's IBM 360 for my project.

So I wrote these punch cards with each possible Orioles lineup through 27 outs 162 times—inputing everybody's data from the 1968 season—which produced more than 300,000 variations. This gave me statistics such as how many runs each player would drive in and how many runners each would advance—basically, what lineup would be the best run producer.

As it turned out, the best lineup would have had me hitting second, as I had hoped for. My program showed we would have scored an additional 80 runs with it—an extra half a run a game. The sixth-worst lineup was the one Earl used the most during the '68 season.

Aside from *Optimization of the Orioles' Lineup*, I was programming other things on Hoffberger's computer simply because I had a thirst for knowledge when it came to baseball statistical analysis. I used to write in the Fortran programming language for numeric computation so I could control data of the opposing teams we were playing—defensive alignments, opposing manager tendencies, and hitter/pitcher matchups for both sides.

Another great tool in the computer program was the random number generator. Every time a guy went up to the plate, it kept in mind what his overall statistics were, so if he hadn't gotten a hit in a while, the chances of him getting one increased. But it wasn't a perfect system. The random number generator would only stay within the year's numbers. And it didn't predict whether he was going to get a hit his next time at bat. Still, it was an excellent resource to have at my disposal.

******

I have to say that I have always been a numbers guy. Names and history were always a challenge, but never numbers. And, lucky for me, baseball has always been a game of statistics.

While at Johns Hopkins, I read with great interest a book written by a professor there, Earnshaw Cook, called *Percentage Baseball*. At the time I was reading the book, which primarily emphasized the significance of on-base percentage, Major League Baseball wasn't even using the term yet. In fact, they weren't even calculating on-base percentage.

So after reading Cook's book I eagerly set up a lunch meeting with him.

During the lunch, he asked rhetorically, "How can you calculate who gets on base the most for your run producers?"

He then proceeded to lay out exactly how I always computed it, but instead of calling it an on-base percentage, I was simply using hits, walks, errors, and hit-by-pitches as a way of tracking how many times a player got on base. I just didn't have a name for it like he did.

Cook had some great ideas, but he also had some that wouldn't work.

"If you're a .250 hitter and you've got two balls and no strikes, don't swing, because your chances are better that you will reach base if you don't," he told me.

"You can't do that, Mr. Cook," I replied. "You would destroy the human element of the hitter. They're not machines."

Other radical ideas he conveyed included that you should have your best hitter bat first; sacrifice bunts are wasteful; relief pitchers should start games and then be replaced by a pinch-hitter in their first at-bat; and starting pitchers should throw the next four innings.

I told him, "Baseball is a very traditional game. Pitchers have a regimented role. When you're a starter in a four-man rotation, you pitch, take a day off, throw on the side, take a day off, and then pitch again. They're creatures of habit. You've got to do it that way. Starting a reliever and then throwing a starter for four innings throws all of this off."

Some of his other philosophies were interesting, but a number of them had flaws that I continued to pick out. Still, we had a great time. He signed a book for me and I was off and running. I thought there was a lot of valuable and thought-provoking information in *Percentage Baseball* that I could consider using.

******

Other mathematical concepts of odds can be related to pitching. I used to help my pitchers by communicating the difference between favorable and unfavorable chance deviation. When you're in a favorable chance deviation as a pitcher, you're throwing the ball where you're aiming it. But when you're in an unfavorable chance deviation, you're missing where you intend to throw it.

One time when Dave McNally was struggling with his control on the mound, I came in from second base.

I said, "Mac, you're in an unfavorable chance deviation. What that means is you're aiming for the corners and throwing right down the middle and that's why you're getting hit. So to get into a favorable chance deviation, aim for the middle because it will go to the corners."

He looked at me quizzically and said, "Dumb-Dumb, get the fuck out of here."

Conversely, Palmer was very rarely in an unfavorable chance deviation. He had the best command—hitting the inside and outside corners with ease—and could go up and down in the strike zone as well as anybody I've ever seen.

Like with McNally, I once visited Jim at the mound with my unfavorable chance deviation speech with the same result.

"Dumb-Dumb, get out of here," Palmer said.

So as you can probably figure out, my nickname, "Dumb-Dumb," was a group decision by a number of my Orioles teammates who didn't know quite what to make of this college graduate with the mathematics degree. It was kind of like nicknaming a fat person "Skinny."

But it's possible that what McNally, Palmer, and some of the other pitchers didn't fully realize was that, as a middle infielder, I can see the catcher's signs when I play behind the pitcher and then see where the ball goes, and thus I know whether they've got their command or not. And from a positioning standpoint, it was important because I played according to the pitch. I would lean a little bit left or a little bit right according to whether or not they hit their spot. It irritated me if they weren't hitting their spots because then I would be out of position. I had to know if they were in an unfavorable or favorable chance deviation in order to know how I should align myself defensively.

Every time I got traded and had to face pitchers I played behind, I knew them like a book—their thought process, when they go away, when they go in, how they set up their pitches.

When Darold Knowles—who used all kinds of pitches—was still a teammate of mine with the Orioles, I told him, "You don't ever want to face me because I'll wear you out. I know your thought process."

And when I eventually faced him as an opponent, I wore him out.

The same with Palmer. The first time I faced him, somewhere in an exhibition game, I hit one over the roof of a house in left field. Then Jim took himself out before I came up again.

Even when I was managing the Orioles and I had Mike Mussina as one of my pitchers, I could tell what was coming. Like with Knowles and Palmer, I picked up his tendencies. For a time, he was getting rocked.

So I told Mussina, "You're too predictable because you use your fastball instead of your breaking stuff. You've got to go back and forth."

He did and he went on to win 19 games that year.

Sometimes, pitchers don't realize that other people are paying attention and they can get in too predictable a sequence.

******

I had a bunch of little programs I used throughout my playing career and continued using when I managed. I did them for Earl through the '72 season and then continued doing them for the Braves after my trade to Atlanta.

In my first job as a manager with the Miami Amigos, I used the programs mostly to evaluate talent. When I put that team together, I knew statistically you needed table-setters in front of your run producers and so forth. I would look at not just a guy's speed, but also things like balls-and-strikes ratio and strikeouts-to-walks ratio. From day one of managing, after knowing all the numbers, that's how I looked for players and how I set my lineups. I could literally set a lineup by looking at my hitters' statistics from the previous season.

I always had computer guys help me with programs throughout the minor leagues, starting with the Amigos in the Inter-American League. The system worked well, as we were in first place with a 51–21 record in 1979 when the league shut down.

Then, when I went to manage the Class AA Jackson Mets of the Texas League, I hired some different guys from a local university to do the same type of programming for me.

Once I came up with the Mets, I had the programs refined and had the programmers in New York give me the output before every series. I continued believing in the numbers those programs produced right through my managerial stint with the Washington Nationals.

Numbers don't lie.

I was the very first person to ever be doing this. Now, of course, it's off the charts. Everybody is tracking everything with all the equipment out there. It's incredible. Today, you can track the speed of a pitch out of a pitcher's hand; when it crosses home plate; and then after the batter hits it, what the exit speed is off his bat and how far it goes. The computers keep track of all of that information.

There was never a question in my mind that this was the direction the game would go in. That's because a computer has a much better mind and better memory than a human being. In fact, it does more than that. It also gives so many variations of the moves different managers make.

What counts do they steal on? What counts do they pitch out on? When do they hit-and-run? How do they use their bullpen?

It's all there.

In managing, everybody can put a starting lineup out pretty easily with all the help you get. But it's how you use your bullpen against their lineup and bench and how you use your bench against their bullpen that's the biggest challenge.

To me, the best managers in baseball are the guys who handle the bullpens and bench because that's the deal. That's where managers earn their money.

What I predict next is that management will have too much data—it's going to be garbage in, garbage out. You have to be looking at specific parts of the data to really analyze talent and your lineup the best way.

I think out of everybody, Oakland A's general manager Billy Beane has probably used data the best in going out and acquiring players. And Billy's teams likely used the programs for their lineups because he usually had table-setters in front of run producers.

And while Beane and baseball writer and statistician Bill James get much of the publicity for what I really started—statistical analysis, commonly known today as sabermetrics—I'm happy they get the recognition they do. Beane should get credit because he was in a very powerful position to use it, and he did. And James' *Baseball Abstract* books in the late '70s and '80s brought sabermetrics to mass audiences. But both were basically doing what I was doing back in the '60s—tracking statistics.

I don't care about who got the most credit for it. I was just proud that others were actually evaluating what I was doing.

It gave validation to what I had started.

seven

October 16, 1969: A Juggernaut Derailed by the Miracle Mets

ON A CRISP, OVERCAST autumn afternoon, the fans at Shea Stadium rose to their feet in unison and roared as I approached the plate in the top of the ninth inning of Game 5 of the '69 World Series. The Mets were one out away from capping off one of the unlikeliest championships not just in baseball, but in all of sports history.

After all, they had been the laughingstock of the National League the previous seven seasons and, aside from maybe a couple of marquee players, had a roster made up primarily of no-names.

Our Orioles team, on the other hand, was even better than the one that had swept the Dodgers in the World Series three years before. We dominated the AL East, winning the division by a staggering 19 games. Our 109 victories were third best all-time. And then we swept a very good Minnesota Twins team in three straight in the inaugural American League Championship Series.

So it was no surprise that Vegas had us as big 8–5 favorites to win the World Series.

Like the rest of the club, I was struggling in the series, having gone hitless in the first four games. Prior to Game 5, some writer told me if I kept going at that rate, I would break Gil Hodges' record for hitting futility when he went 0-for-21 in the 1952 World Series. But fortunately, I avoided any chance of earning that dubious distinction by hitting a single in the second inning of this game to take the heat off me.

And now, batting in that ninth inning, with pinch runner Chico Salmon on first, I represented the tying run and could turn the whole game, and possibly the series, around with just one swing.

I took a first-pitch fastball from Jerry Koosman for a ball just off the plate outside. Ahead in the count, I could look for a pitch in my zone to drive.

Koosman's next pitch was almost in the identical spot, though on this one he nipped the outside corner for a strike.

In staying with his strategy of keeping the ball away from my wheelhouse, Koosman's next pitch was a slow, arcing breaking ball outside to give me a hitter's count of 2–1.

I stepped out of the box—reached down to grab some dirt, spit on my hands, and rubbed them together—pondering whether Koosman was going to stay outside or, thinking I might be leaning, try to sneak a fastball inside on me. As I always did, I would be ready for a fastball and adjust to an off-speed pitch.

The next pitch was what I was looking for, a belt-high fastball that I hit hard—so hard that I thought for sure it was going over the fence. I thought, *Two-run homer. Tie game. Maybe a whole new series.*

The sellout crowd gasped.

But a big gust of wind must have come along at that very moment and blown the ball back in. As Cleon Jones settled under it on the edge of the left-center-field warning track, it was all over—the Mets were world champions. I was dejected, but my feeling of disappointment quickly changed to concern, as what seemed like 50,000 delirious people were running on the field—with smoke bombs going off—as I sprinted toward our dugout. I made it back safely—barely.

I finished the series 1-for-16 with just that one single in the final game. And I made the last out of a World Series nearly everyone had picked us to win.

I guess you can say I've been helping the Mets since 1969.

******

As good as we were in sweeping the Dodgers in the '66 World Series, it just goes to show how hard it is to get back to the Fall Classic.

In '67, we had some key injuries, but none more crippling than the serious concussion Frank suffered when he got kneed in the head in a collision with second baseman Al Weis, then with the Chicago White Sox. Robinson was right in the middle of another Triple Crown–caliber season when it happened. So severe was the collision that Frank suffered a dislocated retina, which messed up his depth perception and gave him double vision for a while.

Palmer was also sidelined for much of the '67 season and all of the following year due to arm, shoulder, and back problems.

But aside from the injuries, I felt that Bauer was not handling the pitching staff very well. We had some good young arms, but when they came up to the big leagues, they weren't being given the proper instruction, a key to winning at that level.

We started that '67 campaign as defending champions, but finished it in sixth place and a very disappointing nine games under .500. After the season, Harry Dalton made some bold and, I thought, smart changes to the coaching staff.

First, he named George Bamberger—the developer of our young and talented arms in the minor leagues—the new pitching coach, replacing Harry "the Cat" Brecheen. "The Cat" was an outstanding pitching coach, but he really babied the pitchers. During a game, he would clean their spikes, get them cold towels—portraying a real fatherly image to them. And, most relevant, he didn't want them throwing every day—instead resting often between starts.

Bamberger wasn't like that. He believed that throwing was like running—you needed to do it every day to stay strong. His philosophy was kind of like Aparicio's in that respect.

Now, make no mistake. Bamberger didn't think pitchers should throw 100 mph every day, but rather just have a daily catch with a nice, easy motion at 60 feet. This work habit built up arm strength and Bamberger could have a starter throw between 130 and 135 pitches a game because they were conditioned to do so.

Today, of course, most teams limit starters to just around 100 pitches because they tire more quickly.

So when I saw Bamberger get promoted and his daily throwing regimen instituted, I knew we would have fewer injuries than what we had the year before. His methods were key in keeping our pitchers healthy—and for the most part they were after he took over as pitching coach. The Bamberger hiring was a pivotal moment for us.

Dalton then promoted Weaver from Triple A to become our first-base coach, replacing Gene Woodling. That move didn't sit well with Bauer, who may have rightfully seen Weaver as a threat to his job.

We were playing better ball than the year before midway through the '68 season, but were still barely over .500 when Dalton fired Bauer and made Earl the manager. Some of the players felt that Bauer had lost the clubhouse and his message just wasn't resonating with the team anymore. Plus, his gruffness was a little hard on some of the guys.

I remember Dalton asking me about the managing situation and I said, "If you're going to make a change, there's only one guy, and that's Earl Weaver. He handles a pitching staff real well."

Weaver and Bamberger would work extremely well together as architects of one of the finest pitching staffs in baseball for many years to come.

With Weaver at the helm, we played a strong second half, finishing with 91 wins. And we were confident we would ride that momentum into the next season.

******

There was tremendous anticipation heading into 1969. We traded Curt Blefary to get Mike Cuellar, who would set an Orioles record for wins that season. Palmer and Robinson were fully recovered from their injuries. Elrod Hendricks became the primary catcher and Don Buford the every-day left fielder. We had great balance between the bullpen with Eddie Watt and Pete Richert and our outstanding starting staff of Palmer, Cuellar, McNally, and Tom Phoebus. We had a strong bench that worked hard to stay ready to play, which was a tribute to Earl's making sure to give them adequate playing time to stay sharp. And, of course, we still had our Gold Glove infield of Brooksie, Mark Belanger, Booger, and myself.

My enthusiasm, however, was dampened when I suffered a freak accident early that spring. I was slumped over, feeding my adopted son Davey a bottle, when my back went out. It just started to spasm violently and I fell to the ground in agony while tightly holding on to my son.

I had my back X-rayed and went to see all kinds of doctors, but they couldn't find anything wrong. So I played through intense pain the entire season wearing a girdle underneath my uniform for stability. In fact, it was so bad at the All-Star Break that I decided to withdraw from the Midsummer Classic—a real disappointment.

I actually wouldn't get any relief until after the season, when I played winter ball in Puerto Rico. I went to Orlando Cepeda, one of my teammates there, and said, "Man, my back's killing me. Do you know what I could do?"

So Cepeda sends me to his doctor, who had all this voodoo stuff and was shining all these blue lights on me. He laid me out on this chiropractic table and really kneeled hard on my back. Then he put this powder all over it. It was all real weird, but I came out of there feeling great. I was cured!

Cepeda and I were always very close. He used to make me laugh when we were playing against Roberto Clemente in winter ball. Cepeda was always positioning the infielders in the holes because he said that's where Clemente always hit the ball.

"Roberto don't know how to hit right at first base or right at second base—he hits in the hole." Cepeda would tell me.

Another amusing thing he did was to always mop his brow with a pair of his wife's underwear. What a character!

Thankfully, the pinched nerve or whatever I had didn't prevent me from having the best year of my career to that point. I hit .280 with 34 doubles, but I was just as proud that I won my first Gold Glove despite having my twists and turns at second base adversely affected by my bad back—at any time I could have really wrenched it.

I give some of the credit for my solid year at the plate to talking hitting with Ted Williams, who was hired as the manager of the Washington Senators that season. During spring training, I was in the batting cage down the right-field line in the old ballpark in Miami. I saw Ted coming with a couple of TV cameramen, ran out of the cage, and said, "Mr. Williams, can I ask you a couple of questions?"

He said, "Sure, Davey."

"Did you squeeze the bat so tight that sometimes sawdust came out of it?" I asked.

"No, just the opposite," Williams replied, shaking his head. "I squeezed the bat like I was holding a bird or a fish. I didn't want to kill it and I didn't want it to get away."

We talked for another 15 minutes about hitting and I told him that I better let him go, concerned I was taking up too much of his time. After all, he did have a team to manage. But he was so gracious, telling me we could talk anytime. So I took advantage of his invitation and spoke to him before every game we played against the Senators that season. I ended up hitting phenomenally well against his team and it was mainly because, after talking with him, I just felt the confidence that he had. I believed I could hit anybody.

And, as a result, I would wear out his staff.

In fact, a couple of years later, Senators owner Bob Short sat Ted down and, I think mainly because of me, told Williams that he would fine him $500 if he caught him talking with opposing players about hitting.

So we carried on our conversations clear of everyone's sight at Ted's bayside home in Islamorada, Florida, over cocktails. It was such a wonderful experience.

Ted Williams was a great hitter and a great man.

******

As the '69 regular season began, we broke out of the gates quickly—taking over first place in mid-April—and never looked back. Frank, Brooks, and Booger put up their usual big numbers, but we had others like Blair, Buford, and Belanger who had career seasons.

Belanger's year especially stood out to me. As a batter who usually hit around the so-called Mendoza Line, which meant about .200, I told him to stop taking so many pitches and be more aggressive. Maybe the advice helped, because Belanger would bat .287 with 50 RBIs from the bottom of the order to go along with his first Gold Glove Award. Mark actually received some MVP votes that year.

With the glove, Belanger was truly remarkable. He had the best and quickest hands of any shortstop I've ever seen. He was so good, in fact, that he didn't wear a cup. He could recognize bad hops and get to the ball before it hit him. He just made all the plays and never got hurt. I guess if I had hands that good, I wouldn't have worn a cup either, but I didn't have the kind of confidence he did.

With Belanger at short, our infield was historically great and I give a lot of credit to Brooksie for that. As the veteran of the infield, he set the example of how we should play by working so hard on his defense—just a work ethic that was second to none. And despite not being fast, Brooksie still made the most difficult, unbelievable plays at third. Like Aparicio had been to me earlier in my career, Brooksie was one of the most influential teammates I ever had.

Over at first base, Booger had great hands for a big man. He could field short-hops and was a big target to throw at. One of my main responsibilities was to occasionally remind Booger to come off the line and to quit eating sunflower seeds while positioned next to the umpire—I'd bring him over a little bit.

Our infielders just knew each other very well, took a lot of pride in what we did, and really helped each other to succeed.

Later on, when I became more of a veteran player, it became even more important to me to help my teammates achieve their potential than my own personal success. That's kind of a weird thing in the cutthroat game of baseball, but I know I'm kind of a weird person.

But it was the same way throughout my career as a manager. It was never entirely about what the team did, but rather about whether I did all I could to develop my guys. Did they progress? Did I protect them? Did I help them? I always felt, everywhere I managed, that I protected and helped my players progress to the point of achieving their full potential. And that way of thinking was instilled in me as a member of the Orioles.

Our star-studded team would clinch the AL East with more than two weeks to play in the season and had a lot of fun in the process. Back in those days, some teams had "kangaroo courts" in which a "judge" would hand down fines for various miscues both on the field and off. It was all in fun and everybody ended up paying fines, with the money usually going to charity.

On the night we clinched the division, court was in session.

Frank was always our judge and relished the role. As intense a competitor as he was, he was a likable and supportive teammate.

You could ask him anything and he typically answered in a cordial way—always happy to help. We all respected him because of the way he played the game, whether it was his defense, his outfield play, or running the bases. He wanted to be the best in the game.

But what really stood out with Frank was his intensity when it came to winning.

One example of this was how he didn't believe in fraternizing with opposing players—even in spring training games!

During one such game, Maury Wills was playing third base for the Dodgers and when Frank was standing on third, he got all over him—just verbally abusing Wills. They had probably long before had some run-in at second base when Wills played shortstop.

Maury finally said, "C'mon, Frank, why are you acting like that?"

The reason was simple—Robinson wanted the opponents to be our opponents and not friends. He wanted us to realize that they were trying to beat us and we needed to go out there and claim what was ours. It always felt like he played with a chip on his shoulder, like, *I dare you to try to knock this chip off me.*

The thing you had to understand with Robinson was that he *always* put the team first.

And what a team player he was.

A prime example of that was his complete disregard for personal statistics. Frank may have been a pull hitter, but if there was a man on second base with no outs, he would always try to hit a ground ball to the right side. Often, he wouldn't just move the runner over, but would bring him home with a base hit.

And as a pure hitter, Robinson was as good as anybody I've ever seen.

One of my favorite stories I like to tell about Frank occurred when we were playing a game in Minnesota. In his first two times up, he flied out both times. After the second one, he told our equipment manager to go and get him some different bats, saying the ones he was using had soft wood in them. Frank added that he had hit those two fly balls on the screws, yet they didn't go anywhere.

We didn't doubt him for a moment.

So in his next at-bat, he brought one of the new bats out to hit with and, sure enough, crushed one about 450 feet.

None of us was surprised.

Frank was simply a remarkable player and the perfect leader of those great Orioles teams.

As far as the kangaroo court was concerned, Frank would hand down fines for practically anything. On that clinching night, I was fined, along with Chico Salmon and Marcellino Lopez, for wearing nearly identical loud suits, shirts, and ties. Like most of the club, we chose those garish wardrobes in anticipation of all the champagne and beer that would be sprayed around the clubhouse if we clinched the AL East crown that night. We were hardly alone—everybody had their worst clothes in their lockers.

Still, the three of us weren't spared by Judge Robinson.

Frank laid down the fines, many named after our players. We had the "Chico Salmon Fine" for players who messed up a fielding play; a "John O'Donoghue Fine" for a pitcher who made a costly pitch; and others for mistakes on the bases or at the plate. The court would always take place after games, with Frank putting on his little gray wig. It may have been a lot of laughs, but it was also a way that we were monitoring each other. You didn't ever want to get a fine for making a boneheaded play.

Because of the way we handled things, everybody loved coming to the ballpark and being around each other. No other team could hold a candle to what we were doing on the field and in the clubhouse.

******

While we were confident heading into the ALCS against the Twins, we knew they were a strong team and a more-than-capable opponent.

They had Harmon Killebrew, a future Hall of Fame slugger who would win the MVP award that year with his 49 home runs—many of them towering, tape-measure shots.

They also had Rod Carew—an all-time great hitter. But with Carew, you also had to really watch out for the bunt. Every one he laid down was so perfect, he could have hit .330 by just bunting all the time if he wanted.

And then there was Tony Oliva—a terrific all-around hitter who batted over .300 and drove in more than 100 runs that season—to contend with.

Still, as good as they were, our pitchers knew how to pitch against them.

As for the Twins' pitching, Jim Kaat was in the prime of a terrific career; Dave Boswell, with his unbelievable curveball, and Jim Perry, the ace of their staff, were both 20-game winners; and Dean Chance, then near the end of his career, still had a sharp, heavy breaking ball.

But despite the formidable staff the Twins had, we all felt they were hittable. And as hitters, we loved playing in their little band box in Minnesota's Metropolitan Stadium—because, top to bottom, we felt like we had a better lineup than they did. We believed that, in addition to our superior pitching, playing there gave us an edge.

As a result, we had great success against the Twins during the regular season—winning eight of twelve games—and our supremacy would carry over into the playoffs.

The first two games in Baltimore were close, hard-fought extra-inning games, but we prevailed in both of them.

Down a run in the bottom of the ninth inning of Game 1, Booger led off with a game-tying home run to send us into extra innings. Then, in our half of the 12th, Blair surprised everyone with a two-out bunt to score Belanger to win the game.

In the second game, McNally was incredible, limiting the Twins to just three hits over 11 shutout innings. We would win in dramatic fashion once again, this time in the bottom of the 11th, when pinch-hitter Curt Motton drove in the game winner with a single to right field to score Booger. That game was the perfect example of how our club went about its business. You had McNally conditioned to go 11 innings and be every bit as effective in his last inning of work as he was in his first, and you had Weaver having everyone on that club—even a bench player like Motton who had fewer than 100 at-bats that season—ready to shine in a big spot.

In the third and final game, we showed how much we loved playing in Minnesota by going on a hitting barrage—18 hits in all—to blow away the Twins 11–2 and win the pennant. "Cakes"— the nickname we gave to Palmer because he always had pancakes on the days he pitched—got knocked around a little bit that day, but limited the damage to just two runs in going the distance.

We all loved Cakes, but occasionally he offended some of us in the field by moving us around. A few times it backfired on us, including in Game 3. The Twins had a bunch of left-handed hitters and, in one instance, he motioned me to play up the middle because he was going to throw a fastball to one of them. But when he turned around and noticed that everyone saw him shade me over toward second base, Cakes changed his mind and threw a change-up instead, which was easily hit in the hole for a base hit.

And it wasn't just the infielders that Cakes maneuvered—Palmer regularly moved the outfielders around, too.

So it wasn't just Weaver that he annoyed.

Anyway, like all great pitchers, Palmer turned in a great effort without his best stuff. And in the ALCS, we gave the Twins more than they could handle in that series.

It was now time to see what all the fuss was about with those Amazin' Mets.

******

Despite what some people may have thought over the years, we never underestimated the Mets.

How could we?

They had won 100 games during the regular season and then gone out and swept the Atlanta Braves in the NLCS.

So we knew, at the very least, that their pitching had to be awfully good to win three straight over a potent lineup like the one the Braves had.

When comparing the teams prior to the World Series, I knew our pitching was at least as good as the Mets', but I thought our every-day lineup was much better. And I felt that we were a deeper, more complete team than they were. It takes 25 guys to win and we had 25 really good players. We had a strong starting lineup with no weaknesses, the right guys coming off the bench to pinch hit, great flexibility in the pitching staff and bullpen, and a superb defense. So everybody's confidence was sky-high.

Still, in Game 1 in Baltimore, we had the task of facing off against 25-game winner Tom Seaver, who was being touted as the game's best young pitcher. The future Hall of Famer had excellent stuff and great command. And even then, at just 24, he was an intense competitor.

But when Buford led off our half of the first by ripping a home run over the right-field fence on Seaver's second pitch of the game, we were off and running.

We really got to Seaver in the fourth when we added three more runs. That would be more than enough for Cuellar, who pitched a complete game gem, and we were 4–1 winners. It was our eighth straight postseason win going back to the '66 Series.

If our confidence was high heading into this Series, after beating Seaver, it was now off the charts.

But it was at this point when things mysteriously started going the Mets' way. Every kind of break in the world you could think of went against us.

Locked in a pitcher's duel between McNally and Koosman in Game 2, with the game tied 1–1 in the top of the ninth, the Mets had runners on the corners with two outs and their weak-hitting platoon player, Al Weis, coming to bat.

Weaver had a decision to make—have McNally pitch to Weis or intentionally walk him to face either Koosman or a pinch-hitter. Earl decided to pitch to him.

Weis made him pay by ripping a high slider for a single to left to score Ed Charles, and the Mets went on to beat us 2–1.

Weaver, of course, was second-guessed for the decision, but I was completely behind him. I always believed—as Earl did—that when you had a base open, your pitcher had the opportunity to make nothing but borderline pitches to get guys out. I feel this is a much better position to put your pitcher in than one where he has to throw the ball over the plate. Later on when I became a manager, I would tell my pitchers in those situations, "Look, you've got a base open, so you can nibble and make him swing at your pitches."

Plus, the thinking here by Weaver was if he intentionally walked Weis late in the game like that, the Mets' manager, Gil Hodges, would have almost certainly used a pinch-hitter off his bench, one who was probably a better hitter than Weis. So I thought Weaver made the right decision.

But this was the beginning of what made the Miracle Mets miraculous—a .219 lifetime hitter stroking the game-winning hit off the hottest pitcher on the planet.

******

The World Series shifted to Shea Stadium for the next three games.

The scene was similar to what we had experienced three years before in Los Angeles—with stars from the stage and screen and politicians in attendance—only this time instead of talking with Frank Sinatra by our dugout like I had in L.A., I had a chat with President Richard Nixon, who was a huge baseball fan. As far as I was concerned, he was the biggest celebrity there.

We felt very confident we would take Game 3 of the series. The pitching matchup certainly appeared to be tilted in our favor with

Cakes going for us against Gary Gentry, a rookie pitcher we felt was a significant drop-off from Seaver and Koosman. Prior to that game in the clubhouse, I remember us saying to one another how we were going to get to this guy.

But actually, Gentry surprised us and may very well have pitched the best game of anybody in the series. It was unbelievable how, with nearly every pitch, he was painting the black by mixing a good fastball with a big breaking ball. Plus, his pitches were hard for us to pick up. Frankly, our scouts kind of underrated him. From a hitter's standpoint, Gentry's stuff was terrific.

However, as well as Gentry pitched, it was Tommie Agee who won the game for the Mets.

Agee got things going for them by leading off the bottom of the first with a home run. But it was his play in the outfield that really stood out, as he saved five runs with two outstanding catches.

In the third inning, he robbed Elrod with a running, fingertip grab by the left-center-field wall to save two runs. Then in the seventh, after we loaded the bases, Blair lined one to deep right-center field and Agee—again running full speed—dived at the last moment to make another terrific catch, this time saving three more runs.

And prior to that, in that same seventh inning, with nobody on base, I hit a fly ball to Agee in which he slipped—kicking up a divot off the outfield grass—got back up, and still somehow had time to make the catch.

In the dugout, we were like, *Boy, the ball seems to blow back toward them and blows away from us.*

And that dynamic seemed to play out the rest of the series. Every single break was going their way.

In the next game, we were down 1–0 in the ninth. Seaver was pitching a gem, but we started getting to him when Frank and Booger both singled with one out to put runners on the corners. Brooksie came up next and hit a screaming line drive to right-center field. If it had split the outfielders and went to the wall, we would have taken the lead. Instead, Ron Swoboda, who usually could hardly catch a fly ball, made a miraculous diving catch. Frank tagged to score the tying run, but we just couldn't get any real momentum going on our side.

I am a firm believer that you create your own momentum, but we were putting some good at-bats up there and coming away with nothing. It seemed like a conspiracy was at play by the baseball gods with the Mets as beneficiaries.

The game moved to the 10th inning and the Mets' Jerry Grote led off by popping the ball up toward short left field. But instead of what would have been the first out, the usually reliable Buford broke late after initially losing the ball in the sun, and it dropped in between him and Belanger for a double.

After we intentionally walked Weis to set up a possible double play, Weaver brought in Pete Richert to face pinch-hitter J.C. Martin. Martin bunted and I ran over to first base to take the throw from Richert. But with Martin way inside the base line, Pete's throw hit him on the left wrist and bounced away from me into short right field to score Rod Gaspar with the winning run.

I questioned the first-base umpire on why interference wasn't called, but there was nothing we could do—it was a judgment call and he apparently didn't see what I saw. Yet all the photos in the newspaper the next day showed that Martin was inside the line and in the way of the throw. The result was yet another break for the Mets, who now led the series three games to one.

Despite the Mets playing like they had angels on their shoulders, we still remained positive about our prospects to get back into the series heading into Game 5. With the team we had, we always felt like we had a chance and never believed we were out of it.

That belief that served us well early in Game 5. In the third inning, we jumped out to a 3–0 lead thanks to a two-run homer by McNally and a solo shot by Frank. It's always a good omen when your pitcher goes long against a good one like Koosman, so we were feeling pretty good about ourselves.

But then, in the bottom of the sixth with us still leading 3–0, the Mets started to get some breaks again. Cleon Jones led off and skipped to get out of the way of an inside curveball. The ball ricocheted into the Mets' dugout. At first, the home-plate umpire Lou DiMuro called it a ball and not a hit-by-pitch. But after Hodges retrieved the ball and showed DiMuro a baseball that was smudged by shoe polish, Jones was awarded first base.

I thought the call reversal was weird because anybody in that Mets dugout could have quickly put a black mark on that ball with his own shoe.

The Mets' next hitter, Donn Clendenon, then hit a home run to deep left field to cut our lead to just one.

An inning later, Weis, who averaged a home run roughly once out of every 250 plate appearances throughout his career, took McNally deep to tie the game. Some of us just shook our heads in disbelief.

After scoring two more runs in the eighth, the Mets jumped ahead 5–3 and would be champions after retiring us in the next frame. Our mighty offense set a dubious World Series record for fewest hits in a five-game series. The Mets' pitching staff ranked as one of the best I've ever seen in that World Series.

The World Series loss concluded a rough year in sports for Baltimore against New York teams, with the Colts losing to the Jets in the Super Bowl, the Bullets losing to the Knicks in the NBA playoffs, and now our Orioles losing the World Series to the Mets.

But the one bright spot that I will never forget was the scene at the airport in Baltimore when we arrived back from New York. There must have been 5,000 fans waiting for us to lend their support. It was a very emotional scene that I thought was unprecedented. The Oriole fans were so great to us after we lost a tough series. I think everybody on our ballclub was moved by their gesture.

I still think we were the better team in the '69 World Series, but sometimes the best team doesn't win.

eight

October 15, 1970:
Mission Accomplished

I WAS SHOCKED.

Everyone was shocked.

To a man, every player in our losing clubhouse couldn't believe the Mets had just beaten us like they did in the '69 World Series. They got all the breaks, the momentum turned completely against us, and all their guys who weren't expected to do anything did big things. And when they started to succeed, they began to feed off one another because it was so unexpected. It truly was a miracle that they beat us, because we were a really great team.

But there was something else at play that we all took to heart. Throughout our clubhouse, most of our guys kept saying essentially the same thing to one another.

"Man, next year we're going to win it all. We've *got* to win it next year."

We decided right there and then that what happened against the Mets couldn't happen again, no matter what.

And just as I was sure we would return to the World Series, I was equally sure the Mets would not be our opponent. I hate to say it, but they were horseshit compared to us.

As eagerly as I awaited the start of the new year, I still had a contract to negotiate. I didn't have an agent, so I acted on my own behalf. So when Frank Cashen, the executive vice president of the club at that time, offered me just a $500 raise, I told him I would rather dig ditches than sign for such a meager pay increase.

"I'm a regular on a pennant-winning team." I told Frank. "I should be paid more than what you're trying to pay me."

I held out—the only thing you could do back then—until he came around with a bigger raise,, which brought my salary up to $25,000. But along with my salary, I was able to convince Cashen to include an incentive clause that would award me a $1,000 bonus for each year that I increased my numbers in at least two of three offensive criteria—batting average, home runs, and RBIs.

I knew my game was going to continue getting better.

As the 1970 season approached, we were in the midst of one of the greatest three-year runs in American League history. And if you add our world championship of '66, it was like a mini dynasty. There is no question that our legacy as one of the best teams of all time was tarnished by losing that World Series to the Mets and then later in '71 to the Pirates. Both of those defeats were horrible things because we should have won them both. In our minds, it was all about what we did in the Fall Classic during that era that would determine success versus failure.

The '70 regular season practically mirrored the one before, as our 108 wins were just one fewer than in '69. We set the tone early by winning our first five games of the season; then were 22 games over .500 at the All-Star break, before finishing the season with an 11-game winning streak, our longest of the year.

And like the season before, we clinched the division title with more than two weeks remaining in the campaign. So with the AL East wrapped up, while we were playing for pride in those final games, I was also playing for my bonus.

Having already hit more home runs than the year before, I

focused my attention on improving my previous season's .280 batting average—which would give me the two offensive improvements I needed.

And this is where it got interesting.

I entered the final game of the year with a .282 average. Earl said he wanted me to sit out the otherwise meaningless game so I could collect my bonus.

But I remembered what my good friend Ted Williams had done back in 1941, when he entered the last game of the season with an average of .404. The Red Sox wanted him to sit out so he would end the year over .400, but Williams boldly insisted on playing. He would go 2-for-3, including a double that broke a loudspeaker, to end the season at .406. To this day, Ted remains the last player to finish above the prestigious .400 mark.

So this was my Ted Williams moment.

I told Earl enthusiastically, "I want to play!"

We were playing against the Senators before a small crowd that day in Baltimore. I was hitless in my first four at-bats and unless I came through in my final plate appearance, I would have blown $1,000—real money back then.

With two outs in the ninth of a 2–2 tie, I came up to hit against Horacio Piña with two men on. And thankfully, I ripped a game-winning single to bring home Merv Rettenmund to win the game and earn my thousand bucks.

The next year, I again hit just one point higher, batting .282 to receive the same bonus. It became a running joke—sort of an awful one because I kept making it by just a single point on my batting average. But I always refused to sit rather than secure that bonus, telling Cashen and Weaver that playing meant more to me than the money.

******

We once again took on Minnesota in the ALCS. The Twins had a different look from the previous year's club, as they had brought up rookie and future Hall of Famer Bert Blyleven and traded for Luis Tiant in an effort to bolster their already solid pitching rotation.

I didn't know too much about Blyleven except that he had a great curveball, but I knew Tiant exceptionally well. In fact, we hated each other.

Tiant was a tough competitor who threw six different pitches from several different arm angles, with seemingly never the same deceptive delivery for any of them. Sometimes when you face somebody that good, it pumps you up to play at a higher level, and that's exactly what happened to me with Tiant. I had such tremendous success off of Luis that it once frustrated him to the point of drilling me in the back with a pitch in a game that I'd homered off of him in.

"That's for you hitting me like that!" Tiant yelled toward me as I jogged to first base.

I hated him for doing that, but loved hitting against him because he brought out the most in me. And conversely, there were a lot of other guys who were lesser pitchers than him that I couldn't hit worth a dime. Tiant, quite simply, elevated my game.

Another change they made was firing their manager, Billy Martin, and replacing him with Bill Rigney.

I guess even though the Twins had won a division title with Martin in '69, they were itching to get rid of him after he punched out and knocked unconscious one of their 20-game winners, Dave Boswell, in a barroom brawl late that season.

But I loved Billy as a competitor and was shocked they fired him. He was just so intense. When I got on base he would start yelling stuff at me—it was relentless. I would motion back at him, bringing out things in me that I wasn't real proud of, but in a way it made the game more fun with him in it.

I mean, how many managers act like that?

Billy was an all-time dandy before, during, and after games and certainly got the most out of his players. So replacing a guy like that with Rigney, whom I wasn't a big fan of, didn't improve the Twins in the dugout. And all the other moves the Twins made to their ballclub didn't help in this series. Unlike in '69, when at least the first couple of games were close, this time around we blew them out in every game.

In the first two games, we pounded out 21 runs in our home away from home—cozy Metropolitan Stadium. I can't say enough how much we loved hitting in that ballpark. And our '70 Orioles team may have been the best offensive club we ever had, led by Booger's 35 home runs, which helped him win the AL MVP award that year.

In Game 1, both Cuellar and Jim Perry got shelled, but our reliever Dick Hall came in and limited the Twins to just one hit over the last four-plus innings to win it for us 10–6.

Dick was an effective relief pitcher with a funny little release. We thought he threw like a turkey, which is why we nicknamed him "Turkey Hall." He was the only guy I knew who could throw high fastballs and high backup sliders and get people out. That was his repertoire. You would think if a pitcher kept everything up he would get rocked, but nobody could hit Turkey.

We all loved Hall—a great guy who was also a terrific accountant. He saved me a lot of money on my income taxes. Those were the days when most of us had regular jobs in the off-season. I have nothing but great memories about Turkey Hall.

In the second game of the ALCS, McNally pitched a complete game gem and I continued my success against Tiant by belting a three-run homer off him in the ninth inning of an 11–3 rout.

McNally, who was a 20-game winner for us four times, was often overshadowed by Palmer because Cakes was a media darling and enjoyed the limelight more than Dave. But McNally was never considered any less valuable to us than Palmer—we thought they were equally important to our success throughout our glory days.

I've long felt that McNally should have received more support for induction into the Baseball Hall of Fame. I loved playing behind him because I knew where he was going to throw the ball. When the catcher called for a pitch down and away, that's where Dave would throw it. That enabled me to lean in that direction when playing second base.

Palmer was easy to play behind as well, because he really only had one pitch—a fastball—that he could pinpoint in and out and up and away against any hitter. So it was no surprise that Cakes pitched his own complete game masterpiece to wrap up the pennant for us in Game 3 with a 6–1 win.

I was really locked in, hitting my second home run of the series—this time off Perry—and led the Orioles in slugging for the ALCS. But I wasn't really impressed with myself to be honest—I just wanted to win ballgames.

I can only explain the dominance we had against those talented Twins teams of '69 and '70 with the fact that they stood in our way of the World Series. I loved competing against guys like Billy Martin and Luis Tiant because they wanted to win as much as we did, but we were the better team and were supposed to represent the American League in the Fall Classic.

Minnesota was never going to stop us.

******

We entered the World Series against the Reds highly confident, yet with a feeling of desperation to win—admittedly an odd combination. But that was because we wanted to avenge the World Series upset in '69 and validate the dominance we had over the American League in '70. In our minds, we had a job to do—we *had* to win.

Unlike the previous year with the Mets, this World Series clearly matched up baseball's best two teams.

The Big Red Machine actually entered as slight favorites. They had guys such as Johnny Bench and Tony Perez—who both hit more than40 home runs—and others like Lee May, Pete Rose, and Bobby Tolan who had career seasons.

We all knew they had a good ballclub, but I can't emphasize enough how there was no question in our minds that we were going to beat them.

And we also knew that with all those right-handed-hitting sluggers, they were going to keep Brooksie very busy at third.

Robinson, as always, certainly was up to the challenge.

Brooksie had a phenomenal series, making more outstanding plays than you could shake a stick at. Whether it was diving to his left or right, he made all the plays. He didn't have a great arm, but the ball got to him so quickly on the artificial turf that his quick release enabled him to throw everybody out. The Reds never had a chance against the "Human Vacuum Cleaner." We simply called him "Hoover."

But even though the World Series would be called the "Brooks Robinson Series" by the writers, there was nothing unusually good about his play. The reality was that Brooks made those plays all the time. You wouldn't believe the shots I saw him field over the years. He just had uncanny instincts.

Of course, the play he made that you see all the time on highlight films was in Game 1, when Lee May hit a bullet down the third-base line and Robinson made a backhand stop and threw the ball from foul territory on one bounce to Booger to get May by half a step. That play helped keep the score tied at 3–3, and we overcame an early three-run deficit to win it 4–3. But the only reason everyone thought Robinson's play was special was because of the situation— he did it in a World Series game.

It also helped that we were playing on artificial turf, which was a relatively new surface in some of the newer cookie-cutter ballparks of that era. When a ball is hit on a dirt infield it can take a bad hop, but on turf the ball may move faster but is a piece of cake to field—you can pick it with your eyes closed. On the bounce throw that Brooksie made to nip Lee at first, it even loked like it picked up speed after skidding on the turf.

Of all the great plays he made in that World Series, the one that sticks out to me was a double play we turned in Game 2 with the Reds again leading early, this time 4–0. Any more damage and the Reds could have buried us in that game to even the series. Lee May again torched one between Brooksie and third base that looked like a sure double off the bat, but Robinson snared it, spun completely clockwise, and got me the ball in time so I could complete the twin killing. It was a game-saving play for sure, and we would go on to score six runs in the middle innings to steal one from the Reds, winning 6–5 to go up two games to none.

The fact is, I learned to play second base as agilely as I did because Brooksie had real small hands and his throws could sink or sail to my left or right. Thus, I had to watch his throws very closely—never taking my eyes off the ball—and catch them using both hands in order to pull the ball out of my glove smoothly. Brooksie taught me how to do all of that and it made me a better second baseman. And because he got me the ball so quickly, it allowed me enough time to make my pivot that Mazeroski and Richardson taught me so well to throw the runner out at first.

I was obviously taught to pivot by the best, but it's hardly even taught at all today—period. I have a real problem with the rule that was passed recently where a runner can only slide straight into a base. If you know what you're doing, like I did, they could slide wherever they want—inside or outside the bag—and not take you out. But now they use video to rule if you slide straight in or not. Good gracious!

And while we're on the subject of rule changes, what is baseball thinking about by making first- and third-base coaches wear batting helmets? Because one guy in the minor leagues didn't watch the ball and got hit?

If you're a first- or third-base coach, you can't be talking to a fielder—you've got to watch the ball. It's pretty amazing to me. The No. 1 rule in baseball is wherever you are on the field, *watch the ball*.

With the way things are evolving, pretty soon the pitchers will have to wear helmets and shin guards.

I also hear there's a lot of talk now about balls and strikes being called from the booth to avoid bad calls. But you know what? Baseball is about knowing your umpire: knowing what he calls and what he doesn't call. And then there's the human element, which is every bit as important. Pitchers, catchers, hitters, and umpires are all going to make mistakes. It's part of the game. We're all humans. We all err. The human element is part of what makes baseball great.

Pretty soon, it's all going to be high-tech and they won't need an umpire behind the plate or others at the bases. Why do they even need them now? With instant replay, officials don't always make the final call on a play anyway.

They say the game is evolving with technology. They think it's great and everybody wants to see more of it. Well, I call that bullshit. I don't think anybody wants it.

With some of the rules the new commissioner, Rob Manfred, and others assisting him are putting out there and considering, it's not even the game of baseball anymore. It's terrible. Somebody who never played the game and doesn't know anything about it has made rules like the sliding one. I hate to say this, but it's not the game I grew up playing.

As someone who loves the purity of the game, it's very upsetting to me.

******

We took a decisive three-games-to-none lead after a 9–3 drubbing by the Reds back in Baltimore. Our offense clicked on all cylinders and McNally continued his dominant postseason pitching with yet another complete game victory. Just as impressive was his grand slam in the sixth inning to give us an 8–1 lead.

As good as the Reds were, we now had an opportunity to sweep them in four straight games—and none of us were the least bit surprised. Even when we fell behind early in the first two games, it never occurred to any of us that we might lose either of those games. We were brimming with confidence and obsessed with winning this World Series. Nobody cared how great those guys were on the other side. We knew we had the complete package—great pitching, defense, and offense—and were going to win. We just weren't going to go down the same road we had against the Mets. It was amazing how locked in we all were.

It really appeared like a sweep was at hand. In Game 4, we took a 5–3 lead into the eighth inning when Earl brought in Eddie Watt to relieve Cakes. Watt got into trouble right away, walking Perez and Bench before surrendering a home run to May to blow the save and give the Reds a 6–5 lead, which they held on to for the win.

Like we always were when we lost, we were shocked, but wanted badly the close out the series the next day.

Game 5 started out much like the first two games, with the Reds taking a sizable lead—this time 3–0 after one inning. And in this one, just like in those other two, we would not be denied. We would score nine unanswered runs and win the game, and the World Series, going away 9–3.

I had a solid finale, going 3-for-4, and finished the Series with a .333 average, but what I remember most about that World Series was how we mirrored our manager, Earl Weaver. Earl was a cantankerous winner and hated losing more than any human being alive. And, aside from all our winning, that's a big part of the reason why he's in the Hall of Fame—because he hated losing so much. I think what made our Orioles team so great was that Earl personified how we all felt.

We all reveled in how he would hide in the tunnel and smoke cigarettes in high-pressure game situations and say, "I can't watch." We fed off that intensity.

So despite trailing early in three of our four wins in this World

Series against the vaunted Big Red Machine, we weren't going to be denied.

And just as we had set out to do in the visitors' clubhouse following that gloomy, final game at Shea Stadium the previous October, we exorcised the demons from the '69 World Series in the process.

This was our finest hour.

nine

October 17, 1971:
Stunned by the Pirates

"YOU TRIED TO KILL me! You tried to *kill* me!" Manny Sanguillen shouted as we both lay on the ground in pain. I had just tagged up from third and barreled into him in Game 2 of the '71 World Series.

"No, no I didn't," I told the Pirates catcher. "I just wanted to try to knock the ball out of your hands because I was out."

The violent collision took place after we already led 4–0 and were on our way to an 11–3 clobbering of the Pirates. It was our 16th straight win and we now held a 2–0 lead in this World Series.

So why would I risk injury in a game in which we already held a sizable lead?

And why do it when I already had a bum shoulder?

Because I didn't know any other way to play. I was always a risk taker. I'd run over anybody, anytime.

I thought, *Hey, they always try to run over me at second, but never can, so what's the big deal in my trying to do the same to them?*

Besides, Sangy could hardly complain. My collision with him wasn't even the most crushing I ever put on a catcher. In fact, two bigger ones occurred around midseason that same year when I bowled over Red Sox backstop Duane Josephson twice—first in Boston and then about a week later back home in Baltimore.

I messed up my shoulder big time in the first one, and the second one just added to my misery. I was sent to the hospital for X-rays and they said everything was fine, but back in those days X-rays didn't reveal what I later found out I had—a subluxation, a very painful partial dislocation of the shoulder.

The problem was, after those two collisions, when I tried to swing and extend my left shoulder where the subluxation was, it would collapse. It would be two years, when I was with the Braves, before I was diagnosed properly and finally understood the reason I was hurting so much.

Worst of all, it put a damper on what was already going to be my best season in the majors. I had 16 home runs at the All-Star break, but only two the rest of the season. I would have hit 30 home runs easily that year with a healthy shoulder because I had finally stopped trying to hit inside pitches to right field—the "Brooks Robinson Way"—like Darrell Johnson had instructed me to do in the minor leagues several years before. Only Brooks could hit well that way.

So I said to myself, *The hell with this. If they throw me a ball down and in, I'm hitting it over the left-field wall.*

Johnson's advice was awful. When I went back to just hitting the ball where it was pitched, I became the slugger I had been before he messed me up.

But it taught me a lesson that I would use later as a manager. Whenever I hired a hitting or pitching coach, I wanted to know exactly what they were thinking, because I didn't want them to mess up my players like I had been messed up.

So with the X-rays not showing a break, Weaver tried to reassure me by saying, "You're fine, Davey. Don't worry about it, you're fine."

"No, I'm not fine," I told him. "My left shoulder collapses."

"There's nothing wrong with you," Earl said more forcefully.

"You're playing."

"Earl," I said, "Play Bobby Grich because I *can't* play."

Grich, a middle infielder, was the minor league Player of the Year in 1971 while playing for our Triple A Rochester club. Ideally, as great as Belanger was defensively at short, our best infield would have been to insert Grich at shortstop, because of his big bat, and a healthy me at second. But with my shoulder injury, I thought Grich was a good option at second to fill in for me at least some of the time.

So in hindsight, would I continue to barrel into catchers—even with an already injured shoulder?

Absolutely! It's part of the game—or *should* be. Anything you have to do to win, you just go for it.

Now, with that being said, I'm paying the price for it today, because I've got joints and other parts of my body that still hurt because of my aggressive play. But you've got to be "all in" when you play the game of baseball or you shouldn't bother playing at all.

******

Following our lopsided Game 2 victory, we traveled to Pittsburgh as everyone's favorite to wrap up the World Series in short order. After the convincing way we won the first two games, it seemed to some like a mismatch.

Los Angeles Times sportswriter Jim Murray wrote, "The Pirates are going back to Pittsburgh now. It's like the elephants are coming home to die."

But the way I saw it, anytime you're playing a team with Roberto Clemente on it, it's no mismatch. Clemente was simply unbelievable in every facet of the game. And the Pirates also had Willie Stargell, one of the game's premier sluggers. But other than those two, nobody on our club knew a whole lot about the rest of their regulars.

Their pitching was sort of a mystery to us, as well. They didn't even have a single 20-game winner on their pennant-winning pitching staff.

Of course, that was the year we had *four* of them—our famous "Four Leaf Clover" pitching staff of Jim Palmer, Dave McNally, Mike Cuellar, and newly acquired Pat Dobson, whom we had picked up in a trade with the San Diego Padres prior to the season. We were the first team in more than 50 years to have four 20-game winners.

Dobson was an interesting study. Before coming to our club, he was a journeyman right-hander who spent a lot of time pitching out of the bullpen. He had a losing record in each of his first four big-league seasons. And he struggled with us early on in 1971.

The problem with Dobson was he wanted to bury every left-handed hitter he faced with a slider down and in.

Well, that down-and-in slider he'd throw often went about 400 feet over the right-field wall.

So one time I took a trip out to the mound with our catcher and said to Dobson, "Look, shit-can that down-and-in slider. Throw it on the outside of the plate—a backdoor slider, okay? Because that down-and-in is going a *long* way!"

"Dobber" lived and died with that one pitch—the slider—his whole career, and threw it to hitters from both sides of the plate. He didn't like to throw the fastball, though when he did, it was effective because it surprised opposing batters who were looking slider all the way. Still, we used to say this about Dobber's repertoire on the mound: "Slider, slider, shake-off, slider."

It was just who he was—a classic breaking-ball pitcher.

Anyway, from that point on, when Dobber started using the backdoor slider against left-handers, he became a very successful pitcher for us.

The addition of Dobson and his slider made our staff tough to face because each of their pitching styles was so different. Palmer threw mostly fastballs, Cuellar loved the screwball, and McNally was your basic fastball/breaking-ball pitcher.

So we started that series with the left-handed McNally mixing his pitches to victory in Game 1 and the right-handed Palmer blowing the Bucs away in Game 2, and looked ahead to Game 3 with the southpaw Cuellar, who complemented his great screwball with a good curveball and fastball.

We felt pretty good about our prospects heading into that third game.

But then we would face a Pirates pitcher who would single-handedly turn the whole series around.

******

Steve Blass was the biggest surprise of the whole deal. Blass painted, I mean *painted*, the inside and outside corners of the plate in Game 3. I thought he was the best pitcher I had ever seen in my life. He didn't make a single bad pitch to any of us—an amazing feat in a game of that magnitude.

Blass was clearly the difference in that World Series—there's no question in my mind. He pitched an unbelievable game against us—a three-hitter—which not only ended our 16-game winning streak and feeling of invincibility, but also suddenly gave the Pirates all the momentum.

And they ran with it.

In Game 4, in the first night game in World Series history, we jumped out to a quick 3–0 lead, knocking out Pirates starter Luke Walker in the very first inning.

We forced the Pirates to turn the ball over to Bruce Kison, a little-known 21-year-old rookie with just three months of major league experience. In our viewpoint, the game had all the makings of an Orioles blowout.

But Kison was unbelievable. He had a high three-quarters and sidearm delivery and we couldn't touch him. We managed just one hit off him in six-plus innings of shutout ball, allowing the Pirates to come back and beat us 4–3 to even the series at two games apiece.

Then, in Game 5, the Pirates beat up on McNally, one of the greatest postseason pitchers of our era, with four runs early to send him to the showers in the fifth. But the story again was the Pirates' pitching, this time with Nelson Briles throwing a gem—a two-hit shutout—to put Pittsburgh a game away from taking the World Series.

Between Blass, Kison, and Briles bringing our offensive arsenal to a grinding halt, we were in a state of shock.

After those three games, we looked at each other like, *What just happened? How did we get beat by the Pirates? We have the better team.* It was like the '69 Mets all over again.

But what was most surprising to us was *how* they were beating us. Anytime you thought about the Pirates, it was about their hitting, and Clemente, and their so-called "Pittsburgh Lumber Company"—definitely not their pitching.

We were the team with the four 20-game winners, not the Pirates.

In Game 6 back in Baltimore, the Bucs would use their sixth starting pitcher of the series, Bob Moose. Moose was used primarily as a spot starter and long relief man for Pittsburgh, so we definitely had an edge by throwing Palmer, the ace of our staff, out there to face him.

With a World Series in the balance, this game was nothing short of a classic.

Moose did everything that could possibly be expected of him, pitching shutout ball into the sixth inning of a 2–0 game until we started coming back. Buford led off the bottom of the sixth with a solo shot to cut the lead in half. And then the following inning, I ripped a two-out single off Pirates closer Dave Giusti to score Belanger with the tying run to make it 2–2.

And that's where the game stood going into the bottom of the ninth inning—deadlocked in a 2–2 tie. Palmer had been tremendous, settling down after a few bumps in the early innings to give us nine strong innings.

We thought we would end the game in our half of the ninth when, with Belanger on first and two outs, Buford hit a screaming line drive off Giusti into the right-field corner. The ball caromed off the side and right-field walls back to Clemente in the middle of the warning track. As the on-deck hitter, I was standing toward the right side of the batter's box getting in position to give Belanger the signal to come home either sliding or standing up. I was anticipating a sure play at the plate.

But Clemente unleashed a missilelike one-hop throw to Sanguillen to keep Belanger at third base. It was one of the greatest throws I had ever seen an outfielder make. After Belanger and I glanced at one another in disbelief, I turned toward the Great One in right field in awe.

With runners now on second and third, I came up to the plate with a chance to win it for us. Facing Giusti for the second time following my earlier success against him in the seventh, he won this battle by inducing me to ground out to short to end our threat.

Clemente's incredible throw had given the Pirates a degree of momentum going into the 10th inning, and they seized the opportunity to build a potential series-winning rally. With Dobson now in the game for us, he surrendered a one-out single of Dave Cash. The speedster then stole second base on a strikeout to Richie Hebner to put himself in scoring position. After an intentional walk to Clemente, Earl brought in his best available southpaw—McNally—to face the dangerous left-handed slugger Stargell. But McNally walked Willie to load the bases for another fine hitter, Al Oliver.

At this point, you could have cut the tension in Memorial Stadium with a knife.

But this time McNally came through, getting Oliver to fly out to center field to end the top of the 10th with no damage done.

That set the stage for a rally of our own in our half of the 10th.

Frank worked out a one-out walk before Rettenmund followed with a single to center to put runners on the corners with Brooks coming up to hit. Then, on a 1–2 pitch, Robinson lifted a short fly ball to Vic Davilillo in center field. Davilillo positioned himself perfectly to catch the ball with all of his momentum going into his throw home. Vic fired a strong one-hopper slightly up the third-base line with Frank chugging home. The throw may have gotten him had it not bounced high off the infield grass between the mound and home plate. The hop forced Sanguillen to leave his feet to catch the ball as Frank slid beneath him to score the winning run. Our guys rushed out of the dugout to mob both Robinsons in a wild celebration.

This game—one of the greatest I was ever a part of with all its back-and-forth emotion and pressure-packed moments—would be hard to beat as far as drama went.

But, incredibly, Game 7 would prove to be just as riveting.

******

We had several things going for us entering Game 7 of the 1971 World Series.

Winning the previous game in dramatic fashion like we did meant a major letdown for the Pirates and gave us the momentum going into this one.

Cuellar was the kind of cool, calm, and collected professional you wanted pitching for you in a winner-take-all game. On the Pirates' side, Blass, by his own admission in his autobiography, *A Pirate for Life*, was "nervous as hell" and "jumpy."

For those who followed trends, each of the six previous games had been won by the home team, so with this one being in our park, how could we lose, right?

But most important of all, we were the defending champions, had been there before, and were the superior team.

Still, it would be the tensest game that I was ever a part of as a player.

Why?

Because we could still lose.

******

Cuellar would set the Pirates down in order in the top of the first, looking every bit like the pitcher who had won 20 or more games in each of the last three seasons.

Anticipating a low-scoring, tight game, we went about trying everything we could to scratch out a run in our half of the inning.

After Blass issued a leadoff walk to Buford, I stepped up to the plate and tried to interrupt the flow of the game. After working the count to 1–1, I stepped out of the box, took a long look down toward our third-base coach, Billy Hunter, took a practice swing, knocked some dirt out of my spikes, and then asked the umpire to check the baseball. All of this was done to rattle Blass because we couldn't touch him in Game 3 and my actions were intended to mess with his rhythm in this one. It seemed to work, as Blass looked a little pissed and out of his comfort zone as he walked completely off the mound and took a deep breath to collect himself.

Back in the box, I then tried bunting for a hit to the left side of the infield. I thought the way Blass' delivery and follow-through forced his momentum toward the first-base side would make it a challenge for him to field anything near the third-base line. But I popped it straight into the air, and Blass caught it easily for the first out. I may not have advanced the runner or reached base myself, but Blass still seemed a little frazzled out there.

And now we had the heart of the order coming up with Booger and Frank.

After Booger fell behind in the count 0–2, Earl got into the act of trying to get under Blass' skin by charging out of our dugout and yelling to the home-plate umpire Nestor Chylak, "8:01! 8:01! He's got to pitch on the rubber in front and not on the side!"

It was typical Earl, trying to say that Blass was cheating by pitching two or three inches off the rubber.

Of course, he most likely did it to get inside Blass' head, because whether Steve was actually on the side of the rubber or not, that wasn't our problem against him. The real problem was that he was making great pitches, with everything he threw going exactly where he wanted. He had an unbelievable slider, and a great curveball and fastball to go with it.

Maybe Earl's little tirade worked initially, as Blass' warmup pitch after the delay sailed past Sanguillen to the backstop.

But if Weaver's actions did appear to unnerve Blass, it didn't last for long, as he came right back and struck out Booger on a perfect slider. Then he lived on the black the rest of the game, getting into a groove every bit as effective as the one he had in Game 3.

Cuellar was dealing that day as well, retiring the first 11 batters he faced until Clemente, shining like the great ones often do in big games, belted a hanger for a long home run into the center-field bleachers to put the Pirates up 1–0.

In a classic pitchers' duel, the game remained that way until the eighth inning, when Jose Pagan doubled to deep left-center field to score Stargell all the way from first to extend the Pirates' lead to 2–0.

But in our half of the eighth, we started to finally break through against Blass. Hendricks and Belanger both singled to start the frame and were moved into scoring position following a sacrifice bunt from Tom Shopay, who pinch hit for Cuellar.

Earl was pacing back and forth in our dugout like he always did in these tight situations.

With the Pirates' infield playing back conceding a run, Buford ripped a sharp ground ball to Bob Robertson near the line at first base to cut the lead in half and move Belanger to third.

In what would be one of the most important at-bats of my career, it was now my turn to try to drive Mark in.

Blass' first pitch was a nasty slider, but I took it outside for ball one. Now the home crowd was really getting into it, sensing that we were in a good position to bring home that tying run just 90 feet away.

The next pitch, another slider, was on the outer part of the plate—not a bad pitch to hit—but I fouled it off on a checked swing. Blass, sticking with his slider, then put one right on the outside black of the plate to get ahead of me 1–2. I thought the pitch may have been a little outside, but when you're dealing like Blass was, the umpire is going to give you that pitch every time.

Then, perhaps thinking I was looking for another slider on the outer edge of the plate, Blass threw a good high inside fastball that really tied me up, but I was able to hold my swing to even the count at 2–2. It took a whole lot of discipline not to commit to that pitch.

Now, in the pivotal moment of the game, Blass threw me a rare "average" slider that was up and right down the middle. I grounded it deep into the whole at short and ran as hard as I could to first. But Jackie Hernandez's strong throw beat me by half a step, and Pittsburgh held on to its one-run edge.

We held serve in the top of the ninth by using two of our 20-game winners—Dobson and McNally—in relief for the second game in a row, albeit not without some drama. Stargell, who had 48 home runs that season, could have busted the game open with two outs and two runners on base, but McNally got him to ground out to me at second base to put out the fire.

Blass remained out there for the ninth inning with no relievers warming up in their bullpen—it was clearly his game to win or lose. We had our big bats coming up in the ninth—Booger, Frank, and Rettenmund. It didn't get any better than this.

During Booger's at-bat, he put a charge into a looping curveball, but was way out in front of it and pulled it foul. If he could have stayed back on it, we may have had a tie game. But, instead, after working the count to 2–2, he bounced out to Dave Cash at second for the first out.

That brought up Frank in what would turn out to be the last plate appearance of his storied six-year stint in Baltimore. And this at-bat brought to mind what my friend Ted Williams used to say— "You get a good pitch to hit once a game—don't miss it."

Well, Frank got one.

Blass hung a slider to Frank right over the heart of the plate—a mistake pitch—but he got under it and popped up to Hernandez in short left field for the second out. Baseball is a game of inches, and Robinson could have just as easily planted that one into the left-field bleachers as pop up like he did.

That left matters up to Rettenmund, who may not have had the power that Booger and Frank had, but was a .300 hitter with some pop. Blass stayed with the slider to get ahead 0–1. Merv then bounced the next pitch—yet another slider—past Blass in what appeared off the bat like it could be a single to center field. But Hernandez moved to his left, fielded the ball from the outfield grass, and got Merv by half a step at first to end our dreams of winning back-to-back world championships.

Blass, an emotional guy, immediately went crazy as he was swarmed by his teammates in celebration. The adulation was well deserved, because he turned in an unbelievable pitching performance. Clemente was named the MVP of the series, but it easily could have been Blass.

And that made what happened to him a couple of years later all the more incredible.

Prior to a spring training game in Bradenton, I watched in bewilderment as Blass couldn't throw the ball anywhere near the plate. Here was a guy who went from "painting" in the most crucial games in the world against us in the '71 Series—just lights out—to literally not being able to throw the ball inside a batting cage. I thought, *How can this happen?*

It was the worst case of the "yips" I've ever seen—just a terrible thing.

I couldn't help but think after his malady really took hold, *How in the hell did this guy beat us? Look at him now.*

******

Despite our supremacy in the American League during the regular season and playoffs from '69 through '71—a three-year level of dominance not seen since the great Yankees teams of the late 1920s—it was horrible losing to the Mets and even worse coming up short against the Pirates.

I mean, how do you lose with four 20-game winners? You've got to be kidding me!

We should have won all three years—no question in my mind.

As great as we were, it just seemed like everything in the world was against us in both of those World Series that we lost. As a player on a team like the Orioles had, you expected to win every time you took the field. But amazing things can happen in a best-of-seven series. With today's wild-card and divisional series, that may seem like a lot of games, but a true measure of a club's worth is over a 162-game season.

Still, despite the one championship, we had a lot to be proud of.

The American League had some great teams during our reign that we had to overcome just to make it to the World Series. Incredibly, we never lost an ALCS game—sweeping the Twins of Rod Carew and Harmon Killebrew in '69 and '70, and then the rising, young Oakland A's of Reggie Jackson, Gene Tenace, and Catfish Hunter in '71, who were on the verge of their own dynasty. And that's not to mention holding off other great organizations like the Detroit Tigers of Al Kaline and Mickey Lolich.

When you can beat teams like those, nothing daunts you. You kind of feel bulletproof.

That's why losing the two World Series like we did shocked us so much.

And we couldn't possibly have realized it at the time, but after losing to the Pirates, our collection of elite players would never again return to the World Series.

The '71 World Series would mark the end of an Orioles dynasty.

ten

November 30, 1972:
The End of an Era

"SHIT! IT'S LIKE COMING to the park every day and opening a box of Cracker Jack!" I shouted after checking the lineup card tacked to the clubhouse wall before a midseason game. "You *never* know what the fuck is going to be in it!"

And it was true. Only Booger and Brooks were fixtures. Nobody else ever knew in '72.

Earl got wind of what I said and wasn't pleased. The next day he held a closed-door team meeting.

Weaver ranted and raved for about 15 minutes, all the while directing his ire my way—looking right at me by my locker.

"Come to play every fuckin' day, *blah, blah, blah*! I make the fuckin' lineup, *blah, blah, blah*!"

He was just chastising me in front of everyone, but had every right to do so. Weaver wasn't going to allow one of his players, especially one who was hitting .220 like I was at the time of my outburst, to get away with what I did. Earl had to maintain control of the clubhouse.

But I was frustrated. I kept trying to tell him I wasn't well, that my shoulder was a mess. But he wouldn't accept that.

When I'd tell him, "Play Grich. I can't cut it. He's better than I am. I'm hurt," he would always say something like, "You're fine. You hit this guy good. You're playing."

I would actually get upset that he wouldn't play Grich because, first and foremost, I wanted to win. But what was even more painful, considering how close I was with Earl, was how he didn't believe me. That hurt me more than anything.

Still, I didn't harbor any ill feelings towards Earl. How could I? Earl and I were good friends going all the way back to my time in the minor leagues when we took ground balls together at short. Besides, he was the best manager I've ever seen. Later on, when I became a manager, I wanted to be just like him, especially with how he superbly used his bench and bullpen—always the keys to successful managing. I owe a lot to him in making me a good manager because I saw how great he was.

I also understood that part of any learning process was to go through both good times and bad times.

The team was going through a transitional period in '72. Frank had been traded to the Dodgers prior to the season. Our rich farm system continued feeding the big-league club—promoting future stars such as Grich, Donnie Baylor, and Al Bumbry that season. Young Johnny Oates was now getting the bulk of playing time behind the plate ahead of Elrod Hendricks and Andy Etchebarren.

As a result, we were playing the role of contender for most of the year and were no longer a team capable of running away with the pennant like we had the previous three seasons. In fact, we held the narrowest of margins within the division chase. Up until the final weekend of the season, we had never been in first place by more than two games or out of it by more than four. We were a part of an extremely tight four-team race in the AL East with the Red Sox, Yankees, and Tigers. In the end, Detroit would clinch the title over Boston on the second-to-last day of the campaign.

To say it was the most frustrating season I ever had in the big leagues would be an understatement. Following the '71 World Series, I put a batting cage up in my backyard to see if the extra swings could help me overcome my shoulder problems and rediscover my stroke. Then, once the season started, I continued getting examined by team doctors, with all of them telling me nothing was wrong.

The pain never alleviated. I could barely swing the bat because my left arm continued to collapse. And nobody, including myself, knew how to fix it.

My average and power were a shell of what they had in the previous season's first half. By year's end, I hadn't been productive in more than a season and a half.

Now the doubts started entering my head. Was I going to be successful again? At 29 years old, was I done?

To be honest, I thought I was through with baseball.

I finished the '72 campaign with a meager .221 batting average and just five home runs. I scheduled a meeting with Frank Cashen.

"Look, I'm done. My career is over." I told him. "I can't swing the bat. I don't think I can play anymore because my shoulder's been bad all the time. Besides, you have Grich—he's a hell of a player. You should trade me—see if you can get any value back."

Then I added a caveat.

"All I ask is that you trade me to the National League."

You may think the reason for that request was so I wouldn't have to play against my beloved Orioles. But it wasn't that at all.

It was because I really liked the aggressive style of play in the Senior Circuit. I thought they played the kind of baseball that I wanted to play. Even though I was hurt, I wanted to go over there and be a part of it because at that point in time, it was a better brand of baseball than what was happening in the American League. They played hit-and-run, stole bases, and did all kinds of things better than what we did in our league.

And I figured that if this might be the last year of my career, then let me go over to the National League and at least see what it's like.

Frank said he would try his best for me.

Coming off the season I had, I honestly didn't think the Orioles would get much for me—if anything at all.

But then an offer came in from the Atlanta Braves. They offered Frank power-hitting catcher Earl Williams—a slugger who had belted 61 home runs over the previous two seasons—and a minor leaguer for me, Dobson, Oates, and Roric Harrison.

On the surface, it appeared to be a steal of a deal for the Orioles. I told Frank, "Do it. Trade me."

My heart may have been with the Orioles—no question about it—but I also wanted to help the team. It really pleased me to find out they could get a good player in return for me. The Braves were probably hoping I could be a semblance of the player I had been at the All-Star break in '71.

So it happened. On November 30, 1972, I was no longer a part of the only organization I had ever known, ending a decadelong association with the Baltimore Orioles. Grich would replace me at second base just as I had replaced Jerry Adair—life goes on.

I knew the thing I would miss the most was the family-type environment created by Orioles owner Jerry Hoffberger. Jerry was the greatest owner in the world—all the others I played or managed under took a back seat to him. It wasn't like he gave us raises or big contracts, but we partied together and genuinely held great affection for one another. We would have run through walls for the guy.

As for all the success in Baltimore—the four pennants and two world championships—it was a phenomenal feat, though when you're living it like I was, it didn't feel remarkable at all. We simply expected winning to happen. So when we lost those two World Series and then didn't make the playoffs in '72, we couldn't believe it.

Did it feel like the end of an era for Orioles baseball?

I wasn't so sure.

But I definitely felt it was the end of *my* era.

| eleven |

September 19, 1973: Chasing Mr. Hornsby

"YOU'LL BE LUCKY IF you hit *15* home runs next year!" crotchety old Astros manager Leo "the Lip" Durocher shouted out at me during batting practice.

"And you'll be lucky if you're still in the fucking game, Leo!" I shot back.

It was the second-to-last game of the 1973 season. Nobody could believe I had hit 43 home runs with the Braves. After all, I had never hit more than 18 in a season and was coming off the worst year of my career.

I was one behind Willie Stargell for the National League home run title and, with two games left to play, thought I had a decent shot to catch him.

But the vengeful Leo didn't forget what I had said to him. Houston was having a rough season and my comment obviously stung.

So in the fifth inning of a blowout with us leading 7–0, he had his pussy left-hander Jerry Reuss smoke me with a fastball to the left shoulder, leaving a welt the size of a baseball and injuring it to the point where I really couldn't swing the bat in those final two games.

While I blame Leo for costing me my chance at the home run crown, I wouldn't take back what I said to incite him. I was always a little cocky. I figured he did what he felt he had to do and I did what I wanted to do. Besides, he insulted me first.

As it turned out, Leo and I were both right. I didn't hit but 15 home runs the next year and he was out of baseball for good.

But to be honest, I wasn't even thinking much about leading the league in homers in '73. Being a math major, I know numbers. But personal goals were never important to me. It's the same way today. When Brian Dozier recently came close to breaking my record for most home runs by a second baseman, I was rooting for him to do it. Records are made to be broken. Dozier looks like a great kid—definitely better-looking than me! I honestly thought, *Man, I hope he does it*. But he fell a few short.

St. Louis Cardinals manager Red Schoendienst was another doubter who tried to ride me.

He once shouted from the bench, "You wouldn't be hitting all these homers if you weren't playing in the 'Launching Pad!'" That was a reference to all the dingers hit in Atlanta. It was a foolish statement, as I was a pull hitter and it was deeper down the lines in Fulton County Stadium than Baltimore's Memorial Stadium.

"I hit more home runs on the road than any of your guys hit all year, asshole!" I shot back.

And I wasn't lying. Their top guys—Joe Torre and Ted Simmons—would both end the season with just 13 homers against the 18 I hit on the road. And he's criticizing me?

I was never a fan of Schoendienst and I assume he didn't like me, either.

But whether it was Red or my "buddy" Leo, when somebody says something that I think is erroneous, or has no reason to create their point of view, I point it out to them. I sometimes don't do it in the most proper manner, but that's part of who I am.

Maybe the reason I got fired five times was because I never shied away from telling people what I thought. And the reaction was often "Adios, Johnson." But that was fine with me, because I always did my best.

******

Almost immediately after my trade to Atlanta, I was examined by the Braves' head trainer, Dave Pursley, who saved my career. He confirmed what I always knew—there was a major problem with my left shoulder.

Pursley sent me to Dr. Jacobs, a specialist in the type of injury I had.

"You've got a subluxed left shoulder," Pursley reported back to me. "You have stretched all the tendons in that shoulder. The only way to fix it is for you to do isometric exercises to put pressure against it. And for the time being, try not to lift your arm over your head."

The isometric exercises were fairly simple. One was to lean against my car door at about a 45-degree angle and push as hard as I could. And when I was home, every time I got near a wall, I would do the same thing. Then, after I reported to spring training, Pursley had pulleys set up for me to work out with. The goal was to build up the outside part of my injured shoulder.

It was working and I was getting better.

Then, in mid-April during a game in San Diego, while taking a swing in my first at-bat, I felt something break loose, like I had broken some adhesions—internal scar tissue—in my bad shoulder, and I felt completely cured.

I ended up going 4-for-4 in that game.

Continuing to feel better and stronger than ever, in mid-May I made a friendly wager with my teammate Darrell Evans, who came storming out of the gates that season with some big numbers. The bet was to see which of us would have more home runs, more RBIs, and the higher batting average at the end of the year. Whoever took at least two out of the three categories would win.

"Give me the difference in RBIs (Evans had eight more than me then) and we'll bet who comes out on top," I told him. "The loser has to buy dinner for four with limo service in New York."

"Sure, sure," Evans said. "You've got it!"

And why wouldn't he take the bet?

At the time, Evans had nine home runs to my five and our averages were about the same. It was a lay down for him—he was an established power hitter who already had a four-home-run lead on me.

Of course, that's when I went on a tear for the balance of the season, finishing with 43 home runs to his 41 and 99 RBIs to his 104. But remember, he handicapped me eight RBIs, so I beat him in both of those categories. So in spite of his having a slightly higher batting average, I won by taking two out of three.

I'm still waiting for that dinner, but it doesn't matter. It was a fun bet.

Evans and I were a part of the best offensive team I ever played with.

We had Ralph Garr, an unbelievable leadoff hitter who would win a batting title in '74 when he hit .353. He was the only hitter I have ever seen in my life who could hit absolutely any pitch with authority—high, low, inside, or outside. It didn't matter. I recall him once hitting a ball neck-high on the outside of the plate and curving it back fair. I had never seen that before. And he was extremely fast, easily our best base-stealer.

We had other guys, such as Dusty Baker and Mike Lum, who hit for average and power. Hitting became contagious on our ballclub because nobody wanted to be left behind.

But when I think back to that '73 Braves team and our offense, it truly all started with Hank Aaron.

It was like Aaron wrote the script for what he wanted to do on a baseball field. I'm not just talking about his hitting, as he was also an outstanding outfielder and base runner—just so instinctual. I was fortunate enough to have my locker next to his in Atlanta. If you didn't learn from watching how he prepared for and played the game, you couldn't learn anything.

Hank was just so dignified. I can only remember one time he ever got mad at me. He was away from his locker and I changed the channel on his stereo. When he came back he got all over me about it. Right then and there, I knew I would never do that again. He simply commanded respect and it was an honor to be his teammate.

In some ways, Aaron's leadership was similar to Frank Robinson's in that they both led by example.

With Hank, I knew from day one of spring training that he was different from any other superstar I had ever played with. At 39 years old, he was still working as hard at his game as a rookie trying to make the club. And it paid off, of course, with Aaron hitting 40 home runs at that late stage of his career.

With Aaron, Evans, and I hitting 40 or more home runs, it marked the first time that three teammates had ever done it in the same season.

But it almost didn't happen.

The Braves wanted the buildup of Aaron breaking Babe Ruth's all-time home run record to drag on as long as possible because it was very good for business. I remember one time after Aaron hit a home run late in the '73 season he was taken out of the game. The Braves didn't even want him playing every day near the end of the season because they wanted to promote Aaron's chase over the winter to sell more tickets.

But with two games left and Hank sitting on 39 for the season, he just needed one more homer to give the three of us—Aaron, Evans, and myself—the record. I was never into personal records, but Evans badly wanted Hank to hit No. 40 and persuaded him to play in the final two games.

"Look, you've got to play," Darrell told Hank. "You have to play because no three guys have ever hit 40 together in one year."

It didn't take Aaron long to comply with Evans' wishes, as he hit his 40th home run in his third at-bat of the afternoon—just two batters before Reuss beaned me in the final Saturday game of the year—to give us the record. It was his 713th of his career, leaving Hank one shy of Ruth. He didn't homer the next day, so the Braves got their wish and could promote the hell out of Aaron for the next six months.

Aaron's performance that weekend made Evans and the Braves very happy.

******

One of the things I really enjoyed about playing with the Braves was how they allowed us all to be more individualistic as hitters. I loved playing under Eddie Mathews. He was an aggressive manager who encouraged us to swing the bat. He almost always gave us the green light—swinging on 3–0 was the norm. And there were no trick plays like the bunt-and-run and run-and-hit like we had in Baltimore. We could just go up there and grip-and-rip, which was very different from the way Weaver managed.

Mathews was a player's manager. One example of this was how he hated spring training exhibition games every bit as much as his players. He just found them to be painfully mundane. In fact, he'd be hammered for some of them.

As the '73 season marched on and I was on my home run surge, I had a bizarre night in which I fought not one, but two of my teammates—one of whom was Mathews.

Eddie was playing me every game through the dog days of summer. He kept coming to me nearly every day, saying, "Don't worry, I know you need a day off. Tomorrow, I promise."

Then I would hit a home run—staying hot—and, sure as shit, the next day I was back in the lineup.

This went on for weeks, with Mathews never keeping his promises of an off day.

In one of those instances, we were playing in Philadelphia a day after I had homered the previous game. I was, of course, in the lineup, but this time went 0-for-4 with three strikeouts. I went back to my room all pissed off. Around midnight, my roommate, Mike Lum, started banging on the door, waking me up from my sleep.

"Where's your fucking key?" I asked as I let him in, not in any mood for this shit.

Lum pushed me in the chest, and I just snapped, smoking him real good with a right hook.

Before long, half the team heard all the commotion and came rushing into our room. Pursley got on top of me and pinned me down.

"No problem! No problem!" I shouted to everybody. "I'm leaving. I'm getting another room. Lum, you can stay. No big deal! I'm going to get me another room!"

I went down to the front desk and got a key for the new room. On my way there, I ran into Mathews.

"Come on, let's go back to your room," Eddie said.

"No, no, Eddie, I have a new room now."

"No, Davey, we're going back to your room."

I had no idea why it was so important to Eddie to bring me back to my original room. It was very confusing and I still don't have an explanation why. We got there and Lum was just as baffled as I was.

Eddie shut the door behind us and says, "Okay, Davey, let's get this over with. Hit me!"

"Hit *you*? I'm not hitting *you*. You're my *manager*."

"No, Davey, let's go. *Hit* me!"

So I softly punched him in the chest with my left hand.

Eddie then cocked his left fist and I gave him the biggest haymaker I had in the world with my right hand—knocking him clear over the fucking bed. I just hit him with everything I had.

Now you can imagine how all hell broke loose. The door burst open and half the team was back to break it up. Pursley again restrained me, this time sitting on me.

Mathews was screaming at the top of his lungs, "Let me up! Let me up!"

I exclaimed, "Let him up! I ain't waiting on this ass kicking! Let's go! *Right now!*"

After a few moments, cooler heads prevailed and, believe it or not, Eddie and I went back to his room and drank an entire bottle of Crown Royal, and that was the end of it.

Mathews said the reason he wanted to clear the air was because he thought I was pissed with him about hitting me fifth or sixth in the lineup instead of higher up.

I said, "No, I was pissed off because 10 times you said I was going to have the next day off and I kept playing after hitting home runs. Then last night I went 0-for-4. That's why I was pissed. I don't give a shit where you hit me in the lineup."

After getting shit-faced with Mathews, I don't even know what room I slept in.

Times were different then. We were gamers. We physically expressed our emotions. You fought and it was over and done with. No hard feelings. Nobody stayed mad. Not Lum. Not Eddie. Not me. That was the deal.

Still, to this day, I feel bad about clocking a guy whom I loved. He may have had a little problem handling the pitching staff—that wasn't his strong suit. But as far as managing us every-day players, he was great.

What's kind of funny about the whole incident was how, near the end of his life, Eddie told a friend, "If I could change one thing, it would be to have just one more chance to kick Davey Johnson's fucking ass!"

That was his dying wish!

******

After my 30th home run of the season, a funny thing was going on back in Baltimore. On the Fan-O-Gram scoreboard at Memorial

Stadium, they actually started tracking my home runs.

It would display stuff like, DAVEY JOHNSON JUST HIT HOME RUN No. ...

This, of course, didn't sit well with the Orioles' front office, but I found it amusing, mostly because my kids had been born there and it's where I grew up and learned to play the game of baseball. I also thought it was great that my old fans were still going to be hearing about me. And so would many of my former teammates who knew the whole scenario I had gone through the year before. But mostly, I was just happy to be healthy again.

Equally satisfying, however, was how the guy they traded me for was driving Weaver nuts. I plead guilty to a little bit of schadenfreude.

Earl Williams was a former Rookie of the Year with power, but wasn't exactly setting the world on fire now that he was in Baltimore. The biggest problem, I heard, was that he wasn't a team player. When I was there, it was a family. We all got together. We all got along. I was told through the grapevine that Williams didn't get along well with others, that he was a complainer. The Orioles had a sense he wasn't a good guy when they traded for him, but were seduced by all those home runs he hit.

So, combine the troubles they were having with Williams with the year I was having, and I knew it was just killing them. And I loved every minute of it. It made me grin the whole year. I was just as happy as a clam.

To be fair, I never blamed the Orioles for not diagnosing my shoulder injury. We have a long schedule and you play with injuries. And, to their credit, they kept sending me to all these doctors who would tell them they couldn't find anything wrong. So, naturally, the team thought I was complaining about some injury that didn't exist.

My only beef with Earl was his not believing me when I told him I was hurting. We had a long history together and he should have trusted me. He should have realized that there was a good reason why I went from hitting 16 home runs in the first half of '71 to getting injured and going straight downhill. But he wasn't the only one. Nobody there believed me.

So there was definitely a degree of satisfaction when I was able to express the talent that I knew I always had in Atlanta by hitting all those home runs.

Did it drive me?

You bet it did.

******

Rogers Hornsby was an idol of mine. He was arguably the greatest right-handed hitter who ever lived. And late in the '73 season, I was chasing his 51-year-old record for most home runs hit in a season by a second baseman.

I wanted to break it. And I wanted to do it within 154 games, the same number of games they played back in Hornsby's day. I wasn't even concerned if I hit one after the 154th because I didn't think it would be fair to break his record in more games.

On September 19, in our 154th game of the year, we were playing before a crowd of around 40,000 fans at Dodger Stadium. Many of them had come out to see if Hank Aaron could add to his total of 711 home runs, but were disappointed by his or, more likely, the club's, decision for him to take the night off. So the fans had to settle for watching me try to surpass Hornsby's mark of 42 home runs by a second baseman.

I was seeing the ball real well as I faced off against Andy Messersmith in the top of the fourth inning with two outs and no one on in a scoreless game. I would work the count full before Messersmith threw me a splitter, which I hit into the Dodgers' left-field bullpen for my record-breaking 43rd homerun of the season.

Or so I thought.

What I didn't realize was that since one of my home runs had come as a pinch-hitter, I was actually now tied with Hornsby for the most dingers while playing second base.

This kind of pissed me off a little because when I hit the home run, I thought I was in sole possession of the record. I thought I had made history. But at least the 43 still gave me the most ever by a player whose primary position in a season was at second. And that mark still stands today.

I wouldn't homer again in our season's final seven games, but the 43 I did hit easily helped make that the best statistical year of my career. If I put up those kinds of numbers today, a lot of people probably would think I was on something. But I wasn't. I just knew how to hit the long ball and was healthy again.

I would receive the Comeback Player of the Year Award following the season. But my true rewards were accomplishing what I thought I was capable of doing and the joy of performing at a high level.

That's all the reward I ever needed.

twelve

April 8, 1974: Hammerin' Hank

IT SHOULD HAVE BEEN a glorious time.

But it wasn't nearly as glorious as it should have been for a man about to break the all-time home run record. Not for Henry Aaron. And not for his teammates.

We felt for Henry. That's what teammates do.

Aaron was a private man. He never shared any of the racist hate mail that came his way by the shoeboxful. Nor did he tell us about the death threats that he received. He never complained about anything. But we all knew what was going on. Henry was playing the hand he was dealt.

And I should know as well as anyone—my locker was right next to his.

During that time, there was a lot of pressure on Aaron. A lot of people didn't want a black man breaking a white man's hallowed record—particularly in the deep South. When we were on the road, Henry would register under an assumed name because of all the hateful calls he would receive. And in some cities, when callers would still manage to get through, he would sometimes stay at a different hotel from the club.

As his teammates, because we knew what he was going through, his home run chase was definitely a distraction because we wanted it over and done with as quickly as possible. We felt that once he hit No. 715, it would eliminate the pressure in his daily life. When you have teammates, you get to know them, you're close to them, you love them, and you know what their struggles are.

We began the season in Cincinnati, which back in those days was always the venue of the first major league game of the season. Henry wasted no time tying Ruth's record, connecting off Reds pitcher Jack Billingham in the top of the first inning for No. 714.

The game was stopped so vice president Gerald Ford, commissioner Bowie Kuhn, and Braves principal owner William Bartholomay could give short speeches commemorating the historic moment.

Aaron's was even shorter.

After thanking Ford, Kuhn, and Bartholomay, with little emotion, Henry said, "I'm just glad it's almost over with."

Aaron would sit out the second game but would begrudgingly play the third, forced to do so because Kuhn insisted he play two out of the three in Cincinnati. The commissioner felt it was in the best interests of baseball, while Henry badly wanted to break the record before the home fans in Atlanta. By going hitless in the third game, he would get his chance.

The atmosphere for our home opener, played before a sellout crowd and a nationally televised audience on Monday, April 8, 1974, against the Dodgers, was electric. And when Aaron came up to the plate in the top of the second, you could have cut the tension with a knife. The cheers for Henry were deafening. But after drawing a walk, the boos directed at Los Angeles pitcher Al Downing were almost as loud.

Aaron would come to bat again in the top of the fourth. He was in his usual cleanup spot in the batting order and I was hitting sixth. So being on double-deck, I had a front-row seat to history.

Downing bounced the first pitch, which again drew the ire of the home fans. But the next pitch was up and over the heart of the plate. Aaron drove it deep over the left-center-field fence and into the Braves' bullpen for No. 715. Fireworks erupted above Fulton County Stadium and a grand celebration began as Henry circled the bases.

As Aaron was rounding second, two young white men who had run onto the field hugged him from each side. With all the threats Henry received leading up to the record-breaking home run, he would have been justified to believe they didn't have the best intentions. But for some reason, none of us thought there was legitimate concern for Aaron's safety. Everyone in the stadium that night just seemed to feel so wonderful. Those two just wanted to jump on the field and embrace him. I'm sure they were prosecuted, but I don't know if either of them confessed to anything other than just wanting to touch the greatest home run hitter in baseball.

Plus, anyone who's been around baseball a long time knows there have always been idiots who run onto the field. To be honest, I'm surprised there weren't at least 20 fans on the field running around the bases with Henry.

By the time he touched home plate, there was no issue. All of his exuberant teammates were there to greet him. To a man, we felt tremendous relief for Aaron, believing that, at last, he wouldn't have all that pressure on him for matters having nothing to do with playing the game of baseball.

In the years since, Henry has always remained classy. He was never a complainer. To my knowledge, the greatest home run hitter of all time may have received just one commercial opportunity—with Magnavox—and he probably didn't make near the money he should have made in doing it.

I don't think he's bitter about anything that ever happened to him—even today.

******

Despite the good vibes that came from Henry surpassing Ruth's record, I was having underlying issues with Braves management—first with Mathews and then later with Clyde King, his replacement after he was fired midseason.

Against my wishes, the club wanted to me to split my time between second and first base. I had led the league in errors at second base in '73 after having just six the year before, but there was a good reason for that—the infield at Fulton County Stadium was the worst I've ever seen.

It was so bad I actually went to the general manager, Eddie Robinson, early in '73.

"We get a lot of rain here and you have the ground crew—*city employees!*—put this Diamond Dry on the infield. Then they drag the infield, roll it, and put calcined clay on top. I understand it's to suck up the water, but it's making the dirt like concrete. Nobody can catch a ball in this friggin' infield. I hear all this stuff about defense, but more bad habits are formed playing on a rock pile like this than anyone can overcome. You've *got* to do something about this."

I didn't stop there, getting more animated.

"Furthermore, look behind home plate," I said. "Look up against the wall. What are those? Those are *weeds*! We call them *weeds*! They haven't even gotten rid of them. Just fix the infield. What you've got to do is have George Toma from Kansas City come in and show the ground crew how it's done."

Toma is not just a legendary groundskeeper in Major League Baseball, but has also been the head groundskeeper in every Super Bowl since the beginning.

I went on.

"Your ground crew doesn't listen to me," I said, my voice rising. "Why don't *you* listen, either? For a $15 million organization, we've got a 10-cent infield. *Call* Toma. He'll show your city employees how to fix an infield because this is *horseshit!*"

I had great hands and was a Gold Glove infielder. You don't just go from six errors to 30 for no reason. In Atlanta, balls would take wicked hops and hit me in the forehead, while others hit soft spots that I would have to collapse on. There would be balls thrown to first base that would hit the ground and go straight up in the air. Other times they would just go *poof* and hug the ground.

But Robinson didn't listen and shot back, "I'm more concerned with your hitting then I am with your defense." Which, of course, made no sense.

So while I was platooning at first base with Mike Lum, Marty Perez moved over from shortstop to play the majority of games at second base.

When I read the writing on the wall during spring training in '74, I didn't want a big beef with Mathews. I told Eddie, "Trade me. I don't want to finish my career platooning."

And the club did listen.

In fact, I was pretty sure I was headed to the Yankees. One of the New York beat writers, Maury Allen, wrote that I would be traded to the Yankees for left-handed pitcher Fritz Peterson. It made sense—the Yankees needed an upgrade for Horace Clarke at second and the Braves needed pitching. But for some reason, the trade never came off.

So I had to learn how to play first base. Nobody helped me. I had grown up as a shortstop and then learned how to play second base from Mazeroski and Richardson. But I was left on my own this time to learn a new position. It was easy to catch the ball, throw the ball to second, toss it to the pitcher covering first, or know when to play behind the runner. The toughest thing about it was learning the footwork when the ball was hit to the left or right side of the infield. You couldn't always judge quickly enough if you should have the left or right foot on the bag.

Ready or not, I started my first game at my new position in May in San Diego. We turned three double plays in the infield and I hit two home runs.

I thought, *Maybe playing some first won't be so bad.*

But then just a month later, while playing first in a game against the Mets at Shea Stadium, my old high school "buddy" from San Antonio—Jerry Grote—ran over my vulnerable, outstretched leg at first base, tearing a ligament. I would have to tape up the injured leg for the rest of the year, and kept trying to play on it, but it was a challenge to hit with any authority. I couldn't really do much more than play first base. So after hitting 43 home runs the year before, I hit just 15 that season.

It was not a good time in my career.

******

Thankfully, baseball was just a part of my life, and not all of it. I had other personal and business interests, as well.

For starters, I often combined two of my loves—flying and golf—during the off-season. I owned a Cessna 182 that I kept near my Florida home at Sanford Airport. I would often hop in my little 1950 Mercedes 190SL, put my clubs in the back, drive to the airport, and fly my plane to play a round of golf with good friends at favorite spots like the Bahamas or New Smyrna. And as a scratch golfer, I flew to and participated in a good number of tournaments as well. Then I would get a ride back to my plane, fly back to Sanford, and drive home.

I learned to fly in San Antonio when I was 19. I'll never forget my first solo flight in a little Cessna 150. I was up there for a while and my instructor radioed me to keep going. Another 10 minutes went by before I called him and exclaimed, "Shit, I'm 20 miles from the airport. I'm coming back! This is my first flight! I can't take this anymore!"

That was pretty scary, but with that experience behind me, I was off and running.

I stopped flying about 30 years ago after a legitimate close call. I landed my plane down in West Palm Beach and this woman was coming right in with me in a Citabria—a single-engine, two-seat, high- and low-wing plane.

I got out of my plane and said, "Hey, how about taking me for a ride in that?"

She said, "Sure."

With the Citabria, a common stunt is to go up 5,000 feet, put it in a little spin, recover, and then do a 360-degree loop. The woman did it perfectly. She then showed me how to do it.

I said, "I'm taking it back up. I want to do this!"

I got the plane up to 5,000 feet, put it in a spiral, and recovered it, but while I began my 360-degree loop, either I didn't have enough gas or my loop was too big. Right at the top of the apex of the 360, we started falling tail down. The plane wasn't doing anything but dropping. I was starting to think I should go for my parachute when, at about just *500 feet*, the plane finally broke and I was able to pull it back up and land it safely.

I got out of the plane and apologized to the woman for all the excitement. Then I went my way, she went hers. Once I got home, I called the airport and said, "You can sell my plane. I think I'm done."

I learned something about myself that day—I was just too much of a risk taker. So I quit flying. But every so often I think about getting my medical exam done and going back up with a plane to fly, but my wife, Susan, doesn't want me doing it. I'm pretty screwed up, aren't I?

On the business side, by this point in my baseball career, I was earning more money off the field than on it. I invested in real estate—anything from hotels to ranches to shopping centers to race tracks. I even took over the note on a 170-acre plot of land on an island from an investor in financial stress—22 acres of which were considered commercial. I would sell those 22 acres to Walmart six years later for $1.5 million.

My philosophy was to not have to work hard for every dollar I earned.

Around this time, one of my partners was my uncle, John Gurtler, a brilliant man despite his telling me he only had a sixth-grade education. His speculative nature was incredible. He once built 93 apartments, which he had painted pink, on the north side of Lake Ivanhoe in Florida. But it wasn't easy. He was originally denied a loan by a bank to build the complex—they told him it was too far out of town. So he went to an insurance company that granted him the loan he needed.

Well, those apartments are located in an area that has now become the center of Orlando. So my uncle's instincts were obviously right on the money.

Knowing I had already done some real estate deals of my own, he came to me with the proposition of buying 100 units in a minority section of Orlando and another 20 units in Parramore, the roughest part of town.

"Here's the deal," he told me. "I'm buying them from a foreclosure bank and I want you to manage them. You won't get paid as a manager, but will be a co-owner with me."

"Okay," I said, "I can do it."

As part of the deal, I also traded some property I already owned to Uncle John for my portion.

It turned out to be a giant headache. There were all kinds of problems. I had to go to court all the time. People wouldn't pay their rent, so I had to throw them out. There were fires. One time there was a dead person in the pool of the complex.

I reached my breaking point.

"I'm selling," I told Uncle John. "I can't deal with this anymore."

So exactly one year and a day after we paid $800,000 for both complexes, I found an interested buyer who offered $1,250,000 for them. I countered with $1,400,000. He accepted my offer.

Uncle John and I split the profit.

I told him I would never do another investment like that one. I was lucky I got out of that one alive!

I parlayed that investment into another, this time purchasing a

72-unit hotel near Orlando that I named Davey Johnson's Second Sack, which you can imagine provided some comedy from my teammates with the double meaning. When Uncle John wanted a piece of that, I traded him properties in exchange for his investment.

When he died not long after that venture, he was worth about $20 million. A devout Christian, he never spent much of his wealth on himself. Instead, after his death, he bequeathed most of his fortune to a charity in a faraway country. And I knew even before he died that that was his intention.

My Uncle John was a great man. I loved him and learned a great deal from him. As a lasting tribute in part due to his influence on me, I'm still involved in real estate dealings today.

thirteen

April 11, 1975:
Sayonara

"SHOULD I GET MY leg operated on?" I asked Braves trainer Dave Pursley after playing through pain the reminder of the '74 season with my torn ligament.

"Oh no," he assured me. "If you don't use it and just relax, in two months it will be fine."

I took Pursley's advice while trade rumors that included my name swirled during the off-season.

After the Braves acquired slugger Dick Allen from the Chicago White Sox for just $5,000 and a player to be named later, there was much talk about my being that player. And it made sense for both teams. Aaron had been traded to the Brewers the month before, which left me as the highest-paid player on the club. The Braves would want to shed payroll after obtaining Allen, who was making $200,000 a season, a huge salary at that time. And the White Sox would want a frontline player for Allen. It didn't take a mental giant to figure out I was the prime candidate to be traded.

However, I was spared from going to Chicago, as that player to be named later would turn out to be a young catcher named Jim

Essian. While things weren't exactly great in Atlanta for me at that time, I didn't want to go to the White Sox. I had other American League teams in mind.

Still, I had the feeling it was just a matter of time before I was gone. I wasn't getting along at all with Clyde King, who was very hard to talk to and wasn't interested in where I wanted or didn't want to play.

The ensuing spring training, when King again wanted to platoon me at first base, I asked Eddie Robinson to trade me. To its credit, the club granted me permission to talk with other teams for which I would be interested in playing.

However, by the end of spring training, no trade had been worked out.

But an interesting conversation took place prior to our breaking camp. We played an exhibition game against the Tokyo Giants and their general manager, Roy Saeki, a smart and good man who spoke English well, approached me prior to the game, knowing full well my predicament.

"Would you like to come to Japan?" Saeki asked me.

"That might interest me," I told him. "I always like new challenges."

Aside from the great Sadaharu Oh, the Giants were a small-ball kind of team. I was confident if I went over there that I could provide the pop their new manager, Shigeo Nagashima—the recently retired superstar who was godlike in Japan—was now looking for in changing the dynamic of their offense. It was an interesting opportunity to ponder, as I would potentially become the first non-Japanese player to ever play for the Giants.

So I kept that option in the back of my head.

The major league season would begin with a black cloud hovering over me. I was in a state of discontent over not starting the first three games against Houston in the Astrodome. In the third game of that opening series, the Astros sent a young J.R. Richard—who had *nasty* stuff—to the hill. But I never got to face him, instead coming up as a pinch-hitter to bat against Dave Roberts in relief. I ripped an RBI double off him in what would turn out to be my one and only at-bat for the Braves that season.

Upset over not starting, I went off on management.

"Sell me, trade me—just get me the hell out of here," I told Robinson. "You guys are *idiots!*"

I could force the issue and address Eddie like I did because I knew I had the interest of the Tokyo Giants in my back pocket.

The next day, Tokyo offered the Braves $160,000 for me and Robinson accepted the deal. But he must have thought *I* was the idiot because I knew I had to clear waivers first.

"I know how this stuff works, Eddie," I told him. "Do you think you're dealing with a *kid?* I'm a free agent now—thanks. You can take that 160 grand and stick it up your ass. I'm not going."

There was no way I would allow the Braves to essentially sell me for $160,000 and then have me work out a far smaller salary for myself with the Giants. I mean, how fair is that? But that was a sign of the times—players were still being treated like the property of the teams they played for.

So Atlanta waived me in order to give me my unconditional release. I passed through with one club claiming me—the Oakland A's. The A's were three-time defending world champs at the time, but they were also a mess under owner Charlie Finley. They went through a bunch of second basemen during that period—just kept releasing one after another. And then there was the embarrassing episode when Finley attempted to put one of those second basemen, Mike Andrews, on the disabled list with a fake injury after he made two errors in a '73 World Series game.

So I decided not to sign with them, clearing the way for me to strike my own deal with the Tokyo Giants.

Finley called me after I declined.

"I really want you to come to Oakland," he told me. "You can play second base for us."

"Thanks Charlie," I said. "But I think I'm going to play in Japan."

Moments later, I received another call—this time from Finley's and my mutual friend, the iconic Alabama football coach Bear Bryant.

One of the A's minor league teams, which Finley also owned, played in Birmingham, and Charlie had tried to bring NFL football to that city with a promise to Bear to give him a 10-year, million-dollar contract to coach the team. So they were friendly.

My relationship with Bear went back to my college days at Texas A&M, where he had coached the football team until 1957—prior to my attending there. I got to know him because he was best friends with a local guy near the college named Smokey who raised dogs. When I signed my first pro contract, Bear gave me a German Shepherd pup from the litter of one of the dogs he got from Smokey.

I maintained a longstanding relationship with Bear through the ensuing years. I admired his stature, the decisions he made—and, of course, the winning. I knew I was way down on the totem pole, but he talked to me and treated me like an equal anyway. I always felt the way people earned his respect and how he gained the respect of others was the biggest thing I learned from him. And it helped that he was one of the greatest evaluators of talent I ever saw.

"Davey, you're an *American*," Bear said. "Stay here in America. *Don't* go to Japan."

"Bear, they offered me a pretty good contract over there," I told him. "I'm going to double my salary. And I need a new challenge. Besides, why would I want to go to Oakland? They had, like, seven second basemen last year. I'm going to Japan, Bear. I'm sorry."

And that was the end of the conversation.

Later that evening, having officially rejected the A's offer to play with them, I was now a free agent. My next telephone call would be to Tokyo.

"I'm a free agent," I told Saeki. "If you want me, you can pay *me* the $160,000."

"We still want you," he said.

"Okay, send me the 160. You can make the check out to me," I told him.

"No, I'm going to send you 50 now, and give you the rest when you get here," Saeki said.

"Okay, that works for me," I told him.

I felt a little guilty about "playing" the Braves a bit to get my big increase with Tokyo. Wanting to be a nice guy, I went back to see Robinson.

"Ed, I've been paid by the Braves for about a month of this season so far," I said. "I'm offering the club back that money. This is for my services."

I then handed Robinson a check for $10,000, shook his hand, and left his office to start a new career with the Tokyo Giants of the Japan Central League.

It was going to be a whole new ballgame.

| fourteen |

April 21, 1975:
Land of the Rising Sun

THE TOKYO GIANTS WERE a juggernaut.

When I arrived there, they had won nine of the previous ten Japan Series. So dominant, they were like the New York Yankees and Los Angeles Dodgers rolled into one. They were the only team that had their own TV station, so all of their games were televised. They had a rabid fan base—always chanting, always moving—and had designated groups that sang, waved flags, and clapped simultaneously. It was a kind of environment I had never seen before.

And for many years, they had the best two hitters in Japan—Shigeo Nagashima and Sadaharu Oh. Nagashima was a five-time Japan Central League MVP and first-ballot Hall of Famer. Oh, a nine-time MVP, led the league in hitting five times and in home runs for an incredible 15 seasons. The duo earned the nickname "ON Hou," which meant "Oh-Nagashima cannon."

Nagashima had just retired and was now the most powerful manager in the league with the Giants. They had a good second baseman named Shozo Doi and a fine defensive player, Kono

Kazumasa, at shortstop, so one of Nagashima's first acts, with the help of GM Roy Saeki, was to recruit me as his replacement at third base. I became the first foreign-born player on the Giants in nearly two decades.

It was a significant new challenge—like going from the American League to the National League—and one I could hardly wait to tackle.

Just hours after arriving in Japan after the long flight, I had my Tokyo Giants uniform on and was taking batting practice for my new club. As I had done my entire career as a player and later as a manager, I wanted to make an impression on my new boss. And while in the cage, Nagashima told reporters within earshot through an interpreter, "Have you ever seen a foreign player in Japan show such enthusiasm?"

But as hard as I worked, the first year was a mostly difficult one for me in Japan.

One of the toughest things about it was how hardly anybody spoke English. Even my interpreter, Ichi, could barely translate. And when he did, he would edit me. So if I said something that he thought was in any way disrespectful, he wouldn't communicate that to Nagashima or anybody else. And, just as bad, he would kind of edit what my critics would say back to me, always trying to keep the peace. That made true communication arduous.

Then there were the conditioning programs they put us through at a practice facility in Kanagawa—a dirt field away from the ballpark down by the Tama River. For the first hour, they made us do flips, cartwheels, and squat jumps in the outfield. Then they had us run sprints as they timed us by stopwatch.

We never had to do any of these drills in the United States. In the big leagues, we mostly just threw, ran, and hit ground balls.

But the Japanese were firm believers in what they called Ōku no renshū, which means "a lot of practice."

Thankfully, I had an ally in Oh.

"Don't run so hard," Sadaharu told me. "Just act like you're running really hard and it's *really* hurting you. *Breathe* hard."

I took that to heart and faked like I was putting in 110 percent—flailing my arms, breathing hard, but not killing myself. Oh's advice really saved me.

But what was strange was how they wouldn't allow me to play any games until I practiced about a week. This, even though I came from the major leagues and was ready to step in there and play right away. Their reasoning was they wanted me to have a "big heart." They believed that when *gaijin*—a word they used for foreigners—first came over to Japan, they had "small hearts."

But I wasn't alone and was actually fairly lucky I only had to wait a week.

We had this really good-looking young player—a left-handed-hitting third baseman right out of college—who looked very promising in spring training.

But when the season started, he wasn't on the roster.

"Where's the kid we signed?" I asked Nagashima.

"He's not strong enough," he told me. "He's got to run for a *month*."

They must have had that kid running 25 miles a day. The club told him if he ever wanted to be an all-star for the Giants, like he aspired to be, he needed to build himself up and get strong enough to play.

The kid had no choice. It was the Japanese way.

******

About a week into my Giants career, I discovered another philosophy the Japanese held that was very different from the Americans. After striking out early in a road game to end an inning, I jogged back to the dugout, grabbed my glove, and trotted out to my position, which was second base in that game.

But there was just one problem. There was already a guy there.

I just assumed this was a change in our defensive alignment, that maybe Nagashima was moving me to third base. But that wasn't the case—I had been removed from the game after just my second at-bat.

The Japanese thought process was that if a player didn't start strong then he wouldn't be able to end strong. So it was better, they believed, to get a player out of a game if he didn't come roaring out of the gates.

Of course, I found this highly counterproductive. I wasn't used to being taken out of a game I started off slowly in. I had a conversation about it with Nagashima and Saeki following the game.

"I'm in a new league and trying to learn how teams are going to pitch me," I told them. "The more learning experience I get, the better I'm going to get."

But my speech fell on deaf ears.

And when I continued to struggle in that first year, it hurt my confidence every time Nagashima pulled me from a game early.

I was also losing a lot of weight. All the exercise they had us doing was taking its toll on me. I dropped from 190 pounds down to just 170.

A few months into the season, with my offensive numbers continuing to drop and the Giants in the midst of their worst season in a generation, Nagashima decided to send me to this palatial house to get worked on.

I asked Ichi, "What's this all about?"

"The coaches have been watching you," he said. "It appears that your muscles aren't lined up properly in one of your legs."

"That's a new one," I said. "This is going to be a real experience."

Once I arrived, I was taken to the middle of the living room and laid out on what they call a *tatami*, a soft, rush-covered straw mat forming a traditional Japanese floor covering. This guy proceeded to twist and pull my legs. It was extremely painful. I left the house as sore as you can get.

It didn't help and probably made things worse for me.

I never complained much about it, understanding that the

Japanese had their own culture and views that I wanted to respect. I didn't want to be what they called a *henna gaijin*, which means "strange foreigner."

But then something happened a few days later I could do little about. An opposing pitcher hit me with a *shoot-oh*—a fastball that rides up and in—that broke a bone in my back and caused me to miss a lot of games.

It wasn't any easier away from the ballpark, either. I was there with my wife and three kids in a foreign country half a world away, and between the language barrier, some of the customs, and the cost of living being very high, it was hard mentally on us.

But it certainly wasn't all bad.

A godsend for us was Nagashima's wife, Akiko. A Japanese businesswoman, she could speak fluent English, telling me she received some of her education in the United States. Akiko showed a lot of sympathy for us and, because we lived just a couple of blocks away from her and Nagashima, she helped get us accustomed to our new way of life.

By and large, the Japanese people were very gracious and friendly. I had a great time getting to know my teammates and strangers alike, as well as our surroundings. It was always an enjoyable day going to Ginza, the most expensive part of Tokyo. The department stores had the nicest clothes and the restaurants offered the best food in town. Of course, everything cost a fortune. But the good news was for every U.S. dollar, you got more than 360 yen back then. So we carried around 10,000 yen notes!

I could spend all day talking about the cultural differences, because there were a lot of them.

One of the more interesting ones was how, in hot weather, they had these places along the road where you could go in and get sugar and water intravenously. I never did that, always concerned about how sanitary it was, but more than once I wondered, *Maybe that's not a bad idea.*

Life there became easier the more I learned Japanese. I got myself a little Japanese book and just kept reading. And if a teammate said something, I could ask, "What does that mean?" Since most of them had been forced to take English early on in their schooling and understood it, they could explain various Japanese phrases in my native tongue.

And once I could talk to the Japanese in their language, I wasn't so much of a *henna gaijin*. I was now just a *gaijin*.

******

A lot has been said about the standard of play in Japan and how it stacks up against Major League Baseball. Speaking as someone who spent enough time in each to form an opinion, I would say every ballclub had two or three guys who could have played in the big leagues. The Giants probably had five. They were that good—great swings, great technique. There wasn't a whole lot of speed, although there were some exceptions. The main thing was how they played what I call "little ball"—hit-and-run, bunt-and-run, and some long drives here and there.

I always felt it was a shame that only foreigners were coming in there and that Japanese players, for so many years, weren't getting an opportunity to play in the major leagues.

Many baseball people allude to how the ballparks are smaller in Japan, but that gets overplayed. Our home games were at Korakuen Stadium, a pretty ballpark that was well-maintained, with the dimensions only about five feet shorter than most major league facilities. Five feet is not going to make much of a difference at all in a player's power production. And because the stadium was mostly under a dome, the wind didn't create a lot of havoc.

There were also challenges that hitters faced in Japan that they didn't in the States. The most significant example was the wider strike zone there, which was a big adjustment my first year with the Giants. Pitchers loved throwing the *shoot-oh*, a fastball in off the plate, and I had to adjust by moving away from the dish a little bit and being quicker with my hands to get the full extension needed to keep the ball fair. In doing so, I could take that pitch away from them.

Another difference I found funny was how common it was for a coach to call a team meeting right in the middle of a game. Everybody would gather around and he would just start talking. And often, the opposing team would do the same thing! The coach might say something like, "Okay, now we've got to change the way we're pitching again because they already know that we're going to do something else."

It seemed more like a chess match than a baseball game sometimes.

******

I would summarize my first year with the Giants as kind of tragic. Along with breaking the bone in my back, I didn't perform at the level I should have.

I was determined to come back in my second year playing better baseball. The learning curve was mostly a thing of the past. I could speak Japanese enough now that I didn't need the interpreter that much. And I felt that I had made the necessary adjustments to the Japanese game.

I came to spring training really early, something that most American players over there didn't do. We trained in Denenchofu, a town south of Tokyo that lies along the Tama River. As I expected, there was a lot of running and, after about a week, we divided into two groups. If you were younger than 28, that group ran together. If you were 28 or older, you ran with the older guys. We would run four-man relays around a regular quarter-mile track.

This was so unorthodox for me, but I was determined not to be labeled a *henna gaijin*. I wanted to do exactly what they were doing. I felt that if I'm their teammate, I'm going to go through everything they do. And if that includes taking part in their version of a track meet then so be it.

This time I had a solid spring, hitting home runs, driving in a bunch of runs, and playing solid defense. I started the year again at third base, but after a couple of weeks moved over to my more familiar position of second for the rest of the season.

The Giants finally brought over another American that year—a onetime solid major league left-handed pitcher named Clyde Wright—and they gave me the duty of making him feel more at home. But actually, he took a lot of pressure off of me because the Japanese thought he was absolutely crazy. In fact, fans and sportswriters nicknamed him "Crazy Wright-oh" because of the way he would throw at opposing hitters and bitch and moan at Nagashima.

In one early-season game, Wright was pitching a no-hitter in the fourth inning. An opposing hitter laid down a perfect bunt to me at third and I didn't get him at first. The official scorer gave me an error to preserve the no-hitter Wright was pitching. Out of the dugout popped Nagashima with the interpreter to take Clyde out of the game. Wright stormed off the mound, went straight to the dressing room, and ripped off his uniform and threw it into the bathtub.

Once the inning ended and I was back in the dugout, I could hear him yelling from the dressing room.

"I'm going home and I'm calling [longtime Dodgers executive] Walter O'Malley and telling him how you guys treat Americans over here!" he shouted at Nagashima.

Saeki rushed into the clubhouse and calmly asked Clyde what the Giants could do to make things right.

After quick reflection, Wright said, "Twenty-five thousand dollars."

And they did. They actually paid him $25,000 to shut up!

Clyde used to tell me afterward, "I should have asked for *more* money."

★★★★★★

Midway through the season, we were playing good baseball and found ourselves in first place. But it was around this time that opposing pitchers were relentless in throwing shoot-ohs at me. As a result, despite my best efforts to get out in front of that pitch, I was getting jammed all the time. To remedy that, our batting practice pitcher threw me a steady diet of shoot-ohs. Consequently, I developed an inflamed neuroma, a big bump on my right thumb by the bone. It was killing me and there was nothing I could do to stop the pain.

The Giants sent me to a doctor and he told the interpreter, "It's going to take 10 days to fix."

So I'm thinking, *Okay, that's not too bad.*

But then the doctor pulls out this *six-inch* needle.

"He's not going to stick that thing in my hand, is he?" I asked the interpreter.

"No, he's going to stick it in your neck for an hour every day for ten days," he said.

I was in disbelief.

"*That's* not going to happen!" I exclaimed. "I'm going to fly to L.A. to see a specialist I know, Dr. Robert Kerlan. He'll treat me and I'll be back."

I returned to the ballpark and went into the clubhouse to take a shower. When I came out, Nagashima was standing in front of me. He ripped off my towel, hunched down at my privates and, challenging my manhood, yelled, "That's a lie!"

It took everything I had in me to keep from hitting him.

"I'm going to L.A. to see Dr. Kerlan," I told him, and immediately got dressed and rushed out of the clubhouse.

Once in L.A., Kerlan examined me right away.

"Boy, you've got bad hematoma," the renowned orthopedic surgeon said.

Kerlan gave me a cortisone shot and told me that in two or three days I would be fine.

But while I was away, the media was killing me. A couple of the Japanese newspapers ran photos of me getting on the L.A.-bound flight with a whole bunch of dollar bills in my pockets.

It was just bad optics and didn't endear me to the fans.

And then it was all made worse after the Japanese forgot to sign my visa to return. It took another five days to get that straightened out.

When I returned to the Giants, one of the coaches told me I needed three or four days of practice before I could play in a game.

Incredulous, I exclaimed, "I'm fine! Just don't mess with me. I'm playing!"

They let me play and in that very first game back, I hit a sayonara grand slam in the bottom of the ninth to win the ballgame. All was forgiven and everybody loved me again.

I stayed hot, hitting nine home runs in my first 12 games after returning from L.A. My teammates were terrific—never giving up on me. But things were never the same with Nagashima, who could just be a very aloof guy. He was never one to give out a whole lot of praise. But I didn't really care. The main thing was he just let me play.

My biggest moment in my two years with the Giants would come with about a week to go in the season. We were in Hiroshima to play a game against the Toyo Carp. A victory that night and the pennant would be ours. We were down a run going into the top of the ninth. *Oh-san*—Sadaharu—homered to tie the game at one apiece. Then I came up next and hit what turned out to be the game winner to put us in the Japan Series.

I was bigger than Hirohito!

******

With four games remaining in the season—just like two years before with Henry Aaron—I was once again a part of a historic night.

I was in the hole when Aaron smashed Ruth's record to become the all-time home run leader, and now I was two batters down the lineup from Sadaharu when he hit *his* 715th to surpass the Babe's mark.

The distinction of being in the same lineup with the first two players—on different continents, no less—to eclipse Ruth's hallowed home run mark made me the answer to one of baseball's best trivia questions. It's probably won a lot of guys beers in bar bets. But for me, I just felt very lucky throughout my career to have played alongside some truly great players all over the world. A lot of guys aspire to only play for one team and retire. But I wouldn't have traded my experiences with different teams for anything in the world—even in Japan, no matter how rough it got at times.

As for Sadaharu Oh, I always thought how appropriate it was that he would forever be linked with Ruth among the all-time great sluggers because Oh-san reminded me so much of Ruth as a player. Both were lefty swingers and both were originally pitchers with great arms. The Red Sox would move the young Ruth to right field and the Giants made Sadaharu a first baseman.

I got asked a lot during that time if I thought Oh-san would have been such a prolific home run hitter if he had played in the United States. There is no question in my mind that he would have been.

When I was with the Orioles and we would play exhibition games against Tokyo, Oh faced McNally and Palmer on several occasions. Sadaharu was on every pitch and I knew back then that this guy would have been a great major leaguer.

So how many home runs do I think he would have hit here?

Well, Oh finished with 860 in Japan, so he may very well have hit at least 700 in the big leagues. He hit the ball to all fields, was an extremely smart hitter, and had tremendous power.

His swing was a thing of beauty—just so graceful. He would slowly lift his front leg, balance it on his back leg, then move his right hip back over his left leg and stride forward with a short, downward stroke to drive the ball. Rockets would fly off his bat. You could almost predict when he was going to do something great.

A true student of the game, Oh not only studied the swings of the best American hitters; he also paid close attention to the bad habits of the poor ones and then would do the exact opposite.

Who does that?

I also found some traits that Oh-san shared with Aaron. Like Henry, Sadaharu was a victim of prejudice in his own country. Oh's mother was Japanese, but his father was Chinese. Thus, because he wasn't pure Japanese like Nagashima, he didn't receive the same adulation and acclaim that his former teammate and manager did.

And while Oh-san, like Aaron, acted like a regular guy, Nagashima was treated like a god.

I can vividly recall walking with Nagashima around a hotel we were staying at while he had two guys following behind him. When he began to perspire, one of them gave him a towel. After using it, he just dropped it on the floor and kept walking while one of the men behind him picked it up. That was just how everybody over there had him raised way up—he could do no wrong.

So it didn't matter that Oh-san had a better career than Nagashima. Japan always felt that a Japanese player was superior to any other player.

Let's just say the Japanese like the Japanese.

It's a mentality I could never grasp. Throughout my long career as a player and manager, I never thought anything about a player's nationality. Either he could play or he couldn't play.

That was all that ever mattered to me.

******

I was riding high as I looked toward our Japan Series showdown with the defending champion Hankyu Braves. I finished the season with 26 home runs, a .275 batting average, and a Gold Glove, and was named to the "Best Nine" of the Japanese League. After that brutal first season in Japan, I had gone from goat to hero.

But things quickly took a turn for the worse.

In the days leading up to the series, we trained in a place near Tokyo called Tamagawa, on yet another all-dirt infield by the river. It was raining. It was muddy. It was freezing. But as they hit me ground balls, I was diving to my left and to my right at anything that came my way. My uniform was soaked, but that's what you did—you had to train hard.

The day before the Japan Series, I paid the price, coming down with a severe case of strep throat.

Tired and sick, I told the club I still wanted to play. And they obliged.

After going hitless in the first game and then again in my first two at-bats of the second game, they took me out of the lineup and played somebody else.

But despite my feeling better after the first two games, the Giants benched me the final five games of the Japan Series. It didn't matter that I didn't play well whether I was sick or not. Again, their belief was if you started slow, you couldn't finish strong. And the word through the grapevine was that I had a small heart and didn't have any fight in me.

The reality, of course, was I wanted to play for those guys as much as they wanted to win.

Conversely, Clyde Wright, after having just a so-so regular season and being largely hated by the fans and media, was now their American hero after winning Game 5 of the series and pitching well in a losing effort in the decisive seventh game.

It was the Japanese way, which was simply, "What have you done for me lately?"

I thought to myself, *How ridiculous is this?*

Right after the Japan Series was over, I said I would return to the Giants only if Nagashima apologized for not giving me a chance to redeem myself in the final games.

But that was never going to happen. Nagashima had to save face.

And despite all the problems the Giants had with Crazy Wright-oh, they re-signed him for the next season because he finished strong. In keeping with their philosophy, they *had* to bring him back.

I told Wright a few days after the series, "I know I can still play. I'm going back to the big leagues."

Despite some of the absurdity I endured with the Tokyo Giants, it was still a great overall experience playing ball with them, learning the customs of the country, and communicating in the Japanese language. You quickly find out that regardless of the differences, the people there have the same wants and desires as everybody else.

I learned to love almost everything there was about Japan.

Except maybe for those six-inch needles!

fifteen

September 6, 1978: The Last Hurrah

"POPE, I *WANT* TO PLAY for the Phillies. I'm worth a hundred grand."

No, that first call I made after returning from Japan wasn't to the Vatican, but rather to Philadelphia general manager Paul Owens, an honorable man affectionately known as "the Pope" because of his uncanny resemblance to Pope Paul VI.

"I'll give you sixty," Owens said. "But you've got to make the club out of spring training."

It was a challenge that I welcomed, so I accepted the deal. Back in the majors and now 34 years old, I really wanted to play for a winner. And I thought the Phillies were going to be the best team in the National League in 1977.

They were stacked.

Of course, it all started with one of the all-time greats, third baseman Mike Schmidt, a real special player who was so gifted in many ways. He was strong both defensively and offensively, was a great pull hitter, had a terrific arm, and was a good base stealer for a slugger. He struck out a lot his first few years in the big leagues, but then really got it together. Mike was also the greatest guy in the world—a lot of fun to be around.

The outfield was terrific. There was Greg "the Bull" Luzinski, a tremendous power-hitting left fielder, who would lead the club that season in home runs and RBIs. In center, Gary Maddox could fly and covered a lot of ground. He would always shade over toward left because Luzinski didn't move well. Maddox also played shallow like Paul Blair, but was four steps faster.

And later on in the season, the club acquired right fielder Bake McBride, a heckuva slap hitter and one of the fastest guys I've ever seen. If he topped one off the infield artificial turf, there was no chance to get him—the fielder might as well just put the ball in his pocket. A slow roller? No chance. A screamer in the gap? Probably a triple.

They had some characters, too—guys such as second baseman Teddy Sizemore, outfielder Jay Johnstone, first baseman Richie "the Gravedigger" Hebner, reliever Tug McGraw, and, of course, Tim McCarver.

McCarver had been in the league since 1959 and, at this late stage of his career, was primarily Steve Carlton's personal catcher. Still, he caught for some of the team's younger pitchers and hated it when they had the audacity to shake off his pitches.

He would call timeout, go to the mound, and confront the pitcher.

His favorite line was always: "Listen, kid, I caught the greatest pitcher who's ever lived—Bob Gibson—and he never shook me off. So what are you doing shaking me off?"

A few years later, I was in a hotel bar with McCarver and Gibson and I couldn't resist a golden opportunity.

"Gibby, I have to ask you something," I said. "Is it true that you never shook off McCarver?"

Looking right at Tim, he said, "No, I shook him off. Whenever he called for a pitchout, I shook him off because I knew he couldn't throw the runner out!"

McCarver just about turned as red as a beet. I couldn't have set it up any better than that.

******

I came into Phillies camp as determined to succeed as ever. In the past, having always been a starter, I used spring training to get myself ready for the season. But now it was different. I was fighting for a roster spot.

Near the end of spring training, I was hitting around .330, driving in a bunch of runs, and playing well at first base—alternating with Hebner. Even though I wanted a shot at second, our manager, Danny Ozark, was committed to Sizemore at second and liked a rookie named Fred Andrews as his backup. But I got plenty of at-bats. When I didn't start, Ozark usually inserted me late in games as a pinch-hitter.

Still, despite my success, Ozark gave little indication as to whether I would make the team.

Then, just before breaking camp, in an exhibition game in Puerto Rico, I came up to pinch hit with two outs in the ninth, with the Phillies down by a run. Facing the best closer in baseball, Rich Gossage, I crushed a home run to tie the game.

After circling the bases and making my way into the dugout, Ozark pulled me aside.

"You just made the team."

"*Really?*" I said. "Thanks! Thanks a lot!"

******

I loved playing for the Phillies. Their fans are the greatest in the world—but only if you're winning. They could be a tough crowd—just brutal when you lost. But we didn't do a whole lot of that in '77, winning an incredible 60 games at the Vet during the regular season.

I was used mostly in a platoon with Hebner at first base, and while I wanted to play every day, I understood how the scenario differed from the one I had had in my final year in Atlanta, when I was moved off second and had to share time with Mike Lum at first. Sizemore was a solid second baseman and helped create one of the best double-play combinations in the game with shortstop Larry Bowa. So I had no problem with the utility role Ozark was using me in. I was just happy to be back in the majors.

I made the most of the opportunity and came storming out of the gates, hitting over .400 through the first couple of months of the season.

In a three-game sweep over the Padres at the Vet late in May, I played a big hand in each of the victories. Pinch hitting for Ron Reed in the opener, I ripped a two-run single in the bottom of the eighth to give us a lead we held on to for the win. The next night, I hit two home runs—the first to tie the game and the second to put it away. I actually almost hit a third, sending Padres center fielder George Hendrick back to the 400-foot mark to make the catch. The effort earned me a standing ovation from Phillies fans. They actually cheered me for making an *out*! It gave me a chill. And then in the series finale, I hit an opposite-field double off the Padres' ace left-hander, Randy Jones, for the game-winning RBI. It was the first time in eight tries that the Phillies beat Jones—which made the victory even sweeter.

After the series, the Pope called me into his office and raised my salary to the $100,000 I asked for over the winter. And on top of that, he added a second year to my contract at $125,000. So instead of sulking over not being an every-day player anymore, my positive approach paid off in more ways than one.

I remained intent on perfecting my new role and helping the Phillies win a pennant. For the first time in my life, I realized that I no longer had complete control over my own destiny. In accepting that, it was a matter of my going through a maturity process.

I talked all the time with first-base coach Tony Taylor, McCarver, and a couple of other veterans in my situation about the art of pinch hitting. The lesson learned was that you better make the most out of that one at-bat. And sometimes that means not always waiting for a certain pitch to pull, but rather just getting a good pitch to hit—wherever that might be in the strike zone—and stinging it. Hit the ball where it's pitched. That's where the bigger strike zone in Japan helped make me a better hitter—you had to be ready no matter where the pitch was thrown.

Taylor, who was an excellent pinch-hitter in his playing days, got me hitting in batting practice like it was a real game—a far different approach from the way I went about practice as an every-day player. This really helped prepare me for coming off the bench late in games. I was mentally ready to go.

But in the midst of my hot steak a third of the way into the season, I got a bad break—literally.

While I was fielding a ground ball off the hard turf at the Vet, it took a bad hop and broke my right thumb. I knew it was broken as soon as it happened, but I didn't want to tell anybody. I figured as long as I could still throw the ball down to second or flip it to a pitcher covering first, everything would be fine. I dealt with it for about 10 days, but could hardly swing the bat.

Soon after, Danny came up to me, realizing that something was amiss as my average dropped to around .320, and said, "We know your thumb's hurting you."

"Yeah, but I'm well now." I told him, not wanting to miss any playing time.

"Well, we're sending you to the doctor, anyway," Ozark said.

Sure enough, X-rays confirmed I had a cracked thumb and the club immediately placed me on the disabled list.

I would sit out the next couple of weeks, but would come back and contribute to our second-half surge.

******

Despite our playing good ball, the Chicago Cubs were on fire. They opened an eight-and-a-half-game lead in the NL East—25 games over .500—near the midpoint of the season. At the time, it appeared like they might actually have a shot at ending decades of misery by winning their first World Series since 1908.

But when the dog days of August arrived, the Cubs faded badly and we were as hot as the balmy Philadelphia summer—going 22–7 for the month, taking over first place, and never looking back. We held off a surging Pittsburgh Pirates club to win the division by five games and secure the best record in the National League.

The Cubbies?

Well, they finished *20* games out—a collapse of enormous magnitude.

To celebrate our division crown, I went out to dinner with Carlton and McCarver. During that season, the three of us were living in a hotel on Philadelphia's historic "Main Line," an affluent suburb in the western region of the city.

We often dined together, anyway, but this, of course, was a special occasion.

Carlton, one of the best pitchers in baseball, was making tons of money and was the wine connoisseur of our group. He would always insist on buying us hundred-dollar bottles of wine.

"We can order cheaper than that," I would tell him.

But we were buddies, and Steve wanted us to have the best.

******

The best-of-five NLCS opened in Los Angeles against a Dodgers team that was never challenged during the regular season, having run away with the Western Division crown and handily dethroning the two-time defending world champion Reds in the process.

Under outspoken rookie manager Tommy Lasorda—who never met a camera he didn't like and claimed to "bleed Dodger blue"—and All-Stars such as Steve Garvey, Dusty Baker, Reggie Smith, Ron Cey, and Davey Lopes, the flashy Dodgers were the embodiment of Hollywood. They weren't just very good, they also loved to entertain the crowd with their hugs, high-fives, and curtain calls in front of their dugout after home runs.

But we managed to take the crowd out of Game 1 early. Luzinski hammered a two-run homer off Tommy John in the first and I knocked the Dodgers lefty out of the game in the fifth with a two-run single to give us a 4–0 lead.

With our ace Carlton on the mound, we were feeling pretty good about our chances until the bottom of the seventh. Steve loaded the bases and then surrendered a grand slam to Cey to tie the game at five apiece.

Dodger Stadium was in a frenzy.

But after Garvey singled to finish Carlton's night, our bullpen of Gene Garber and Tug McGraw shut the door from there, not allowing another Dodger to reach base. We settled things in the ninth when Schmidt singled home the game-winning RBI off Elias Sosa to give us an all-important win on the road.

After dropping the second game, we returned to the Vet with a sizable home-field advantage. We felt we had the Dodgers right where we wanted them.

Down 2–0 in the bottom of the second, our 58,000 boisterous and intimidating fans grew louder and louder after some borderline pitches went against an obviously rattled and unglued Dodgers starter, Burt Hooten. So unnerved was Hooten that he walked four straight Phillies—the last three scoring runs to give us a 3–2 edge. Having completely lost his composure, Lasorda had no other choice but to remove Hooten—his arms flailing in the air towards the home-plate umpire Harry Wendelstedt in protest—from the game.

Ironically, Hooten's meltdown and removal turned out to be a blessing in disguise for Los Angeles, as Rick Rhoden kept us in check by pitching four-plus innings of scoreless relief.

In the meantime, my former Braves teammate Baker, who had a terrific series, tied the game with a fourth-inning single off our starter Larry Christenson.

And that's where things stood until the eighth when we broke through, as we did in Game 1, on Sosa. After Hebner doubled to start the frame, Maddox singled to give us the lead. Then our catcher, Bob Boone, reached on a throwing error by shortstop Bill Russell with Gary scoring to give us a 5–3 lead.

So we were feeling really good about our chances with Garber out on the mound to try to close out the Dodgers and give us a decisive 2–1 edge in the NLCS. And Gene didn't disappoint— getting two quick outs to start the inning.

But here's where things turned ugly for us.

All season long, without any doubt, whenever we had a lead in the ninth, Luzinski would get taken out of the game and replaced for defensive purposes by Jerry Martin. But in this one particular game, Ozark left Greg in there after looking at his scorecard and seeing that "the Bull" was due up third in our bottom half of the inning. His thinking was that if the Dodgers tied the game, he would still have a big bat in the lineup.

This was terribly negative thinking.

You just *can't* think that way.

So after Vic Davalillo came off the bench and bunted his way on, the Dodgers brought up another pinch-hitter, Manny Mota, representing the tying run, to the plate.

Well, you could have seen this coming.

On an 0–2 pitch and the sellout crowd on their feet, Mota sent a high fly ball—really more like a *pop fly*—to left field that, with Martin out there, would have been game over. But with Luzinski, who didn't get back to the wall in time, it glanced off his glove, hit the fence, and "officially" (maybe the official scorer was a Dodgers fan) went for a run-scoring double to cut our lead to 5–4. Greg simply butchered it. Any other outfielder in the game would have gone back and made that catch easily.

Ozark's decision to leave Luzinski in left would turn out to be the worst of his career.

The opportunistic Dodgers quickly capitalized when Lopes ripped a game-tying infield single off the glove of Schmidt and then took a 6–5 lead after Russell singled him home.

We would never recover, going down quietly in the ninth. We were simply stunned.

When it was over, you could have heard a pin drop at the Vet. The day forever became known in the annals of Philly baseball as Black Friday.

It almost didn't matter that we had Carlton, our 23-game winner, going next. Los Angeles now had all the momentum. When a game shifts like the one in Game 3 did—and we helped do the shifting— it's a major downer. We should have won that game and the pressure would have been solely on the Dodgers. Now it was all on us.

Sure enough, on a cold, dreary, and rainy night in Philadelphia, Carlton wouldn't have his best stuff—surrendering four runs early—while Tommy John went out and pitched a complete game gem in the finale.

Our season, one that had showed so much promise, was over.

******

As the '78 season began, it became apparent that my playing time would diminish even more than the year before. With the addition of Jose Cardenal, it was getting very crowded over at first base.

I felt the need to visit the Pope.

"If for some reason I don't perform well this season, and you want to trade me, I want to go to the Cubbies," I told him.

Owens agreed.

Why the Cubbies?

Simple. I always dreamed of spending at least part of my career with them so I could play every home game at Wrigley Field—a beautiful ballpark.

The Phillies were once again a highly talented team, and we spent most of the season in a two-team race with the Pirates.

I was still a part-timer at first and gave Schmidt rare breaks at third, but my most significant contribution to the team was as a pinch-hitter. In fact, I became the first player in major league history to hit two pinch-hit grand slams in a season. But that distinction wouldn't last long, as Mike Ivie of the San Francisco Giants equaled my record later in the season by hitting two of his own. To this day, Ivie and I share the record as the only two National League hitters to hit two pinch-hit grand slams in the same year.

But my season—and career—took a turn for the worse in a late-June game in Chicago.

In the eighth inning, with our club clinging to a 4–3 lead, I tried to score from second on a Jerry Martin single to left. Dave Kingman fielded the ball and came up throwing home. I only knew one way to play and as the ball came in ahead of me to Cubs catcher Larry Cox, I lowered my shoulder to barrel him over. But Cox ducked really low and bumped my feet, sending me into a forward flip where my heels almost hit the back of my head. The collision was on every highlight film for a long time.

I knew right away that I had done something terrible to my back on that play. I started having shooting pains down my legs and whenever I went to bed, I couldn't sleep very well.

About a month later, coming to the realization that I wasn't going to be able to help the team with a bad back, I went to see the Pope.

"I think I'm done," I told him. "I'd love to finish my career with the Cubbies if you can pull off a deal with them."

I was also hoping that lightning might strike twice. After my career-threatening shoulder injury with Baltimore, I was able to recover and resurrect my career with the Braves. I thought this time maybe the Cubs could fix my back and the same thing would happen with them.

The Pope was able to honor my request quickly, sending me to Chicago for a young pitcher named Larry Anderson.

******

On September 6, Philadelphia visited Wrigley for the first time since my trade to the Cubbies a month earlier.

In the first of a two-game set, I watched from the bench as the Phillies took a 6–0 lead into the eighth inning. Schmidt opened the frame with a single and then, going against an unwritten rule of stealing a base with a big lead late in a game, swiped second. Our pitcher, Rick Reuschel, reciprocated by sending a purpose pitch over the head of McCarver.

This didn't sit well with Tim and he became even more steamed after striking out.

Reuschel finished the inning, but was due to lead off in our bottom half of the eighth.

Knowing I always hit Carlton pretty well throughout my career, our manager, Herman Franks, told me I was pinch hitting for Rick.

"Hol-y shit!" I said, believing the Phillies would retaliate for Reuschel's purpose pitch by plunking me for sure.

As I walked to the plate, McCarver took off his mask and winked at me.

Buddies or not, the first pitch is going straight for my coconut, I thought.

But, instead, Carlton threw me an outside fastball—nowhere near me. I breathed a sigh of relief and thought, *Maybe I'm not going to get beaned after all.*

The next pitch was a downward slider that I pulled deep down the left-field line, but foul. After missing with a couple of fastballs, he threw me another slider—his "out" pitch—and I was ready for it, slamming the ball over the ivy-covered left-field wall for a home run.

As I rounded second, Bowa shouted at me, "McCarver told you

what was coming! He told you what was coming!"

"Check the record books," I shouted back. "He didn't have to!"

I had no way of realizing it at the time, but that would be the last homer of my major league career—a blast off of Hall of Famer Steve Carlton.

I hit over .300 in my two months with the Cubbies, but my back kept getting worse and worse. I knew I was going to need to get it operated on.

When the season was over, the Pirates offered me a contract, but I turned it down, telling them I wanted to begin the next phase of my baseball career.

I wanted to become a manager.

| sixteen |

April 1, 1979:
Hola, Amigos!

"DAVEY, HAVE YOU EVER considered the idea of being a player/manager?"

The inquiry came from Joe Ryan, co-owner of the upstart Inter-American Professional Baseball League's Miami Amigos at baseball's winter meetings following the '78 season.

My immediate thought was, *This would be great—a new challenge.*

Whether it was going from the American League to the National League, playing over in Tokyo, or coming back to the United States to help the Phillies win a title, I've always liked exploring new challenges in my life.

The Inter-American was a pan-Caribbean Triple A level minor league that didn't have affiliations with any major league clubs. But while their teams could concentrate on just winning ballgames instead of developing players for a big-league organization, they were also run independently and responsible for their own expenses—which was risky business.

So it definitely had its pros and cons.

But the league intrigued me. And so did the idea of becoming a manager.

Managing was always something I saw myself prepared to do after my playing days were over. When you're a middle infielder, you're in charge of defensive alignments, coverage of second base on steal attempts, and calling cutoffs. So you're kind of like a manager on the field because you're involved in so many aspects of the game.

I also considered myself a student of the game—always intrigued by watching the way different managers used their bullpens and benches. I had a healthy hunger for knowledge, whether I agreed with the managers I observed or not—everything I saw went into my mental file. And I was fortunate enough to have played for managers in whom I witnessed mostly good decision making.

After telling Ryan that I thought I would be interested in the post, we were later joined by the other Amigos owner, Ron Fine.

"I'm up for it," I told them. "I like baseball in Latin America. I practically grew up in Miami with the Orioles at their spring training complex. This seems like a natural fit for me. Let's do it!"

******

I ended up having three roles with the Amigos, as Ryan and Fine added assistant GM to my player/manager duties. So in putting together the squad for the following spring, Ryan would tell me which players were available and I would invite them to one of the two tryout camps I held—one in Miami-Dade, the other in Sanford.

When the roster was finalized, we had a very good club with some interesting characters.

We had a highly talented, Cuban-born former big-league pitcher named Oscar Zamora, but because he owned a shoe store, he could only join the club for weekend home games.

Then we had the colorfully talented Tyrone brothers—Wayne led the league in home runs and would later win a car as a contestant on *The Price Is Right*; and Jim won the batting title with a .364 average.

But none of them was as talented, bizarre, or tragic a figure as one of my outfielders, Danny "the Sundown Kid" Thomas. Like Zamora, he had once played major league ball, and because he was a member of the Worldwide Church of God, he also missed time due to religious observance—prohibiting him from playing from Friday night until Sunday.

But Danny's scheduling conflicts were hardly the greatest challenges I had with him.

While leading the league in home runs in early June, Thomas got into a major beef with an umpire for calling him out for missing third base. Danny was so wildly out of control that I had no choice but to suspend him for a couple of games. But that didn't seem to help matters. His tantrums with umpires continued to the point where he kept getting ejected from games, forcing my hand to release him.

Thomas clearly had psychiatric issues, and they would lead to a sad end just a year later. While serving time for a rape charge, Thomas hanged himself in a jail cell.

It was a tragic end to a once-promising career.

******

Despite the sometimes uphill battle of dealing with different personalities, tropical rains, exchanging different currencies, and visa and airline issues in the Inter-American League, it was still the game of baseball played in nice ballparks. You never think much about the negatives when you're really engrossed in what you're doing like I was. Besides, I believed this was an opportunity for me to do something I thought I could be pretty good at.

As for the game itself, the baseball-loving Caribbean fans loved the product. At its core, it was minor league baseball with some flair.

The highlight of any Amigos home game for many fans was

when our so-called Hot and Juicy Girls from our sponsor, Wendy's, would come out in these tight, skimpy outfits and run on to the field to dust off the bases and home plate—a *real* crowd-pleaser.

Our season, and my managerial career, kicked off in the beginning of April at Miami Stadium, a park we shared, ironically enough, with the Orioles' single A team. But there was just one minor hitch—our new Amigos uniforms were stolen the day before the opener and we had to temporarily wear jerseys that read "Miami Marlins."

My first year managing would be a mostly enjoyable one, and the Amigos were easily the best team in the league.

I also hardly felt like a rookie manager.

With the starters, I put to use Bamberger's strategy of using a four-man rotation by having them pitch a game, take a day off, throw on the side, take a day off, and then start their next game.

With my relievers, I followed the way Weaver used to handle his bullpen, having them throw off the mound every two days from the start of spring training well into the beginning of the season. That was the best way for them to work.

I put those routines into play with my coaches and watched how the pitchers would react to my decisions.

It was the same thought process I used with my hitters. Whether it was putting together a starting lineup, deciding whom to pinch hit for, or how I used double switches, my goal was always to put my players in situations where they would succeed.

Another thing I did was act as positively as I could with my guys, while at the same time being straightforward with them about my observations of their play. I found out right away that first year that players really appreciate honesty.

But the most critical thing I discovered was to be right *all the time* in your evaluation of your players. They know very well what the pecking order should be. If you, as a manager, don't know it, then you can quickly get some guys pulling against each other.

It was extremely important to bring logical thinking into every ballgame because the players seemed to thrive and play well under it. It also took a lot of pressure off of me, so I just built on that as I kept going forward. This was a team with a sprinkling of older players who were trying to get back to the big leagues and younger players looking to move up. I was in the fortunate position to help get them where they wanted to be.

******

As the season approached the midway point, I could hardly walk. I had a doctor examine me and the X-rays of the L5-S1 disc in my lower back gave the appearance that somebody had taken two big bites out of my spinal cord.

"That's where your disc is pushing against it," the doctor told me.

I benched myself for the rest of the season, effectively ending my role as a player from my player/manager duties. Surgery was planned at the conclusion of the season. So from that point on, I focused solely on managing the Amigos.

But then a few weeks later, the league was dealt a major blow.

Two of our clubs—San Juan and Panama—folded because their owners were undercapitalized due to low attendance figures. It was a disaster, with many of their players left stranded across the Caribbean with little or no money to get home.

The loss of two of the league's six teams put the Inter-American in utter disarray and just a couple weeks later—on the last day of June—it disbanded.

With a record of 51–21 and a full 15 games in first place, we were declared champions in the most bittersweet of ways. The failure of the league broke my heart.

So for the next couple of months, instead of signing, training, developing, and managing players, my new role would be to try to sell them off to teams in Mexico, Japan, and the major leagues.

After we arrived back to Miami following the premature end

to the season, I got right to work. My first call was to the Phillies.

"You've got to see this pitcher Porfirio Altamirano," I told them. "He throws in the high 90s."

The Phillies sent down some scouts, and Porfirio was just incredible. He threw 93 pitches and I think 87 of them—mostly fastballs in the 90s—were for strikes.

"So what do you want for him?" one of them asked.

"I need $50,000," I told him.

After conferring another one asked, "Is $25,000 enough?"

Having little choice, I said "Sure."

It was, after all, a fire sale.

I ended up selling about $150,000 worth of players—anybody who was worth anything—which pleased Fine and Ryan a great deal.

After dismantling what I believed to be the best Triple A team in existence, I went home and got my back operated on.

And then pondered my next move.

seventeen

October 30, 1980: Meet the Mets

"WE HAVE A DOUBLE-A team in the Texas League," then–Mets scout Joe McIlvaine called to tell me. "Would you have an interest in managing for us?"

I had taken a year off from managing minor league ball following laminectomy surgery so I wouldn't have to endure the long bus rides. I focused instead on my real estate interests and on volunteering as the coach of the University of Central Florida's intramural baseball team.

But now I was ready to get back in the saddle.

"Yeah, I'd be interested," I told McIlvaine.

I thought, *My parents and all my brothers and sisters live in San Antonio, so this would be ideal.*

But then I was really disappointed when I found out that the Mets' team in the Texas League was actually in Jackson, Mississippi—about a 13-hour bus ride to San Antonio.

Still, I wanted back in.

"We can offer you $17,500," McIlvaine said.

I got him to come up to $18,000 and we had a deal. It was a

fraction of what I was earning in real estate, but I loved baseball and truly missed the action.

The Jackson Mets had a tough travel schedule—with most of it done during the night—and we had to make regular stops along the side of the road because we didn't even have a pisser in the bus.

But that was the least of my concerns.

One of the problems we had coming out of spring training in 1981 was that we only had maybe one or two decent prospects on the club. When you don't have prospects, it's really tough. But then we made a trade to obtain outfielder Marvell Wynne from the Kansas City Royals—a very interesting young player.

And we had some good young pitchers, such as Terry Leach, Rick Ownbey, Brent Gaff, and Doug Sisk.

But by and large, we didn't have a lot of speed, we didn't have home run hitters, and we didn't have high-average guys, so we had to find creative ways to score runs.

The one thing we could do, though, was put the ball in play. That allowed us to hit-and-run and stay out of double plays. So whenever we got guys on base, I put the hit-and-run sign on every time.

Still, despite our efforts, we started the season a dismal 2–15.

But I believed in our guys and, at the lowest point of the season, wrote on the clubhouse wall, WE WILL WIN THE TEXAS LEAGUE CHAMPIONSHIP. SIGNED, DAVE JOHNSON.

I meant what I wrote. I liked the character of the club—we had some real grinders.

And the club didn't disappoint. We went on to play good ball in the second half of the season, qualified for the playoffs, and then beat a very good San Antonio Dodgers team—with future big-league stars such as Orel Hershiser, Tom Niedenfuer, Steve Sax, and Greg Brock—in the finals.

It was a great finish to a challenging season.

The executives of our club were clearly pleased with the job I did.

"Davey, we'd like to have you come back and manage Jackson

again next year," Lou Gorman, the Mets' vice president of player personnel, said to me following the season.

But I wanted a new challenge and turned him down.

Soon after, a more intriguing opening within the organization arose—that of special assignments instructor. When that job was offered to me, I accepted.

My new role would allow me to see prospects at all levels of the Mets' system—which would help me tremendously when I took over the big-league managing job a couple of years later.

There were no limitations placed on me. I could talk to pitchers, infielders, outfielders, and hitters—it was really fun.

Ultimately, though, I had more meetings with managers about the way they were handling players than I did with the prospects themselves—often over things I didn't agree with.

I recall one time I was in Shreveport, Louisiana, and Billy Beane was on the same Jackson team as Darryl Strawberry. Late in the game, our manager, Gene Dusan, had Straw hit for Beane.

I was really upset.

"You can't take a prospect out of the game in that kind of situation," I told Dusan. "And you especially can't replace one prospect with another. That's not the way you build character on the team. Now, if you had Darryl pinch hit for somebody who was just a "filler" on the club, that's another thing. But you can't hit Straw just because the situation arises where you'd like a left-handed batter up there. It's not the way you develop good talent."

But I understood why Dusan did what he did—he wanted to win. It's tough on a lot of young managers in the minor leagues. They all figure that they have to coach these guys and make decisions in such a way that they'll win ballgames. They believe the only way to get promoted to the next level and become a big-league manager is to win at all costs and not worry so much about what they are really there for—to develop talent. But that's a really hard thing for a young manager to hear and accept.

And then there's another side to it, as well. We had a new

director of minor league operations, Steve Schryver, in that '82 season. Schryver used to put pressure on the minor league managers because of his own career ambitions—not a completely uncommon occurrence in professional baseball.

I used to have some real heated arguments with him after he would yell at a manager or a team—something like, "You're not playing up to your potential! You guys should win this division!"

He figured if the whole system had a great winning record, then he would instantly become a candidate for a general manager's job.

We had a big difference of opinion on that.

I once told him, "Winning is the byproduct of developing players the right way. You develop the wrong way and you might win a few more minor league games, but the organization as a whole won't get anywhere."

The reality is that sometimes you're going to win ballgames and other times you're going to lose, but the name of the game is how many players you nurture and develop into major leaguers. When you see a guy has a lot of good talent, you have to have patience and be optimistic with him. You should never get down on him about his weaknesses, but rather stress his strengths. Even when he fails, you just have to remain upbeat.

The Mets, at that time, had a great deal of talent throughout the minor league system, in part due to all the high draft picks they had received after years as cellar dwellers.

But one prospect stood out among all the others—a skinny 17-year-old who pitched for our Kingsport Rookie team in the Appalachian League named Dwight Gooden.

Dwight was teammates with a couple of other top pitching prospects, Floyd Youmans and Randy Myers. The three of them were fun-loving guys, always full of energy.

The first time I saw Gooden pitch, he was getting some side mound work in along with Youmans and Myers. I watched each of them for about 10 minutes. They all had great stuff, though Youmans and Myers would miss the catcher's target roughly two out of five times—just all over the place.

Then this kid Gooden comes in, puts that catcher on the outside corner down, and just starts popping the mitt with a 95-mile-per-hour fastball. Then he moves the catcher inside and does the same thing—just locating the ball. Then he throws some curveballs, hitting the glove wherever it's positioned.

Once he was finished, I asked him, "How do you grip your fastball?"

"I grip it across the seams when I want to put a little giddy-up on it," Gooden said. "And then I grip it with the seams when I want a little lateral movement."

Utterly impressed with the composure, maturity, and intellect of this 17-year-old as a pitcher, all I could do was nod and say, "That'll work."

Soon after, we had a simulated game prior to the start of the season. I was calling balls and strikes from behind the mound. It was Dwight's first time pitching in a gamelike setting since being signed to a rookie ball contract. Gooden punched out the first two guys easily by pitching them away. But then he had to battle the three-hole hitter. Dwight started him off with a fastball and the batter put a good swing on it, fouling it straight back for strike one. Then the catcher called for a curveball, but Gooden shook him off, wanting to throw a fastball inside to see if he could beat him there. But again, the batter was on it—this time pulling it foul. So with two strikes, and the hitter looking dead-red for a fastball, Dwight threw him a nasty "Lord Charles" curveball to strike him out looking.

The guy never had a chance.

At 17, Gooden was reading hitters and showing us all what he could do.

In a word, he was special.

That same spring, the Texas Rangers offered the Mets pitching prospects Ronnie Darling and Walt Terrell for outfielder Lee Mazzilli—the steal of the century for our organization. But initially,

Mets GM Frank Cashen hesitated in making the deal because of Mazzilli's popularity with the fans.

I was completely dumbfounded.

I told some of our scouts rather emphatically, "If we don't make that trade for those two, we're *crazy*! If we can still get that trade done, *do it*!"

Of course, Frank ultimately pulled the trigger, and we would have both of those young pitchers in the big-league starting rotation the next season.

I had a sense that greatness could be just a few years away for the Mets.

It was time to get back into managing.

******

I had two offers to manage at the Triple A level for the '83 season—one from the Mets and the other from the rival Cardinals.

My heart was set on the Mets' Tidewater position because I had already been in the system for two years and I liked the idea of going to Norfolk, Virginia, a city not too far from Baltimore, where I had kind of grownup with the Orioles.

But I must admit the Cardinals made it interesting.

After the Mets verbally offered me the Tidewater post, I became entangled in a little bit of a contract dispute with Schryver—who was lowballing me in our salary negotiations.

By contrast, the owner of the Triple A Louisville Cardinals, A. Ray Smith, was offering me significantly more than the Mets with better perks.

Smith was all over me to take the job. It's one thing for the owner of a Triple A club to want you, but it wasn't like I was contacted by anybody from the Cardinals' big-league club. And that weighed on me.

So I was pleased when Lou Gorman stepped into the Mets negotiations and we could finally get together on a contract that was equitable for both sides.

From there, we were off and running.

When I took over the Tidewater club, we had a mix of players like Clint Hurdle, Wally Backman, and Ron Gardenhire who had major league experience trying to fight their way back up, and other, younger players like Kelvin Chapman, Marvell Wynne, and, of course, Strawberry, who hadn't tasted big-league life yet but felt they were ready to.

There could have been real discontent on a ballclub like that, especially if the players' roles weren't clearly defined. That's where the manager comes in. It's his responsibility to inform each player what he should be doing and then get player to agree with his assessments.

Is he starting the right guys? Is he hitting them in the right order? Is he evaluating talent properly?

Those are all questions the players are going to ask themselves in sizing up their manager.

The thing that I put the most emphasis on with my ballplayers—even more so than their natural talent—was their makeup. I was most concerned, above all else, with whether a guy was going to give me 110 percent—no matter what—every time he went out there. I could care less if he's in a slump or whatever.

The question I would ask myself was always, *Is he going to give me all he's got?*

So by defining each player's role and having him bust his ass every game, it also makes for a happier ballclub because all they really want is an opportunity, and I would provide that to the guy who deserved it most. And if things worked out, they would *all* get big-league jobs or, at the very least, get noticed because they were expressing their talent at a high level.

Another important thing about managing any ballclub is knowing your players. Whenever you hear a manager say, "I treat everybody the same," it's the biggest crock of baloney in the world.

Everybody's different. Everybody's psyche is different. And

everybody's motivation is different.

Some guys you have to pat on the back more; with others, you've got to kick them in the pants.

A club may very well have the same rules for everybody, but not everybody is treated the same. It really just comes down to this—you're treated according to your success and the more you have, the more you're treated the way you want to be.

A perfect example of this was with Darling, one of my pitchers on that Tidewater team and later with the Mets. Ronnie was a real smart guy from Yale and a gifted athlete. But after he won a game for us at Tidewater, and was feeling pretty good about himself, I knocked him down a peg and said, "You should have been in the major leagues a couple of years ago."

I wouldn't do that with every player, but sometimes, with the really bright and talented ones like Ronnie, they would understand and work harder at their craft.

In Ronnie's case, I think he was set back in the minors because of some bad advice.

When I managed against him in the Texas League, he was throwing at a high three-quarter-angle and his fastball was basically unhittable. Then, he would throw a slow curve or another off-speed pitch and our guys had no chance.

But the next year, a pitching coach in the Rangers' organization told him, "If you could get your arm more over the top, you'll have a better breaking ball."

It was terrible advice.

When I got him at Tidewater, I noticed something very different from the dominant pitcher I had seen a couple of years before in the Texas League. We were in Syracuse, New York, and he was throwing on the outfield side of first base to a catcher. Ronnie's fastball was as straight as a string and his curveball wasn't that great, either.

I walked over to him and said, "I remember you high and three-quarters—not over the top like that. Go back to your old ways."

Ronnie listened and started throwing again. The difference was remarkable.

"That's one of the best fastballs I've ever seen," I told him after a few pitches.

And it was—the ball just had so much movement.

Later on, when I got him in the big leagues, he threw to a high pitch count because he was always trying to paint the corners with that fastball of his that moved all over the place. When we got Gary Carter in '85, I told my catcher, "Carter, look—give them inside and outside, but just sit down the middle and have him throw to your glove. Don't worry, he ain't going down the middle with his fastball—I can tell you that. It'll move to the corners naturally."

As a result of just having Carter set the target in the middle of the plate, Darling went from throwing between 100 and 120 pitches through five or six innings to finishing some ballgames with fewer than 100.

Ronnie, of course, would go on to have a terrific career in the big leagues.

******

Of all the talent we had on that Tidewater team early in the season, the biggest spotlight was always on Strawberry—the No. 1 pick in the nation just three years before.

But after just 17 games, Cashen succumbed to the pressure the media and fans were putting on him to promote the young phenom out of Crenshaw High School up to the major league club.

I thought this was a mistake.

Straw may have been a great talent, but I thought he was still learning who he was. Plus, he had the pressure of knowing he was the No. 1 draft choice in the country and was now playing in New York. If you come to New York, you better know exactly who you are and be able to express your talent to folks.

And to me, this 21-year-old wasn't ready yet.

But after a terrible start to yet another season, New York was desperate to get a winner on the field. With the promotion of

Strawberry, they were trying to create some excitement for a fan base that had grown tired of losing.

To his credit, Straw did hit 26 home runs in taking home Rookie of the Year honors, but there's no telling how much that pressure early in his career affected him later on.

With Straw and our 19-year-old shortstop, Jose Oquendo—another player who wasn't ready to be called up to the Mets, but was anyway—both gone, we struggled much the same way my Jackson team had a couple of years before. At one point, Tidewater lost 14 straight games.

But I believed in my players and gave the Tidewater team a similar vote of confidence to the one I gave Jackson. At a team booster club dinner, I told the audience, "Not only are we going to win the playoffs, but we're also going to take the Triple A Little World Series!"

I wasn't blowing smoke—that doesn't cut it. And I knew that if they felt like I did, we could do this. You can't accomplish anything unless you believe you can.

We got hot in September and had the fourth-best record in the International League—good enough to snare the final playoff spot.

As manager, I pretty much had final say on whom I was going to take on the postseason roster. So I promoted Gooden to the club, after he finished 19–4 with 300 strikeouts at Single A Lynchburg that season.

I never had a doubt he could handle the promotion. I recalled how, in an organizational meeting earlier in the year, some of our scouts didn't want Gooden to even make the jump from Kingsport to Lynchburg—concerned that he might struggle.

I raised my hand and said, "Hey fellas, if Doc could go to Triple A right now, A ball is going to be nothing."

With Gooden in the rotation, I thought my pitching would hold down our first opponent, the first-place Columbus Clippers—a terrific offensive team that included Don Mattingly—and we'd scratch out a few runs and have a good shot at beating them.

Doc actually lost his one start in that series, but we took it anyway—three games to two—advancing to the Governor's Cup to take on the Richmond Braves.

Against Richmond, Doc was back to his brilliant self, hurling a five-hitter in a 7–1 victory to give us the International League title. I knew by his winning a game like that it would help him grow as a professional.

From there, we advanced to the Triple A Little World Series, a double round-robin tournament played at Cardinal Stadium in Louisville, Kentucky, between the champions of the American Association, Pacific Coast League, and International League.

We would take three of our four games to win the series over our competition—the Denver Bears and the Portland Beavers.

Again, Gooden was simply phenomenal, pitching a complete game victory over Denver.

After leading Tidewater to a Triple A Little World Series victory and knowing the entire system the way I did, I thought that Cashen would have no choice but to hire me as the next Mets manager.

And if he did, I was going to do everything I could to convince him to let Dwight Gooden come along with me.

| eighteen |

October 13, 1983:
Bringing the Magic Back

"I HAVE A LIST of 10 skills I look for in a manager," Cashen said to me during my interview in an Atlanta Fulton County Airport lounge. "Fearless, intelligent, good communicator, energetic, tough, dedicated to player development, patient, hardworking, cooperative, and positive."

"Yeah, I got all those," I told him. "Anything else?"

Frank, my GM when I played in Baltimore, gave a slight grin at my cockiness, which he knew all too well, then moved the talk to salary.

"We can pay you $50,000 a year."

I kind of laughed and said, "Frank, I can't take that job for less than a hundred grand. It's *New York City!*"

After getting close enough to the figure I wanted, we had a two-year deal, but I told Cashen, "I'm only going to deal with one general manager. Not you *and* Lou Gorman. I'm only going to deal with you, Frank. I don't want two different opinions getting filtered into the organization."

At the time, Gorman was the Mets' VP of player personnel, but more important to me, he was like the chief deputy to Cashen.

Frank agreed that I only needed to report to him.

Of course, it all became a moot point when Gorman left the Mets to accept the Red Sox's general manager job just prior to spring training. Another team vice president, Al Harazin, and McIlvaine, who was now director of scouting, would absorb Gorman's duties.

If I seemed direct or even brash during my interview with Cashen, it's because I was confident he was going to offer me the job. In fact, I believed he didn't have a choice. There was a lot of young talent in the minor league system and nobody had a better knowledge of it than I did.

I have long believed that, ideally, the prerequisite to becoming a first-time manager should be to manage in a team's minor league system and see how the organization reacts to your judgments and how they deal with you so you'll get constructive feedback from them before going to the big-league level. I felt like that was what I did and it made it easy for me to transition to the major leagues.

The announcement of my hiring was made in Philadelphia at a press conference during the '83 World Series.

"I'm really happy to be here," I told the reporters. "I like working for smart men and Frank Cashen is a smart man for hiring me."

In an unconventional move, I announced the hiring of Frank Howard, the manager I had just replaced, as one of my coaches. Although I didn't agree with him on some of the ways he managed the ballclub, I thought he was an outstanding coach. He would relentlessly work with the outfielders—who usually never got enough practice.

A few days after the press conference, I made another hire that could be perceived as uncommon. I brought on a young data processing manager named Russ Richardson. I wanted offensive data on how every one of my players hit against every National League pitcher and information on how every Mets pitcher did against every hitter in the Senior Circuit.

I would learn so much from this data. For example, I learned that the switch-hitting Backman had a harder time swinging right-handed than he did left-handed.

I also wanted Russ to get me information on all the other National League clubs—like on what counts they like to steal or hit-and-run on. Richardson would spend the next several months over the winter preparing this data for me and enter it into what I called my "manager's book." All of that information was going to be much better than trying to use my memory all the time.

I also had Russ prepare a "pitchers' manual," which would tell me things like who my various pitchers' regular catcher was, how many pitches they typically threw, and how far into games they went. All of that data was important. I was basically a systems analyst at that point.

I was going to be baseball's first big-league manager to embrace sabermetrics.

******

One of the primary ways I wanted to change the culture of the Mets and their moribund path was to stress working on fundamentals—something the last-place club hadn't emphasized in previous years.

During my first spring training as Mets manager, we worked on some bunt plays I picked off from the Cardinals, the wheel play, and all kinds of defensive alignments. I think a tight structure set up at spring training allows extra work time for the guys who don't do things very well. The instruction and practice they receive are just part of the learning process that helps them become major league–level ready.

I leaned heavily on field coordinators, which enabled me to be at different stations during spring training. Even though I had interviewed all my coaches and knew them well, I wanted to see how they were interacting with players and, conversely, how my players took to that interaction. That's how you gain cohesion on a ballclub.

One of my pet projects that spring was with one of our second basemen, Wally Backman, who had bounced back and forth between the majors and minors, but excelled for me at Tidewater. He was a little guy, so low to the ground that I used to joke that when he crouched into his fielding position and farted, dust would kick up off the infield dirt.

I would preach to him, "Wally, there's no 'hands up.' You should be a great fielder because your hands are so close to the ground."

He worked extremely hard to get "softer" hands and ultimately became one of the most sure-handed guys in baseball.

I actually saw a lot of myself in him. Backman was a gamer—always getting his uniform dirty—and was driven by trying to find ways to beat you.

We had another second baseman in camp, Brian Giles, who had twice the talent—good speed, good power, good arm, smooth—but his makeup wasn't half as good as Backman's. Wally would be our starting second baseman coming out of spring training. It was an easy decision for me.

I didn't think Backman would go into managing, but when he did, I thought he would be pretty successful because of the way he played the game. I feel for him that some of his off-the-field issues from many years ago have apparently kept him from getting a big-league job.

One of my other missions that spring, of course, was to head north with Doc on the big-league roster. I knew how good he was—he had such great command. If I had to be picky, maybe his only drawback was how he was a little slow to the plate because of his high leg kick and lengthy follow-through. This made it easier to steal bases off him.

Still, I would think, *Those base runners could steal all day long if they wanted, but they ain't gonna score. Nobody's stealing home!*

Early in camp, I brought the specter of promoting Gooden to Cashen.

"He's ready, Frank," I told him. "At least keep an open mind."

But Cashen was noncommittal and I knew exactly why. One of his big bugaboos was what happened with another one of our talented young arms three years earlier. At just 21 years old, Tim Leary was lighting it up at Double A Jackson, going 15–8 with a 2.71 ERA. Then, early in the '81 season, Frank brought him up to start the third game of the year on a frigid day in Chicago. Leary lasted just two innings, leaving the game with a bad shoulder because of the freezing weather. Tim would miss the rest of the season.

So Cashen clearly remembered that, and thought, *Oh, I took a young kid out of Double A ball, I brought him up to the big leagues, and he hurt himself trying to do too much.*

Frank didn't want to make the same mistake twice.

By the end of spring training, despite a stiff back, Doc showed everyone his stuff was more than major league ready.

I practically pleaded with Frank.

"I'll take care of him," I told Cashen. "Trust me. I won't abuse him."

I simply never had a doubt that Gooden could handle the big stage—even as a teenager. I had him as young as seventeen in the minors. Dwight was a young man who loved the game—that was apparent early. He was always happy, came from a great family, and pitched for a great high school coach. I didn't see any behavior out of the ordinary that would lead me to think he would consider any other path than to take care of himself.

Frank finally acquiesced—but under one condition.

"I don't want him hitting left-handed," Cashen told me. "I don't want to expose that great right arm of his."

I was actually a little upset about Frank's order, because Doc was a good switch-hitter.

"Nobody is going to hit him," I countered. "He can hit them back anywhere he wants—and with a much *harder* fastball."

But that's the way Cashen wanted it and I couldn't override him on that.

Still, I got my ultimate wish.

Doc was coming to Flushing.

******

One of my goals was for the club to get younger—especially with all the talent we had on the farm.

Some of that work was done for me prior to spring training.

Dave Kingman, a 35-year-old power-hitting outfielder who had a bit of a reputation as a bad teammate—but a guy I had enjoyed playing with on the Cubs—was released just prior to camp.

And then there was the case of 39-year-old Tom Seaver. The Mets icon, who returned to the club in '83 but was mysteriously not protected from the annual free-agent compensation pool following the season, was signed by the Chicago White Sox in January after one of their pitchers, Dennis Lamp, left them to join the Toronto Blue Jays.

It was a public relations nightmare, but I think the reason the Mets let him go was because he was making too much money. I actually didn't have a say in the matter, because if I had, I would have wanted to keep him. I always admired Seaver. He was a hard worker and we'd had some interesting conversations together the previous spring in St. Petersburg, where the club trained.

He was special and knew more about pitching than anybody I knew.

There were other veterans, however, whom I felt we needed to rid ourselves of.

One of the things I knew when we headed north was that I was taking three veteran pitchers—Craig Swan, Mike Torrez, and Dick Tidrow—whom I didn't think would last for very long.

"If they don't cut it after two months, I'm going to insist that we release them," I told Cashen.

All three of them had enjoyed fine careers, but were clearly close to be being done.

Swan, a longtime Met, was coming off a dismal 2–8 season with an ERA of 5.51; Torrez led the National League in losses, earned runs allowed, and walks the year before; and Tidrow, a relief pitcher, was a guy we signed as a free agent after he had a subpar campaign with the Chicago White Sox.

Sure enough, my intuition was right. Swan would give up an average of more than eight runs over ten games; Torrez opened the season just 1–5 with an ERA of 5.02; and Tidrow had a 9.19 ERA in 11 appearances.

We would release Swan and Tidrow in early May and Torrez in June.

I really wanted to give the kids a chance—particularly our young arms. So with those older pitchers gone, we had one of baseball's youngest staffs in place. Aside from the 19-year-old Gooden, there were Sid Fernandez (21), Darling (23), Terrell (26), Ed Lynch (28), and Bruce Berenyi (29), who came over in a deal with the Reds at the trading deadline.

If there was anything I felt strongly about—and differed with many other managers on—it was how I ran a young pitching rotation.

The most important thing was not to overuse them—never asking them to do too much for you. A lot of that was always tied to pitch counts. I would see a guy who, for the first six innings, had a great curveball, but was now leaving the ball up. That's an indication of a tired arm, and I would quickly take him out of the game.

Another one of my hard-and-fast rules was to always put a young pitcher in the position to get a win. I watched how other teams managed young talent and would often shake my head at how they used them. I would often see a kid with a one- or two-run lead after six innings and marvel at how he'd be allowed to go out and pitch the seventh inning. Maybe he still had a friendly little pitch count, but I wouldn't let a pitcher, after six strong innings, get in a position where he could get the loss. I wanted to make sure, whether we ended up winning the game or not, that the kid knew he had pitched well enough to win so he could build on that his next time out.

Additionally, if there was a time when I thought the kid was going to have a tough matchup against a certain pitcher or opposing team, and I could give him an extra day's rest, I wouldn't hesitate.

Building a young starting pitcher's confidence was equally as important to me as taking care of his arm.

I felt the same way about the relievers. I had to have faith that they could deal with different hitters and lineups. I didn't like situational guys I could only bring in for one hitter. I wanted the guys to feel like I had more confidence in them than that.

Of course, I grew up at a time when most teams only had 10 pitchers on their staff. When it went to five-man rotations, it was sometimes 11—but never beyond that. Then, when I managed the Nationals, there were 12 pitchers. It gets to the point where, with all those pitchers, it's easy to overmanage, and I think that hurts players in the long run because then they start thinking, *Well, I can't do this or do that.* It becomes a big negative.

On that '84 Mets team, we had three relievers used out of the pen—Doug Sisk, Tom Gorman, and Brent Gaff—to set up our primary closer Jesse Orosco. Like the starters, they were young as well—all in their midtwenties.

It would be pitching coach Mel Stottlemyre's and my job to nurture this special group of young arms.

******

Early in the season, Cashen took a seat in my office—concerned about something he had just observed.

"We have a disjointed clubhouse," he said. "Should we make it smaller?"

"No, Frank," I said. "Everybody just needs to know his role on the ballclub and they'll be fine."

"Well, Keith (Hernandez) likes to do crossword puzzles and he's a Civil War buff, and…"

"Who cares about that?" I interrupted. "Just let everybody do their own thing."

I basically wanted the guys to come to the ballpark and enjoy being in the clubhouse. I wanted it to be fun for them and even more comfortable than being in their own homes with all their kids running around. And if there was ever an issue, I would always tell Keith and later Gary Carter, "You guys handle it." I didn't want to be the one monitoring minor clubhouse problems. And I never wanted to have an environment where there was a whole lot of policing going on.

Keith was a big help to me that first year—both on the field and as a clubhouse presence. He was the true captain of the Mets before I made it official following the '86 season.

And as a player, they didn't come any better.

Defensively, Keith was the best first baseman I've ever seen. I don't know how anyone could be any better at fielding ground balls and throwing to different bases. And he was like having an extra coach in the infield, with his visits to the mound to talk to a pitcher—slowing down the pace of the game.

At the plate, he was a pure .300 line-drive hitter. And he wasn't just smart and talented, but he loved the game and made it fun. He enjoyed playing little games with the opposing pitchers. When he knew they were trying to make him hit into a double play when runners were on first and second or when the bases were loaded, he would tell me something like, "They're going to try to throw me down and away and that's just where I want it. I'm going to hit a line drive over the shortstop's head."

And then he would do it.

And if he knew a guy was going to try to jam him, he would use a little bat that was two inches shorter than the ones he normally hit with. Well, he would take "shortie" up there, get around on the pitch, and sometimes drive it over the right-field wall.

Other times, when he wasn't feeling right at the plate, and with a man on, he would tell me he was swinging first pitch and to put the hit-and-run on. It was just so enjoyable having him on the club. I didn't have to coach him on anything.

We had other capable veterans, too—players whom I was definitely interested in keeping on the ballclub. Guys like Mookie Wilson, an electric, 100 percent gamer; George Foster, a winning ballplayer with tremendous power; and Hubie Brooks, a very underrated third baseman and hitter who drove the ball to all fields with authority. Brooks was also an especially fun guy to be around.

And then there was Strawberry—a player with unlimited, yet not completely realized, potential—now in his second year. I really tried to be like a father to him in a lot of ways. And one of the things a father has to be is firm—especially when a son does something you don't like.

I once told Darryl, "You can't stay out late. You can't drink all night. And you can't have sex all night. You've got to cut it to one out of three."

I realize he was probably doing all those things to help him deal with the pressure of being a young superstar in New York. And it didn't help when, like in Doc's case as well, his homeboys were saying stuff like, "You've outgrown us. You're not my friend anymore because you're bigger than me."

I wasn't going to go out looking for him and drag him out of places. He was a grown man. But when that kind of behavior had him coming late to the ballpark or not hustling on the ballfield, I had to do things like fine him. But even with the fines, I tried to be fatherly. We used his fines as donations for charities so he could help others while writing it off on his taxes.

We practically supported an entire orphanage with his fine money.

But I think what really held him back was his thinking that because he was the No. 1 pick in the country, in his mind, he was as good as he needed to be. It's not that he didn't work hard—he did—but I don't think he wanted to be the greatest player he could be. He didn't strive to lead the league in hitting or home runs or any category. The telltale deal was when he hit 39 home runs in '87 but sat out two of the last three games. He didn't care about reaching the 40-homer plateau.

Anyway, Straw was still an awfully good player and one of the building blocks in making our club a winner.

******

I knew we had the makings of a really good ballclub. We weren't perfect, but I had a strong feeling we would be very competitive. But you never know for sure what it's going to take to win a division title.

Going in, I thought there were some clubs that were better prepared than us—the Cubs being one of them.

After we surprised everyone and spent much of the first four months of the season in first place, the Cubs caught us in early August—setting up a big four-game showdown at Wrigley Field. But maybe we were just too young for greatness, as the veteran Cubs swept the series. My guys didn't pitch badly, but were simply outpitched. Their staff made very few mistakes against us and were far more advanced pitchers. I'm not saying they had better stuff, but they knew how to pitch. They had been working at their trade for a number of years, so when the pressure got on them, they knew right away how to respond. My younger guys had a little harder time with that.

But I wasn't down about it. I knew that '84 was a growing year, that we would get better, and that we would learn. It was all about establishing a contender.

It takes 25 guys to win a championship, and we were short in some areas. It's not having the best eight or nine guys in the league, it's having 25 good players who come together as a team because they are all important. Everybody must be a part of a winning club. If you have a few guys who maybe were in a little over their heads or had a little age on them, like we did, it's hard to cover those holes without abusing other players.

But the harshest reality for us in that NL East race was a seven-player trade made on June 13 between the Cubs and the Indians, with the principals in the deal being Cubs outfielder Joe Carter and the Indians' Rick Sutcliffe. It was an incredible in-season pickup for the Cubs. Sutcliffe would start 20 games for Chicago and go 16–1. Despite pitching the first two months of the season in the American League, Sutcliffe was so outstanding that he was still awarded the National League Cy Young Award—edging out Gooden for the honor.

The Cubs really won the division on that fateful June day.

And it should have never happened.

"You can't let that trade go through," I strongly advised Cashen. "You *claim* that outfielder!"

I told Frank to claim Carter because the Cubs' general manager, Dallas Green, hadn't passed him through waivers prior to making the trade. It became common knowledge around the league that he had made a grave mistake.

"Claim him, Frank. I could use him," I said.

"No, I can't do that," Cashen responded.

Those were different times when general managers didn't want to make another GM look bad by not getting waivers ahead of a trade. It was kind of like if Frank did it to Green, then when Cashen might want to slide something by, the other general managers would call him out on it.

Still, I knew the impact Sutcliffe could have for the Cubs and told him so.

"Just *claim* the guy," I said again. "I don't want Sutcliffe going to the Cubs."

But Frank let it happen and it might very well have cost us the division.

In early September, the Cubs came to Shea for a critical three-game series. We were seven games out and needed a sweep to have a prayer of catching them.

In that first game, Doc was sensational, pitching a one-hit complete game shutout with 11 strikeouts. A win the next day against Sutcliffe and we would pull to within five.

But the Cubs' new ace was up to the task, tossing a 6–0 shutout to end our hopes. Sutcliffe had beaten us three times down the stretch to simply demoralize us.

We finished the year with 90 wins—18 games over .500—a great campaign when you consider we got outscored by 18 runs. And it was the first time in eight seasons that the Mets eclipsed 70 wins. It may have been the finest job of my managerial career.

And we got the fans back, drawing nearly two million of them after years of Shea looking and sounding like a mausoleum.

The '84 season was a lot of fun for me, personally. I had a radio show and guys would call to second-guess everything I did—giving me a chance to show them all how dumb they were!

Another thing I did was stay away from reading the tabloids when things would go badly. I wanted to always remain positive.

Not winning the division was hard, but it's all about looking at things logically. Our offense wasn't as consistent as it could have been. My pitching was good, but it was going to get even better as time went on. And I was working with basically half a bullpen—dividing four relievers with varying degrees of effectiveness into A and B groups to avoid overuse.

But again, Sutcliffe was the key—if the Cubs hadn't picked him up we probably would have had enough to take the NL East.

I pointed out a few areas to Frank where we needed to improve, and he was all ears. Near the end of the '84 season, we picked up right-handed-hitting third baseman Ray Knight, who would help against opposing lefties—an Achilles' heel for us. Plus, he would give us veteran leadership in the clubhouse.

But there was still more work to be done. We still needed another big bat in the middle of the order and an experienced catcher to mentor our young pitching staff.

As it would turn out, help was right around the corner.

nineteen

December 10, 1984:
The Final Pieces

FRANK CASHEN HAD JUST gotten off the phone with Expos GM John McHale. There was a sense of urgency in his voice.

"McHale called asking if I had an interest in Gary Carter," he said. "What do you think?"

"Yes, *of course* we do!" I exclaimed. "Gary would be a definite upgrade hitting in the middle of the lineup, and he's the best catcher in baseball."

I was instantly intrigued over the prospect of getting Carter, who was coming off one of his best seasons ever—a .294 average, 27 home runs, and a league-tying 106 RBI. Any time you had the chance to get a guy who's as good a catcher as he was—a big target who received and threw the ball well and called great games—*and* had thunder in his bat, it was exciting.

Plus, by putting a right-handed power hitter in the middle of the lineup between Hernandez and Strawberry, he would fit right in.

"What would we have to give up?" I asked.

"They want Hubie, Fitz, Youmans, and Winningham,"

Frank said. "And we also get a good-looking prospect who plays shortstop—Argenis Salazar."

The Expos were asking for an awful lot. I liked all the guys they wanted. I had managed each of them at one time or another. Hubie was the crown jewel of the trade for them—already a good player who I felt was going to really come into his own and be a star. I hated the idea of losing him.

I didn't mind dealing Mike Fitzgerald so much because we were getting an every-day catcher to replace him. But the other two were among our top prospects. Floyd Youmans reminded me a little bit of Doc—they were both from Tampa, were the same age, and both threw hard and had great stuff. The difference was that Youmans was a little wild and didn't have Gooden's command. And Herm Winningham was a good young player—a left-handed batter who hit .354 in the Texas League before we promoted him to the International League that year.

We would basically be giving them four guys who were ready to play on their big-league club.

Still, I thought we *had* to make that deal.

"Let's do it, Frank."

"Okay, Davey," he said, "But Carter has a no-trade clause in his contract. As you know, he's very popular with the Montreal fans and his wife and kids are happy up there. So you may have to get on the phone and help me persuade him to play for us."

"No problem, Frank."

After hanging up, I was already rehearsing in my head what I might say to Gary.

I would have told him, "There's no better place than New York City. When you make it there, you can make it anywhere. You would be immensely popular. We're building a great fan base—really packing them in. It's going to be nothing like those small crowds you've been playing in front of up there in Montreal. New York's a great city. You'll really love it!"

I also knew that Gary was a TV hound. He liked to smile in

front of the cameras, and coming to New York would be perfect for him. There weren't going to be just the one or two interviewers he was used to up north. There would now be *hundreds*, and if he wanted to talk to each and every one of them, it would be fine with me because it would take the pressure off of everybody else.

Later that night, Frank called me back.

"You don't need to talk to Gary—he's in," Cashen said. "But McHale wants to keep Salazar."

So now it was just Carter for all those guys.

But after a short pause, and realizing the immediate impact a superstar like Gary could make on our ballclub, I told Frank, "Let's still do it."

After the deal was made official, I told reporters, "It will be a thrill for me to pencil Carter's name in the lineup. I'm a much smarter manager already!"

It would be a blockbuster trade that shook the baseball world.

And make us the immediate front-runners in the NL East.

******

It can't be overstated the impact the Carter trade would have on our ballclub. Everybody knew that he was a perennial All-Star catcher who was a big run producer. But until you have him on your team, you don't realize the other intangibles he brings along with him.

What a lot of people didn't know about Gary was how he kept a book on every hitter in the league—noting their strengths and weaknesses. It was really well done, and he demanded that each of our young pitchers knew how he wanted them to pitch each hitter.

As a result, Carter made all the pitchers better.

"Kid" was, like Hernandez, a leader on the club whom players gravitated to by his simply leading by example.

He also was an iron man. This was a guy who, in his first season with us, had loose cartilage in his knees, cracked ribs, and banged-up fingers, but would still fight with me while he lay in pain on the trainer's table because he didn't want to sit out a day game after a night game. And most of the time, he'd talk me out of it, which wasn't easy to do because I didn't want him to get hurt any worse than he already was. Gary was a tough man.

But for as big as the Carter deal was, it was just a part of our push to address all of our weaknesses.

The same week we picked up Gary, we acquired Howard Johnson from the Detroit Tigers for Walt Terrell. HoJo may have only been a part-time third baseman with the Tigers on their '84 World Series championship team, but I always liked switch hitters who had some pop—and he fit the bill. I also knew he had a really strong arm.

That spring, before an exhibition game with the Tigers, I spoke with their Hall of Fame skipper, Sparky Anderson, about HoJo and all he said was, "He's a great player and great kid."

But something didn't seem right in his answer. I wondered why Sparky played guys like Manny Castillo and Tom Brookens over Howard in the World Series. I wish I would have asked him, though I got the feeling it was a confidence issue with HoJo's play in the field.

When Johnson came over to us, he had a funny little way of throwing the ball over to first. I addressed this with him.

"Howard, I don't want you aiming it over there," I said. "Just cut it loose. I don't care if you throw it 10 rows up behind first base. As long as you cut it loose, I'm not going to be upset about any ball you throw away."

It worked. By doing just that, HoJo's throws actually became more accurate.

Up until that point, Howard felt that being a power-hitting third baseman who could run and steal bases was his identity—that's who he thought he was. But I knew he could be a good defensive player for us as well. In fact, when Sid Fernandez—a strikeout/fly ball pitcher—started, I had enough confidence in HoJo to sometimes play him at shortstop.

But while I always thought HoJo would turn out to be the star he eventually became for us a couple of years later, I platooned him with Knight throughout the '85 season. And there were two primary reasons for this.

First, Knight was a veteran and a great mentor to the younger guys. He was a lot like Carter in that he never wanted to sit out a game. I remember that when Ray arrived with a bum knee that spring training, I talked to him about it.

"Maybe I'm going to need to put you on the DL, give you some time to rest it up because I don't want you to go out there hurting it worse," I said.

"Skip, I'll play right through it," the former Golden Gloves boxer told me. "I'll be fine."

"Well, just take it easy," I said.

I appreciated Knight's toughing it out because the other value he gave us was his right-handed bat in the lineup. Even with Carter and George Foster, we still had a predominantly left-handed hitting lineup. And off the bench, I had other left-handed bats like Danny Heep, a good hitter whom I desperately wanted to give more at-bats to keep him sharp; as well as Clint Hurdle, an outfielder whom I helped turn into a versatile backup third baseman and catcher. And then we had the best pinch-hitter in baseball, Rusty Staub, who also batted from the left side.

Although HoJo was a switch hitter, he had problems at times hitting left-handed pitching. So we needed more right-handed hitters to offset the parade of left-handed arms teams like the Cardinals used against us. And with Knight out there, if they came in with a righty, then they'd have to face HoJo. So they would have to pick their poison.

Following that '85 season, we solved the same issue over at second base, picking up the right-handed Tim Teufel in a trade with the Minnesota Twins. I pushed hard for Frank to make that deal. Tim was a solid hitter with some pop for a second baseman, and would be an upgrade over the right-handed second basemen we had in Kelvin Chapman and Ron Gardenhire. So now I had another solid platoon with Teufel and Backman.

And then we had the best-looking right-handed pure hitter I've ever seen ready to come up from Tidewater in Kevin Mitchell. Mitch was called "World" because he could play everywhere, and I envisioned him as another potent bat from the right side to complement all of our lefty swingers.

Up until the point of acquiring some right-handed bats, it was like I was playing a game of chess against Cardinals manager Whitey Herzog in the way he used his bullpen against us. I thought he used it superbly. He had two hard-throwing lefties and some power righty arms. He was picking his matchups. I had to fix where he went, "check," and I'd go, "check to you," and he'd go, "checkmate."

With guys like Knight, Teufel, and Mitchell, we working to eliminate any edge the Cardinals may have had on us.

But the '85 season did produce yet another left-handed swinger who would become an important cog in our offense—Lenny Dykstra.

By the end of May, the injuries on our ballclub were piling up. Gardenhire had back problems and a pulled hamstring, Foster had a bad knee, Carter had cracked ribs, Mookie had a bad shoulder that would require surgery, and Strawberry had badly injured his thumb while making a diving catch. Straw would also require surgery and, like Wilson, would miss two months of the season.

That paved the way for "Nails" to come up from Tidewater.

******

Lenny was just Lenny and there was nobody quite like him. Everybody loved him for it. I never saw any animosity toward him by our guys. Was he cocky? Of course he was. But the one thing you can be in New York is cocky if you can go out and produce. That's much better than if you're not cocky and you don't produce.

And Dykstra made an immediate impact, homering in his first

game up with us. But his game was more about getting on, stealing bases, and crashing hard into center-field walls. He played with reckless abandon, which endeared him to the fans right away.

Lenny was also a giant headache for pitchers. They never knew what he was going to do at the plate. They would think, *Is he going to bunt? Is he going to slap the ball the other way? Is he going to open up and pull one?*

He always had such a squatty, small strike zone—as he hovered right on top of the plate. He was like hell to pitch to because if you came in on him too much you were going to hit him. And if he got on base, he was a terror. We're talking about a guy who stole more than 100 bases in the minors two years before.

I never had a problem with Lenny and his cockiness on the ballfield because he knew what the hell he was doing and could back it up with his ability.

That's a whole different story, of course, from what happened to him after his playing days.

"Skip, I got car washes now," he told me. "I got all the cash that I need."

I said, "Good for you. You need it."

So then he sells them and goes into brokering.

"Man, they're writing you up as some genius," I told him.

But I knew he was a gambler, and when he started playing the market, buying shorts, and trying to do everything conceivable to turn whatever he had into a billion dollars, I knew he was in trouble. He was doing something he didn't know a whole lot about—just pure gambling.

I played a good deal of golf with Lenny when he was with the Mets. One time he bet me 50 dollars a hole, but wouldn't take any shots despite the fact I was a scratch golfer. Lenny lost a bunch of holes and then went, "I'm not playing in the next hole, but the hole after that I'm playing you for a 100!"

Let's just say Lenny didn't have any problems with confidence.

******

Another weakness on the ballclub I felt we had to fix was in the bullpen. Our '84 team really only had one effective late-inning left-handed reliever in Orosco. I wanted to get him some help—with the preference being another southpaw. This was my top priority in the pitching department.

Of course, we also had Doug Sisk, who saved 15 games for us in '84. But Sisk was an interesting study. He had a closer mentality, with a nasty sinker and a little teeny slider he was working on. Sisk was very hard to hit.

Still, despite tremendous success in his first two seasons with the Mets, Dougie was heart-attack city—always getting himself in and out of trouble. He was the one that got me on Rolaids. Believe me, I kept them right on the bench behind me. When I had him warming up, I was already taking them. He knew I was taking Rolaids when he pitched, and we had some fun with it.

But, conversely, Sisk had nerves of steel. The booing and even the death threats he received by idiot fans for his wildness in '85 didn't outwardly bother him. I'm sure it bothered him inside, but you would never know it.

On the mound, he never got frazzled. I recall one time I brought him in with a three-run lead and he walked the first three batters he faced. But he got out of the inning without giving up a run after inducing a pop-up and a ground ball double play. He was capable of doing that. Sisk was a big part of our success when healthy and was very durable.

But he really struggled for us late in '84 and in '85, and later, we found out why—he had bone chips in his elbow. Once he took care of that, he was damn near unhittable again in '86 and '87, with an ERA in the low threes. I stayed with him, never losing faith. I wasn't worried about Sisk like the fans were.

And I should thank him. Because of Doug, I started doing Rolaids commercials.

But we had to do something to compensate for his off year.

I thought we caught a lucky break when the Houston Astros released lefty reliever Joe Sambito, a once outstanding closer, early in the '85 season. We quickly snatched him up, signing the free agent just two weeks later.

But when Sambito struggled, and with Calvin Schiraldi out with a broken toe, I started using a rookie right-handed reliever— Roger McDowell.

McDowell had missed the entire '84 season at Double A Jackson after surgery for bone spurs, but was back in spring training that year and impressed everyone. The first day of camp, I watched him for the first time while standing behind the cage. A lot of our hitters couldn't touch him. I never saw such a nasty sinker. He threw it right over the top and the bottom just fell out. He had great command over that pitch, running it in, running it away, sinking in, sinking away. Roger could tell you he was coming right down the middle with it and you would still have a hard time hitting it. Most batters would swing right over it.

Like I had over Gooden the year before, I had to fight Frank to allow me to bring McDowell north with us.

"Look, I'll take care of him—I'll *baby* him," I pleaded to Cashen. "I'll rehab Roger by treating him like a starter out of the pen. I'll pitch him a couple of innings, then give him a day off. Then I'll let him throw on the side, then I'll give him another day off. And then I'll use him for a couple more innings."

Cashen agreed, and I stayed true to that regimen with Roger basically until the All-Star break. But after that, I approached Frank again.

"I'm taking the wraps off him!" I exclaimed.

With all the success McDowell was having, Frank had to agree.

Roger basically took over Sisk's role and became my go-to guy whom I brought in the sixth and seventh innings. Because he threw mostly sinkers, with enough rest, I could sometimes push his outings to three innings. Sometimes I felt bad when McDowell pitched multiple innings and then, if a left-handed hitter came up who might be a threat to him, I'd bring in Orosco to close it out for the save. But Roger was my workhorse and arguably my most valuable reliever, even though Jesse led the club in saves.

McDowell pitched in 62 games and had 17 saves that year. He didn't walk many guys and had a very low hits-to-innings ratio. Roger would be the mainstay in our bullpen, and the complement to Jesse, that we desperately needed.

******

As for our stable of good, young starting pitchers, I knew they were going to keep getting better.

Sid Fernandez, who struggled a bit in spring training, got a chance to come up to our club after a rash of injuries to our other pitchers, and really impressed. Here was a guy who went from having a lack of confidence to making a few adjustments and tossing a one-hitter over six innings against the Phillies in one of his first starts up.

The one thing Sid always had going for him was how tough he was to hit. When he threw the ball, it was like it was coming out of his jersey—just in so close to him. Then, if he threw the curveball over for a strike, the hitter had no chance. And he had a riding fastball that he kept up in the zone that was near impossible to hit on the ground.

I think the biggest thing that helped Fernandez, though, was being around our other young pitchers who were still learning to pitch—Darling, Doc, Rick Aguilera, and Tim Leary—and his interactions with Carter. Gary had a huge influence on him.

But as far as the adjustments he made, Sid had a little bit of a problem I helped him work out. Fernandez had this big, long leg kick before firing home. A runner on first could read his movement real easily and steal on him. So one day I went up to him during a workout to discuss this issue.

"Sid, let me ask you a question," I told the southpaw. "You know what a sidestep is?"

"No," he answered.

"Well, let's just say the runner's going to steal," I began. "When delivering, pick up your right foot and put it back down just six inches forward before releasing the ball. When you get a man on, why don't you just use that approach?"

Sid agreed and it turned out to be a great remedy for his problem. The thing about Fernandez was he was all upper body. When he pitched he was all shoulders. So once he started doing the sidestep, his motion jumped on the hitters more quickly because now they couldn't set themselves and the runners couldn't steal. So everybody was neutralized.

When Sid joined the walking wounded with an Achilles tendon injury, we brought up Aguilera. We truly had an embarrassment of riches in the young pitching department, and Rick fit right in.

Aggie was a high-three-quarter-guy with a good moving fastball, a good slider, and an excellent splitter. He would end up getting 21 starts, so he effectively was one of our starters for a half a season and really shined.

Another pitcher who we got to bring up was Terry Leach, a guy who basically had a rubber arm. A tremendous competitor, his sidearm, slingerlike delivery brought his hand so close to the dirt that it almost hit the ground. In turn, his delivery made his breaking ball go up, while his fastball acted like a big sinker.

Leach did well for us, highlighted by a shutout he threw in August, a period in which our staff tossed three of them in four days.

The only time Terry encountered some difficulties was when an opposing lineup featured primarily left-handed hitters, because Leach was a mostly low-ball pitcher and that's just where a lot of lefty hitters like it. So his best chance in those situations was to throw his curveball up in the strike zone, which isn't really a good location because it comes in to a hitter. But, being the competitor Terry was, he battled out there and became a really good pitcher for us.

Eddie Lynch, the veteran on the staff, was one of the more respected members in the clubhouse and ate up a lot of innings. He was a workhorse who helped keep us in the pennant race when so many of our other pitchers when down with injuries.

Ronnie Darling, of course, was really coming into his own in '85. After Doc, he was clearly our best pitcher. In fact, Ronnie would have been the ace on most staffs in baseball. He started the same number of games as Doc, going 16–6 with an ERA of under three.

But in '85, *nobody* on the planet was better than Gooden.

In all my years in the game, I never saw anything quite like it. His earned run average was microscopic at 1.53. His record was 24–4. He struck out 268 hitters in 276 innings. He didn't give up many hits—an average of around seven a game.

Every game Doc pitched at Shea was an "event." It felt like the entire city stopped when he took the mound. We'd have 50,000 fans in the stadium, screaming and hollering on every pitch. Fans brought placards with "K" printed on them, hanging them along the rafters whenever Doc struck someone out. Now, of course, fans hang "K" signs for nearly every strikeout pitcher, but it was Mets fans who began that trend with Gooden.

The toughest thing for me was when I came out of the dugout to pull Doc from a game. The fans booed me mercilessly.

But I figured out a way around that.

I told Doc, "Wait until the relief pitcher gets here and you and I will walk back to the dugout together."

"Yeah," Gooden said. "I get cheers."

So this was one way I got cheers instead of boos—by leaving the mound *with* Doc.

Gooden was so successful in '85 that, following the season, the league changed the balk rule because of him. Doc used to bring the ball down in the stretch, hit his belly, bounce up, and throw the ball home. Now the umpires were saying you had to stop completely at the belt. But my argument all along—which got me tossed from a spring training game—was that the old way was really a stop because of the change of directions from the belt to going back up.

But I obviously lost that debate.

On a different matter, with Doc still just 20 years old, the front office was very concerned I was burning him out.

Mel Stottlemyre—one of the best pitching coaches in baseball—and I used to talk about that all the time.

It was always, "Do you think we're having Doc throw too many innings?"

Gooden would complete 16 games for us that year, a number that is unheard of today. But back in Stott's era, that figure was nothing out of the ordinary. You had guys back in the '60s and early '70s throw 300-plus innings and nothing was ever said about it.

Even in '85, you had Tommy Lasorda over in L.A. throwing Fernando Valenzuela around 160 pitches in some games and just as many innings as Doc.

In the final analysis, I thought we were careful with Doc. I never let him go above 130 pitches in a game and, if he got tired, wouldn't hesitate to hook him early.

Gooden was just a remarkable athlete.

There wasn't anything he couldn't do.

******

Nelson Doubleday, the president of Doubleday and Co., the entity that acquired the Mets in 1980, would buy a 50 percent stake in the ballclub along with Fred Wilpon after selling his publishing company to Bertelsmann A.G. in 1986.

Nelson was a very likable and wonderful human being whom I took to immediately upon joining the Mets. He lived out on Long Island and was a member of both the Piping Rock and Meadowbrook golf courses. As an avid golfer, I made sure wherever

I rented a place to live that it would be right in the middle of them both. That was because, on off days, Nelson gave my coaches and me carte blanche to use either course.

"If you need anything in the pro shop, just sign for it. I'll take care of it," Doubleday told me.

On certain occasions, particularly at Piping Rock, Nelson would come out and greet us on the greens in his golf cart with his golden retriever in the back to bring us coffee laced with brandy.

We loved Nelson. There was nothing we wouldn't have done for him. We'd have run through a wall for the man.

Wilpon, who was team president and owned a small share of the team when I was hired, was also very supportive.

"If there's any move you want to make or anything else, let me know and I'll help you with Cashen," he said to me my first week in a very nice way.

I took Fred up on that and used him to help me influence some of the moves I thought Frank should make. The Teufel trade was one of them.

Another was for a left-handed pitcher in Boston named Bobby Ojeda.

Although we were loaded with good starters, Sid was the only southpaw I had in the rotation. And with all the young talent, I thought there was a good chance Lynch would soon be edged out. So aside from another left-hander, I thought we could use a veteran to anchor the staff.

At first glance, Ojeda's career numbers didn't jump out and scream "ace pitcher" at you. But I believed he had a chance to become just that for us.

Here was an ultracompetitive guy who had a great change-up, a good curveball, and command of his fastball. Those kinds of pitchers, ones who can throw three good big-league pitches, can enjoy a great deal of success.

The fact that he was basically a .500 pitcher with the Red Sox didn't bother me in the least—because I understood why. Everybody

Andrea, my "little surfer girl." Of all my children, Andrea was the most like me, with a fierce competitive spirit. She was taken from me too early due to complications from schizophrenia. (Davey Johnson Collection)

From the time I began little league, I knew I wanted to be a professional baseball player. It was an obsession. Here I am at 12 years old (top row on the right) with the Winter Park Giants. I may have been a skinny little kid, but I was 9–0 as a pitcher while hitting nine home runs—two of them off future major leaguer Jack Billingham. (Davey Johnson Collection)

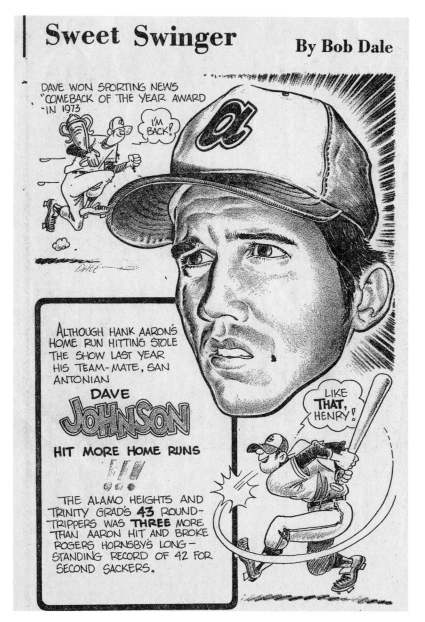

My best individual season was in 1973, when I belted 43 home runs—42 as a second baseman to tie Roger Hornsby's all-time mark at the position. The record still stands today. (Cartoon by Bob Dale, San Antonio Express-News artist)

My loving mother, Florence, was an outstanding swimmer, setting a southern record while at the Florida State College for Women in the 100-yard crawl. Her encouraging demeanor had a major impact on the way I managed my ballplayers as a manager. (Davey Johnson Collection)

Being a scratch golfer is just one of my passions away from baseball. I've also been a successful land investor, pilot, scuba diving instructor, and mathematician. I believe in living life to the fullest. (Davey Johnson Collection)

As a member of the Atlanta Braves (pictured with Houston Astros first baseman Lee May). Teaming up with Henry Aaron and Darrell Evans, we became the first three teammates to ever hit more than 40 home runs in the same season in 1973.

I grew up a Dodgers fan, so having the chance to manage the club was a dream come true. But despite improving the team's fortunes, I never was in sync with general manager Kevin Malone (pictured on the left) and would eventually tell the Dodgers managing partner, Bob Daly, that I could no longer work for him—that it was either him or me. I was actually relieved when Daly chose to fire me—I wanted to return home to care for my sick daughter, Andrea. (AP Images)

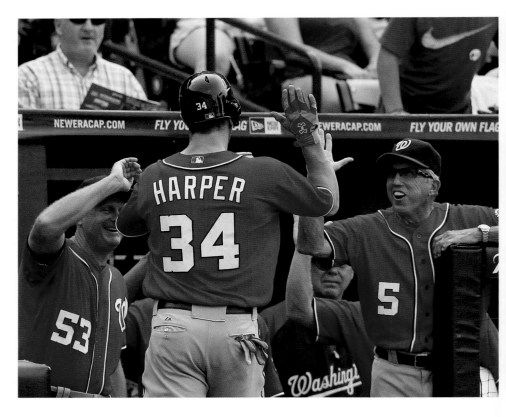

After 11 years away from managing in the big leagues, I returned to pilot the Washington Nationals and guided them to the city's first baseball playoff berth since the Senators in 1933. The club featured two budding superstars—Stephen Strasburg and Bryce Harper—both of whom I knew when they were kids. I presented Harper with a baseball skills tournament trophy for hitting the longest home run—more than 400 feet—when he was just 16. When Bryce (pictured above after hitting a home run) entered the 2010 draft the next year, I advised the Nats to make him the No. 1 pick in the nation. I'm glad they listened. (AP Images)

Relaxing at home and enjoying life in Winter Park, Florida. (Erik Sherman)

In 2016, we celebrated the 30th anniversary of the 1986 Mets World Series Championship. (AP Images)

thinks in Fenway that a southpaw has to pitch away from right-handed hitters because of the Green Monster. But that's actually not true. A lefty pitcher needs to throw in on those hitters because guys can go up there and hook balls on the outside part of the plate over that green wall. Other right-handed hitters could also take that outside pitch and drive it to the vaster right field at Fenway.

Pitching in with hard stuff wasn't Bobby's strong suit. It's no lefty's strength in that ballpark unless they can really pitch in. I should know. I played there enough when I was with the Orioles and know full well how the successful pitchers pitched there.

So when we got Ojeda from the Red Sox after the season in an eight-player deal with the principal from our side being Calvin Schiraldi, I believed we had really solidified a tremendous pitching staff.

******

As for the NL East race in '85, with the Cubs decimated by injuries and showing their age, it was the Cardinals who stepped up and were now our chief rival in the division.

Two weeks into September, we were deadlocked in a first-place tie with St. Louis as we entered a three-game set with them in New York.

It also marked the first game back at Shea for Hernandez since he testified at the Pittsburgh drug trials, proceedings that put a spotlight on Major League Baseball's cocaine scandal of the early '80s.

Keith had admitted to doing cocaine while a member of the St. Louis Cardinals and was a little nervous about what the fan reaction would be toward him that night.

I spoke to him about it prior to the game. My message was very short and simple.

"We missed you," I told him. "That's a fact. Now we're home."

As it turned out, the fans gave Mex a standing ovation as a sign of their support for him. Their reaction nearly drove him to tears.

He was also dealing with a divorce and custody battle over his two daughters, so that season was particularly difficult for him personally.

But to be honest, I was never worried about Keith.

Mex was always happiest on the ballfield and most content in the clubhouse. He was a Civil War history buff, always reading books about it. And we had a light clubhouse with some real characters like Straw, Mookie, Rusty, HoJo, Wally, and Carter. It was a happy and fun place and everybody, especially Keith, liked coming early.

I think when times were tough for him, his baseball life may have acted as an escape from reality. And no matter what happened off the field, it never affected the way he played on it—which was usually outstanding.

And that series with the Cardinals was no different.

Keith drove home the game's first run and later scored on a HoJo grand slam in the opener—a 5–4 win.

And then he singled in Mookie with a walk-off RBI single in the finale to put us up a game in the standings with a little more than three weeks remaining in the season.

But after our series with them, St. Louis went on an impressive roll, winning 15 of 18, which included two separate seven-game winning streaks.

We played pretty well, going 11–7 over the same stretch, but with just six games to go in the season, we found ourselves three lengths behind the Cardinals as we traveled to St. Louis to play a critical three-game series against them.

We needed a sweep or else our season was basically over.

Herzog was going for the kill in the first game, moving his ace, John Tudor, a guy who had owned us all year, up a spot in their rotation to face Darling. The New York media was all over me to move Doc up a spot to counter Whitey's move.

But I wouldn't do it.

I had confidence in all of my pitchers. Besides, I didn't want to say to Ronnie, "Look, you're not good enough to pitch this first game. You're going to pitch the next one."

That's like saying I didn't have the confidence in him to get us off to a good start. It's a mind game, really, in that you want them all to think they're the best.

Besides, we had to win them all anyway, so it wouldn't make any sense to bring Doc back with less rest than he would normally have had.

As it turned out, Ronnie was more than up to the challenge, matching Tudor through nine scoreless innings.

And it all worked out in the end when Straw broke a scoreless tie in the 11th with a moon shot off of reliever Ken Dayley to give us a 1–0 victory. We were relieved and elated—and still alive.

As a result of my faith in Darling, I had a rested Gooden ready to go in the second game with us just two games out. The media was now calling me a genius.

Doc may not have had his best stuff in that second contest—giving up nine hits—but it was good enough for a complete game 5–2 victory over 21-game winner Joaquin Andujar.

Now just a game out of first, I had no other viable option than to pitch the young rookie Aguilera in the biggest game of our season. But I really didn't have a problem with that because Rick was a heck of a competitor and had great stuff. I felt he could cut it.

And things looked good for us early.

We were already up 1–0 when we loaded the bases with one out against Cardinals starter Danny Cox with Foster and HoJo coming up. HoJo had hit the grand slam in the last series against him back at Shea, so we were hopeful that history might repeat itself. But this time, Cox got out of the inning without any further damage done.

A missed opportunity for sure.

Aggie pitched decently over six innings, but St. Louis won it 4–3 and now led by two games with three to play.

They would clinch the title two nights later.

We finished the season with 98 wins—an eight-game

improvement over the previous campaign—despite a ton of injuries, most notably to key guys like Straw and Mookie, who were out for long stints. But if we grew up in '84, then I think we got better and more balanced in '85.

And we were no longer the little brother to the Yankees in New York. We owned the back page of the tabloids and were drawing 50,000 screaming fans a night down the stretch.

But most important to me, with the final additions we would make in the off-season, we had addressed our shortcomings. So if we indeed were involved in baseball's version of a chess match with Whitey Herzog's Cardinals, we could now say, "Checkmate."

We sure as hell weren't going to fall short again.

| twenty |

March 1, 1986:
Ready to Dominate

IT WAS THE FIRST day of full-squad spring training and I had a message for my ballclub.

"We're not going to just win the championship," I told them. "We're going to *dominate*! We've got all the pieces together, boys—now let's go do it!"

A lot has been made of that brash proclamation I made that day in St. Petersburg, but it was easy for me to say because I thoroughly believed in our ability and how good we were going to be.

I had taken over a last-place team that had won just 68 games in '83. Then we won 90 games in my first year, but still had a few holes. So we made a few trades and got better, winning 98 in '85. But we still had some areas we needed to patch up—which we did—that would enable us to beat the best team in the league at that time, the St. Louis Cardinals.

We simply had a great club that just kept getting better and better. We did the things we needed to do to win. Putting this team together wasn't easy. It was a challenge. In that way, we mirrored the city. New York's a challenging place to work and play. But that would make winning there all the sweeter.

So in coming to spring training in '86, I felt with the experience my pitchers had, the time my position players now had playing alongside each other, and the final pieces we had picked up in the off-season, if we *only* won the championship and *didn't* dominate, it would be all my fault.

We just needed to do the things that we were capable of doing—simply 24 guys doing their job. It wasn't a big deal. I didn't give a lot of speeches and none of them were very long, including this particular one. And if my talk put the spotlight on me and off my players, then all the better. I always tried to take the pressure off my players anyway.

Overall, spring training went well—everybody worked hard to get ready for the season. But there were a couple of issues that were troublesome.

Lenny, whom I saw as one of my table setters with Wally, came to camp overweight like he wanted to be some big home run hitter.

"Lenny, you've got to start running in the outfield," I told him. "You can't carry that much weight around without getting hurt."

He followed my instructions and took the weight off, but he was always fixed on becoming a slugger. And that was reflected in his approach to hitting. Occasionally, he would try to set a pitcher up by taking pitches right down the middle in his first couple of at-bats. That was Dykstra's way of getting a fat pitch right down the middle in his third at-bat to try to drive out of the ballpark.

It was always a constant battle with Lenny to get him to accept his role as a leadoff hitter and not a guy trying to hit home runs all the time. When I had him in the Instructional League, I was in the batting cage working with another kid who had the exact same issue as Lenny.

"Line drives," I told the kid. "Get on top and hit line drives."

So Lenny walks by and goes, "Let me in there. Why didn't you tell me to do that?"

Dykstra then proceeded to hit one rope after another.

The thing about Lenny was if I was telling somebody else what he needed to hear, he might listen. But if I talked to him directly, he often didn't heed my advice. I knew that about him.

Another issue I had to deal with that spring was with the front office.

During one of our first spring training games, I noticed that Gooden's pitching motion had noticeably changed.

"What the heck is going on here?" I asked Stottlemyre.

"Well, the front office wants him to do this," he told me. "Frank wants to change his delivery so he's looking more at the target. He doesn't want Doc to hurt his arm or anything."

"Oh no!" I exclaimed.

Gooden had a big bounce coming down, so Mel told Doc to hold himself up higher and go from there. He also cut down the turn in his delivery. Doc used to have a huge turn. But by altering Doc's delivery, I thought he lost a little effectiveness. I hated to see them change his motion the way they did. And I told Frank so right away after the game.

"You don't have to worry about his arm," I practically pleaded with Cashen. "I'll continue to be careful with him."

But Frank was adamant about doing everything he could to save Doc's arm.

We finished the Grapefruit League season with a .500 record—13–13—which, of course, is meaningless. The purpose of spring training is to get your club ready for the season and keep everyone healthy—which we did.

Not everybody agrees with that philosophy, of course—like the owner across town. George Steinbrenner wanted to win every last battle, including exhibition baseball games. The Yankees ended up with the best record in the American League that spring. But it wouldn't lead to a title in the AL East during the regular season.

With the Mets, it really helped to have the feeling that not only were we good, but we were better than all the other teams in baseball. I don't think that's bravado, but just stating the facts.

Our club was built to win it all, and I could hardly wait for the season to begin.

******

We would come storming out of the gates in April, taking over first place for good on April 23 and then sweeping a four-game series in St. Louis. It was devastating to the Cardinals, but we had put together a team specifically to beat them.

The Cards were still a very fine club—they had speed, switch-hitters all throughout their lineup, a great bullpen—but now we could favorably match up against anything they threw at us. If they went one way, we could go the other way and win the battle. In previous years, St. Louis had that edge on us.

I will never forget when, after the sweep, a reporter showed me a clip that quoted Herzog saying, "Nobody's catching the Mets."

And that was in *April!*

That series set the tone for the rest of our season. We knew we were good coming out of spring training, but you've got to show it by how you play—and we did. And when you go on the road and beat a very good ballclub like the Cardinals, that just adds to your determination of how good you are. It reaffirms the fact that everybody knows you're talented.

After leaving St. Louis, we kept on winning, closing out the month with an 11-game winning streak and a five-game lead in the NL East.

We stayed hot, basically winning an average of two out of every three games we played up to the All-Star break. Our success was due in large part to our starting pitching, which was the best in baseball as far as I was concerned. Our four starters—Gooden, Darling, Sid, and Bobby O—were a combined 41–10. We had built a 13-game lead over the second-place Expos—simply running on all cylinders.

Keeping the team focused with the big lead was never an issue.

The guys came to play hard every day.

Instead, one of my most pressing tasks was the handling of the pitching staff. We kept a close watch on pitch counts, and if I felt I needed to hook a pitcher early because of the number of pitches he threw in his previous start, I didn't hesitate. The aforementioned four primary starting pitchers had between 30 and 34 starts, with Aguilera contributing 20. When you can spread out assignments like that, it means the manager takes pretty good care of his staff. And that was my whole point I had with Frank about Doc—I was always going to make sure I protected him.

But with the changes Cashen instructed Mel to make with Doc's delivery, there is no question in my mind it had an adverse effect on his performance that season.

It's hard to compare any season to the one Doc had in '85—it was epic. But despite finishing the '86 season with a record of 17–6, there was a fairly big drop off in his numbers as the year wore on. In his first 12 starts, Gooden was 8–2 with a 2.11 ERA and four shutouts. But in his last 21 starts, he was 9–4 with an ERA of 3.29. His strikeouts were way down and his walks significantly higher.

Doc had always been about ripping. Here's a pitcher who comes into baseball, lights out, phenomenal, and every other superlative you want to add. And now the organization is changing the rules, messing with his rhythm and making him look more toward home plate instead of delivering in that twisting motion. It's like having a guy hit .400 a couple of years in a row and now, all of a sudden, you're changing his stance.

While still very good, Gooden was no longer the same dominant pitcher. It might even have caused him to start doing drugs.

Maybe Doc thought, *Man, I guess something's wrong with me, 'cause now I gotta do something different.*

Rhythm is so important in pitching. But the front office was convinced his new delivery would save his arm in the long term. I felt strongly against it, that it was the worst thing that could happen to Doc.

With Gooden no longer the undisputed ace of the staff, Ojeda stepped into that role for us in '86. Bobby was simply phenomenal. He was a tough pitcher who had a great change-up, located his pitches well, had a good curveball, and didn't give up a lot of hits or walk many batters. And when you put him in a rotation like we had, following a flamethrower like Doc and a pitcher whose ball was all over the place like Ronnie, he's extra difficult to hit because he could pull the string on his off-speed stuff like a yo-yo out there. The three very different styles really messed up opposing hitters, not just in their series with us, but also in their series after that.

Not surprisingly, the more our lead continued to increase, the more fun the guys had coming to the ballpark. And perhaps no two players were enjoying themselves more than McDowell and HoJo. Aside from their contributions to the ballclub on the field, they were motivated to give as many of their teammates and coaches the hotfoot as they could, with Bill Robinson victimized the most. They tried to get me a couple of times, but I was always looking around for them. The closest those two got with me was getting a match in my shoe, but I moved away before they lit it.

McDowell just had so much energy and was really the ringleader of giving hotfoots. HoJo was an amateur compared with Roger. But it was just a way for the two of them to have some fun.

Other teams began to take notice of how much we were enjoying ourselves while we were kicking ass. But baseball is a damn hard job. Every day you're out there competing with other teams trying to take you down. I've often been called a "players' manager" for allowing my guys to enjoy themselves, but I never took that label as a bad thing. As a former player, I could relate to what my guys were going through.

And furthermore, I think all managers should be looking out for the best interest of their players and protecting them from bad press. If they made a mistake, I would never chastise them in the media.

Some managers kept a distance between themselves and their

players. I didn't see the point.

Still, all the hotfoots, the curtain calls at Shea, our swagger, and our perceived arrogance put a big bull's-eye on us—both on the field and off. I guess opposing teams and their fans felt like we were rubbing our success in their faces and that got on their nerves. The Cardinals even had a nickname for us—"pond scum."

On July 19, a few of the guys—Ojeda, Aggie, Straw, and Darling—took Teufel out to celebrate the birth of his son at a place called Cooter's while we were in Houston. Darryl left early, but the rest of them stayed until around closing time. The problems began when a few of the bouncers—who were off-duty cops—got jealous and treated them a little rough.

My guys didn't overreact. They didn't do anything where I was going to fine them or anything like that. But their altercation with those off-duty cops served as a reminder that they were in the limelight and that we all had targets on our backs. There were people out there who didn't like us because, first, we were from New York and, second, we were in first place.

After the four of them spent the night in jail, I spoke to each of them in my office individually. I didn't berate or get on any of them like the old dictator managers would. Again, being a former player, I understood all the things they were going through in trying to have a good year.

I basically told them all the same thing, trying to keep it positive.

"You've got to try to stay out of trouble, get re-signed for next year, and relish the opportunity to play in New York on a winning team. It doesn't get any better than that."

We were also marked men on the field—to which our four bench-clearing brawls in '86 would attest. Things would happen in ballgames—big home runs, curtain calls, etc.—that would irritate the other team. We tried to monitor what was going on as much as we could to avoid confrontation. For example, I never told a pitcher that season—or throughout my entire managerial career for that matter—to hit anybody. But inevitably, when an incident occurred, the other team would get fired up and do something to us first. And if something happened to one of our guys that might cause injury, we were right out there, ready to fight back.

Our first sparring partners were the Dodgers in late May, after Tom Niedenfuer beaned Knight immediately after serving up a grand slam to George Foster.

Then, in early June, we got into it with the Pirates after Bill Robinson accused pitcher Rick Rhoden of doctoring the baseball.

A month later, we brawled with Atlanta when Braves pitcher David Palmer hit Straw with a pitch after surrendering a first-inning, three-run homer to Carter.

But the most hostile of them all occurred a couple of weeks later and just days after the Cooter's incident, on July 22 in Cincinnati. It was also one of the strangest games I ever managed.

We were about to lose when, with two outs in the ninth, Mex hit a routine fly to the Reds' Dave Parker in right. But when Parker attempted a "snatch catch," he dropped the ball, allowing two unearned runs to score to tie the game.

The game remained deadlocked when, in the bottom of the tenth, Eric Davis stole third. But after Davis slid hard into the bag and thought Knight tagged him too hard, they started going at it, with Ray clocking Eric with a right hook. The fight resulted in the ejections of Knight and Mitchell on our side, and they joined Straw in the clubhouse, who had been tossed four innings earlier.

So now I had to do some major juggling, moving Carter to third and alternating my two primary relief pitchers—Orosco and McDowell—between the outfield and the mound. The guys loved it. It was fun for them and fun for me. Roger may have actually been the best outfielder I had anyway. All throughout the year, he was always shagging fly balls during batting practice. And Jesse was pretty good at it, too. So I wasn't really worried about any balls dropping in out there. I just had to make sure I followed the rules. You can only make that outfielder-pitcher switch once an inning.

But in the end it was all worth it, as we won the game 6–3 in

14 innings and moved a season-high 14 games up in the standings.

A fallout from the brawl was how Foster remained on the bench while his teammates were all on the field. A few of the guys didn't take his inaction very well, feeling like he didn't have their back. And some didn't really buy into his explanation of our setting a poor example for young fans with all of our fighting.

I actually didn't take it the same way those players did. George was just a very mild-mannered, nice man. I could understand why he didn't always want to fight.

A few days later, in a move that had nothing to do with his sitting out the brawl, I replaced Foster in the regular lineup with a platoon of Mookie and Mitchell, which prompted George to call me a racist as we were getting off our team bus at our hotel in Chicago.

I was stunned.

I thought, *How am I a racist if I am replacing you with two other black players?*

His comment really stung—and *still* does to this day. It really hurt me because I've never felt like I had one racist bone in my body. I've never looked at a guy's color at any point in my career. As I managed through the minor leagues, I had Latino players tell me they were really happy I was their manager because they said others were a little prejudiced against them. They knew I was different—that I just liked good ball players.

Foster's comment was a personal betrayal by someone I liked a whole lot and respected for what he had accomplished in his career.

But I think, in retrospect, here was a man who was now on the downside of a great career. I always enjoyed an excellent rapport with him and, when he struggled, we used to go to the cage and talk hitting. I would tell him how good he was and what he did well. If I sensed he was lunging a little bit too much, I would tell him to make a certain adjustment and he'd go on a tear. George would come out of our hitting sessions feeling great, but when you're near the end of the line and you're no longer a mainstay in a lineup, it's hard on a veteran.

I had already begun using different players in left field to basically give him some rest. He was getting slower and his bat speed wasn't what it had once been, either. It came to the point, as much as I hate to say it, that we became a better team when I could use Mitchell more in left field in place of Foster.

I felt like I had no choice but to suspend George. If a player calls me a racist and I don't address it strongly, that almost says I must be one. And I didn't want in any way, shape, or form for anyone to think I was a racist. Equally important, I just didn't see any validity in the statement he made when I was playing guys such as Mitchell and Mookie in his place. The only thing I can think of is maybe because I was playing Dykstra in center and moving Mookie to left in some games, he felt that he was really being replaced by Lenny.

Still, I couldn't let him get away with what he said. I had to take action.

"George," I told him, trying to keep my composure. "I'm going to have to suspend you."

I didn't know if the suspension would be for 10 days or some other number until I spoke with Frank, who had other ideas.

"I think it's just better that we release him," Cashen told me.

And that's just what the club did. We let George go on August 7. I guarantee you it was the toughest thing I ever had to do in my Mets career.

I've seen George since and we were fine. He was a little aloof with me, which was understandable.

But I may never get over what he said to me all those years ago.

In a season filled with great moments, that was the lowest.

******

Of course, Foster wasn't the only one who wanted more playing time. In fact, keeping all my platoon players content was, without question, my single biggest challenge of that '86 season.

None was more direct about it than Teufel, who came right up to me and said, "Davey, I should be the every-day second baseman."

I'm pretty sure Backman felt the same way about himself.

Certainly Dykstra and Mookie both believed that they should be the regular center fielder. And then you had the battle at third with HoJo and Knight.

Even our backup catcher Eddie Hearn was having a really good year swinging the bat, but Carter never wanted a day off.

And then I had a couple of backup outfielders—Danny Heep and late-season acquisition Lee Mazzilli—two guys who would be regulars on a lot of teams whom I needed to find playing time for.

I even tried giving Mitchell some time at shortstop to get him some at-bats to replace Rafael Santana, a sure-handed fielder who wasn't a great hitter.

I mean, I had guys champing at the bit to get in the lineup. I had to figure out different ways to get them in there.

It's safe to say that everybody on that ballclub felt that they should be playing every day. After all, they were *all* good players.

I tried hard to communicate to each player what his role was and how he could possibly expand it by his production on the field. And when all things were equal with the player with whom he was competing for playing time, I would make clear to him why I might use one over the other in creating the best hitting matchups. My job, as I saw it, was always to try to put every player in situations where he could excel.

I think one of my biggest accomplishments was getting a great hitter like Mitchell, a guy without an every-day position, 364 plate appearances. But I also got Heep, a fifth or sixth outfielder, into 86 games and got him 227 at-bats. Mookie, who alternated between center and left field, had more than 400 at-bats even after missing the first month of the season with a severe eye injury. And Lenny had nearly 500 at-bats while sitting versus most southpaws. Even Hearn saw plenty of action, getting into nearly 50 games.

I basically wanted everybody to feel like they were contributing to the ballclub. And that wasn't easy with a team filled with All-Star-caliber players.

What *was* easy, however, was managing a club filled with gamers. I instilled early on what I called the "Strawberry Rule," which basically meant if they didn't run hard on a ground ball and the infielder bobbled it, it's a $500 fine. Or, if they hit a fly ball to the outfield, weren't hustling, and the ball dropped in and they weren't on second, it was another $500.

But I hardly ever had to invoke the Strawberry Rule, as we had professional ballplayers who *always* played hard. Guys such as Mookie, Lenny, Backman, Knight, and HoJo were especially full-out, playing at 100 percent. We put pressure on the other guy, and if he made a mistake, we took full advantage of it.

We had a 24-man roster other teams could only dream about.

******

We would clinch the NL Eastern division title on September 17 behind Doc's complete game, 4–2 victory over the Cubs. I was very pleased we won it at Shea for our fans after just getting back from a five-game road trip. It was a thrilling night, with a near-sellout crowd into every pitch as we got closer and closer to finishing off Chicago.

Even Mex, who was as sick as a dog, entered the game at first in the eighth inning just so he could be on the field for the anticipated celebration. And the party started in earnest when the fans began storming the field a split second before Keith had even squeezed the webbing in his glove to catch the throw from Wally for the final out. It was pure bedlam, and I was just relieved my guys got off the field relatively unscathed.

With nearly three weeks remaining in the season, we didn't let up. I didn't take my foot off the pedal—like trying out rookies, as other teams might have done. I had so many guys who were interchangeable whom I needed to keep sharp. And because of the strength of my roster, there was never a big drop-off no matter whom I put out there—*ever*.

As a result, we rallied to the end, winning our final nine of ten otherwise meaningless games.

We would finish with 108 wins, which tied the '75 Reds for the modern-day National League record for most victories in a regular season. Our club reminded me a great deal of the Orioles team I played for from '69 through '71, from our starting pitching to our outfielders right down to how both clubs had a weak-hitting shortstop who played great defense.

I used the word *domination* to describe how we would crush the competition on that first full day of spring training. But did I believe we would finish 21½ games up in first place and 28½ games over our archrival St. Louis Cardinals?

The answer is *absolutely*!

That's because when you put a club together, you judge not just the talent on your own team, but also the talent on the other teams and how you match up.

So when we made the trades and call-ups we had to make to address our remaining weaknesses against our competition—most notably the Cardinals—the end result was exactly what I anticipated happening.

So it was now on to the NLCS to take on the Astros, the one club in the league that I thought was very similar to ours. They had played us tight in the regular season, as we took 7-of-12 against them. I knew going in that it was going to be a tough series, primarily because of their outstanding starting pitching.

But little could I have imagined exactly how tough—*and exhilarating*—a series it would be.

twenty-one

October 15, 1986: It Doesn't Get Any Better than This

HOUSTON'S STARTING STAFF AND bullpen, over the final 12 games of the season, had pitched to a microscopic ERA of 1.34 with five shutouts. Legendary fireballer Nolan Ryan was still in the prime of a Hall of Fame career. Crafty left-hander Bob Knepper had our number all throughout the regular season. And their No. 4 starter, Jim Deshaies, had a winning percentage of better than .700.

But none of that mattered.

When it came down to the one pitcher we wanted no part of in a potential do-or-die seventh game, Mike Scott stood alone. And we would battle the Astros the entire series to avoid such a scenario.

Scott showed the baseball world why we felt the way we did beginning in the very first game of the NLCS.

Mike thoroughly dominated us in the opener in the Astrodome with a combination of high fastballs and unhittable "scuffed" balls that moved violently down in the strike zone—as if the bottom had dropped out of them. He struck us out 14 times in going the distance for a 1–0 win. But just as meaningful, he had totally gotten inside our heads—particularly that of Carter, who fanned three times and complained bitterly to home-plate umpire Doug Harvey over the unnatural movement of Scott's pitches.

Gary was never one to get as angry and frustrated as he did in that game. And I think when some of the other guys in our lineup saw him react the way he did, it definitely had an effect on how they approached Scott. For one thing, we swung at more high pitches out of the strike zone simply because they were fastballs. No one wanted any part of the scuff ball.

I believe this was a mistake in our judgment. We should have waited out the high fastball because a lot of times they weren't even strikes. There was no doubt a lot of our guys were pressing.

But as difficult a defeat as that was, we knew it was a best-of-seven series and it was just one game. And really, the margin of difference wasn't that great in the opener. Doc pitched seven strong innings, only yielding a solo home run to Glenn Davis in the second inning. And we actually had some balls the Astros tracked down that, had they fallen in, would have completely changed the outcome of the game. I don't think anybody—except maybe Kid a little bit—was down at that point.

We knew we matched up well against Houston—it was just going to come down to who would execute best. But to avoid seeing Scott two more times, we knew how important the second game was going to be.

And we were ready.

We jumped on Ryan for five runs our second time through the order and Bobby O. scattered 10 hits over nine innings to give us a big 5–1 win.

Ryan was known for scuffing the ball at times, as well. But I guess he wasn't scuffing that game.

When opening on the road in a postseason series, your minimum goal is to at least split the first two games. And we accomplished that in a very loud, hostile environment.

Now we were going home.

******

Although we were back at Shea playing before our fans, we would have a tall order in facing southpaw Bob Knepper. With the exception of Mex and Straw, I went with an all-right-handed-hitting lineup. And that meant sitting my two scrappy table-setters—Lenny and Wally.

Knepper was a "pitcher's pitcher," not a thrower. He had great movement on his fastball, which he threw a little harder than Bobby O. Knepper also had a nasty little off-speed pitch and a good change-up to go with it. Plus, he kept the ball down.

One of the reasons for his success was his ability to run the ball away from right-handed hitters. And he kept them honest by coming in when he had to.

Ronnie started for us and struggled early. A wild pitch and a hit batsman helped the Astros take a quick 2–0 lead in the first. Then they tacked on two more in the second after Darling walked a batter and then gave up a two-run homer to Bill Doran to give Houston a 4–0 edge.

Darling had a great fastball, but was in love with his off-speed stuff and—as he sometimes did—was trying to be too fine with his pitches. As I've said, I always believed with the natural movement of his pitches he was best served by aiming the ball right down the middle of the plate and it would find the corners.

Ronnie would settle down and, as we had done so many times during the regular season, we rallied back from behind in the sixth.

With a run already in, Straw came up to hit with two men on. Darryl was struggling at the time versus southpaws, often pulling off the ball a little bit. But our batting coach, Bill Robinson, who considered Straw one of his special projects, gave him two pieces of advice that day—to keep his right side in and to always be guessing fastball against Knepper because he wasn't going to connect off his off-speed stuff anyway. Bill was a great instructor—I agreed with everything he taught those guys.

So when Knepper threw Darryl a fastball in, he was ready for it, driving it high and deep beyond the right-field auxiliary scoreboard to tie the game.

The sellout crowd, quiet for most of the afternoon, was now in a frenzy. We definitely had the edge at that point, until we handed Houston the lead right back in the seventh. Aggie walked the leadoff hitter, Doran, Knight committed a throwing error on a Billy Hatcher ground ball, and Denny Walling's force-out at second gave the Astros a 5–4 lead.

And that's the way things remained until the bottom of the ninth.

We faced the very real prospect of going down two games to one and facing Scott in the next contest and, if necessary, a seventh game. A loss here would give a clear advantage in the series to the Astros.

With Knepper gone by the eighth, Houston now had right-hander Dave Smith in the game to close it out. This enabled me to use Wally, whom I had inserted in the top of the inning to replace Teufel at second, as my leadoff hitter. Backman's mission was to get on base by any means possible.

Wally would drag bunt the ball up the first-base line, running just barely inside the base line to avoid being tagged out by Glenn Davis. Astros manager Hal Lanier came out to argue Wally was outside of the base line, but that's a judgment play and probably would have induced an argument either way first-base umpire Dutch Rennert called it.

I sent Heep up to pinch hit for Santana and, while he ultimately flied out to center, Wally did move into scoring position on a passed ball during the at-bat.

That brought up Lenny, who had entered the game two innings earlier. All I wanted out of him there was a single to tie the game. I had worked with him on situations just like this one where he wouldn't try to hit the first pitch he saw out of the ballpark. Instead, he would work the count, get on base, hit the ball up the middle, or go the other way. But he always had it in the back of his mind that if he got his pitch—a fastball down and in—he could hit it a long way.

And Lenny got it right where he liked it on the first pitch, but was swinging from his heels and fouled it straight back. That's when he took a quick glance toward "Uncle Bill" in the first-base coach's box and saw him motioning to take something off his swing. In doing so, he would have a better chance of hitting the ball out of the ballpark. It's like Ted Williams always said, "If you swing 100 percent, your timing's 80 percent. If you swing 80 percent, your timing's 100 percent."

For as many antics as he had, Lenny knew what he was doing at the plate. He was a smart hitter. I loved watching him play. He knew how to get on, he knew how to set pitchers up, and he knew what he wanted to do before he even went up there.

Dykstra made the adjustment and got out in front of the next pitch—a forkball down and in—and lofted it high and deep down the right-field line. The ball just kept carrying and carrying until it disappeared just beyond right fielder Kevin Bass and into our bullpen for a game-winning home run.

It was pure bedlam on the field and in the stands as Shea went crazy. It was now edge Mets, with us up two games to one.

Despite all of Lenny's skills as a prototypical leadoff hitter, ever since the first time I saw him, he wanted to be a home run hitter.

Well, at least on that day, I'm grateful my skinny center-fielder was.

******

So now it was on to Round 2 against Scott and his scuff balls.

Unfortunately for us, it was the same result as in Game 1. He again went the distance, only this time allowing just three hits without walking a man.

The heart of our order—Mex, Kid, and Straw—combined to go 0-for-11.

Since we were at Shea, I had our very own batboy, Mike Rufino, collect as many of the balls he pitched as possible—23 in all. And, sure enough, they were all scuffed in the same spot.

I submitted them to the National League office and president Chub Feeney. Of course, he didn't do anything. I mean, what could he do? He wasn't going to award Game 4 to us.

And I knew during the game that Scott would likely not get caught or ejected. He was pretty good about concealing how he was scuffing the ball. It's possible he had something in his glove that he used while he rubbed the ball up. Or maybe one of his infielders was scuffing it. I didn't know for sure. So I told my hitters to ask the home-plate umpire to look at the ball and, hopefully, he would toss the scuffed ones out of the game.

Gamesmanship has been a part of baseball forever. Gaylord Perry, a Hall of Famer, made a career out of throwing an illegal spitball. He even wrote a book about it. The spitball would act the same way as a scuff ball, as the bottom would drop out of both pitches. But I imagine it was easier to command a scuff ball over a spitter because of the grip.

In any case, more than ever, we didn't want to face Scott again. But while winning the next two was critical in ensuring that, we weren't thinking about *both* games. We knew we had to win the next game to go back to Houston up 3 to 2. That was all we were really thinking about.

Because Game 6 would get all the attention—and rightfully so—the fifth game often gets overshadowed. But it should rank right up there with the greatest displays of pitching in postseason history.

Ryan struck out 12 and gave up just two hits and a run through his nine innings of work. His command was a lot better than in Game 2 and his pitches had more movement. Plus, I thought maybe he had gotten a lesson from Scott.

Doc was equally as impressive, going *10* innings and also giving up just one run.

We would win it in the 12ᵗʰ when Kid got his revenge on reliever Charlie Kerfeld—who had "showed up" Carter in Game 3 by fielding a comebacker and holding it up for a moment before firing it to first—by hitting the game-winning single off him. I was extra happy for Gary because he had really been frustrated at the plate the entire series.

Game 5 was the longest ever played in NLCS history. As it would turn out, that distinction would last but one day.

******

You hear a lot about how Game 6 was one of the most nerve-wracking, intense games ever played.

But, personally, I thought it was one of the most fun.

Well, maybe the first eight innings weren't so much fun. After all, we were down three runs to Knepper as we entered the top of the ninth.

But to a man, we knew somehow, someway, we could find a way to score three runs to tie it. We had done it all year long. And as we accomplished it this time, there was just so much energy in our dugout you wouldn't even believe it. We knew we just *had* to win that game. The last thing anyone wanted was to face Scott the next day.

I brought in McDowell to protect our lead and he was nothing short of phenomenal, pitching five innings of one-hit ball through the 13ᵗʰ inning. I don't think I had ever used Roger more than four innings in relief, but these were the playoffs—you go the extra mile. When looking back, his performance was unparalleled by any other player in this game for the ages.

We would finally break through in the top of the 14ᵗʰ, when Backman singled home Straw to give us a 4–3 lead.

I brought in Jesse in the bottom half of the inning in a save situation.

Orosco retired Doran with a strikeout to open the frame. We were now just two outs away from the World Series.

You could have cut the tension with a knife on our bench. But to be honest, I wasn't really the least bit nervous. During any game, I get so involved with player moves, strategies, and just being so totally into it that I don't want to miss anything. And this game—as critical as it was—was no different. It's like a hitter being in the zone. Managers get into zones, too. It's like they see behind their head. There's nothing they're not catching.

I also think it's much harder to be on the bench during a game like that than play in it. All you can do is watch. For the players on the field, sometimes it's even *easier* to perform under those intense circumstances because your level of concentration is so high. And when your concentration is that high, your performance tends to peak.

Part of our intensity and battling in that game boiled down to not wanting to let our fans down. We felt that we had the best fans in the world. We knew that they were watching us and we didn't want our great run to that point in the season to come down to one game.

So with us now just two outs away from winning the game, Billy Hatcher came up to hit. In well over 400 plate appearances that season, Hatcher had but six home runs.

Feeling pretty good about the situation, I turned to Mel, who looked extremely nervous.

"Relax, Stotts, it don't get any better than this."

Then, *boom*! Hatcher connected on an inside fastball, driving it high and deep down the left-field corner. It would hit the screen of the foul pole. Tie game.

I turned back to Mel again.

"I take that back."

The score remained tied until the top of the 16th, when we broke through yet again, this time scoring three runs to take what seemed like a commanding 7–4 lead.

But, again, Houston battled back, scoring two runs of its own in the bottom half of the inning. I had already decided that, no matter what, I was sticking with Jesse the entire inning—win or lose.

With two out, Kevin Bass walked up to the plate with the tying and winning runs on base.

Mex and Carter went to the mound to talk with Jesse.

"Don't throw him any fastballs or I'll *kill* you!" Keith shouted at Jesse.

I looked over at Stotts, now white as a ghost.

"C'mon Mel. You knew it had to come down to a one-run lead in the end."

Orosco, throwing nothing but breaking balls, would go full on Bass, before striking him out swinging.

Jesse, who won three games in relief in that series—a postseason record—flung his glove a mile high in the air, then caught a leaping Carter in his arms as the rest of our team piled on in a raucous celebration on the mound.

That game—that entire series—took a lot out of them not just physically, but even more so emotionally. They were just so drained and relieved it was over.

I get asked a lot about how I thought we would have fared in a seventh game against Scott. While I can assure you that none of us wanted to go there, I always felt we would have found some way to beat him—probably by a really low score, like 2–1.

But I'm sure as hell glad we didn't have to find out.

******

A lot has been made about our infamous plane ride back from Houston. So let me set the record straight once and for all. It was the women, for the most part, who trashed the plane—*not* the players.

Having wives and girlfriends on team flights was generally a no-no. But the club allowed it just this one time because the feeling was that they had supported us all season long.

As far as airplane etiquette, our guys—even the so-called "Scum Bunch" (Sisk, Orosco, and Heep, among others)—knew better.

With the Scum Bunch, in my first few trips with them after becoming manager, I noticed they were leaving too many cans of beer where they were sitting.

So during an ensuing flight, I took a walk to the back of the plane.

"Here's a garbage can," I said. "You boys fill this up so it's easier to clean up back here instead of making a mess."

And that was the end of it. There was no problem.

The other guys got along well, and often put the seats down and played cards.

But when the wives and girlfriends got on that flight after we won the pennant, all the rules vanished.

Actually, the plane wasn't as trashed as has been widely reported. But it was bad enough that United Airlines sent the Mets a bill for $5,000 in damages. And Cashen wanted the players to pay it.

But I wouldn't have it.

Prior to the start of the World Series, I held a team meeting. I held up the invoice and told them the front office wanted them to ante up the five grand. But I stood behind my guys.

"I didn't think it was that bad," I told them. "You're not going to be responsible for this. I'll take care of it. I'll pay it."

I simply didn't want them to be punished for their wives and girlfriends trashing the plane.

Instead, I wanted them to focus on the job at hand—winning a World Series.

twenty-two

October 20, 1986:
The Day Off

"YOU'VE GOT NO WORKOUT tomorrow," I announced to the club on the plane ride up to Boston.

"I don't want you to pick up a baseball. I don't want you talking to the press. Just take the day off and relax. We'll get 'em next game."

There was no doubt in my mind that we had lost the first two games of the World Series at home to the Boston Red Sox, in large part, due to a hangover effect from the extreme intensity and emotion of Game 6 of the NLCS. The guys were physically and mentally spent—and it showed.

In the first game, our offense was listless—losing 1–0 to Bruce Hurst—and we wasted a great effort by Darling in the process.

Game 2 featured the much-anticipated, marquee matchup between Roger Clemens and Doc, but both pitchers struggled and were gone by the fifth inning. Gooden was really off—not looking like he was as into it as he normally was and sweating more than usual. I didn't think the magnitude of the game put any undue pressure on Doc because he had always dealt with big spots well— much like a 10-year veteran—since the day I met him. He could have just been a little gassed from the NLCS and perhaps the 250 innings he'd pitched during the regular season had finally caught up with him.

But when Doc had everything going for him, he was *still* the best pitcher in baseball. So when he got rocked in Game 2, it was a big blow to our psyche.

The guys badly needed a day off. But they *especially* needed a day away from the media.

I knew what it would be like. There would be cameras and reporters lined up everywhere, to the point where you wouldn't be able to blow your nose without somebody taking a picture or writing about it. I knew hearing the same questions over and over again about how we lost the first two games of the series wasn't going to help anybody.

And then there was this: how many times would they have to hear that only one team in the history of the World Series had lost the first two at home and come back to win the Series?

What would be the benefit of that?

Plus, with the day off, I thought they would come out fresher for Game 3.

Of course, the move didn't go over well with the press. And it's something I could never have pulled off today.

I mean, can you even imagine what kind of fine or suspension I would receive if I tried something like that now?

But it worked—and paid immediate dividends the next night.

If you're a baseball fan—or a player—you couldn't ask for a better venue than Fenway Park. That old ballpark just drips with history. Babe Ruth, Ted Williams, Jimmie Foxx, and so many other all-time greats have played there. And to be in that park playing in a World Series, before their avid fans—who were a lot like ours—was going to be a thrill. Everybody on our club, to a man, was excited to be there.

Lenny started things off with a bang, hitting just Oil Can Boyd's third pitch of the game—a fastball down and in, *what else?*—down the right-field line by "Pesky's Pole" for a home run. It was our first lead and, for that matter, first extra-base hit of the series. But most important, it was *exactly* what we needed and picked us up immediately. Our entire bench walked over to greet Nails as he approached the dugout.

Then, after Wally and Mex singled, Kid drove home Backman with a double up the left-field gap to give us a quick 2–0 lead.

A few of our guys were really riding Boyd pretty good from the bench, yelling out things like "Shit Can" instead of "Oil Can." It was just kind of the normal, relatively harmless bench-jockeying stuff that had gone on in baseball for decades. The Red Sox pulled the same crap on our pitchers, though it didn't bother any of them. But it was common knowledge that the high-strung Boyd was a bit of a loose cannon and had a reputation for being thin-skinned and rattling easily. And it was evident by his body language and how hyper he was early in the game that some of the riding was getting inside his head.

After Straw struck out for the 17th time in 29 at-bats in the postseason to that point, it brought Ray Knight up to the plate with Mex and Kid still in scoring position with just one out.

Ray had been very upset that he didn't start the previous game. But my reasoning was simple. In addition to putting HoJo, who could bat left-handed, into the lineup to face the right-handed Clemens, I wanted to send a message to Howard that, even though Ray had been the primary third baseman during the season, I had all the confidence in the world in him—unlike Sparky Anderson, who basically kept him out of the '84 World Series.

So Ray came into my office at around noontime prior to Game 3 and pleaded with me to put him back in the lineup—despite the Red Sox throwing another right-hander at us.

"Skip, you've *got* to play me," Knight said. "I've *got* to be in the there."

After some more back-and-forth and hearing his argument for playing, I finally acquiesced. Knight had talked his way into the lineup.

"Okay, Ray. You're in there, baby!" I exclaimed with a grin. "You're my third baseman tonight."

So with Knight up against Boyd, he would hit a routine two-hopper to Wade Boggs at third. But when Boggs came home with it, Mex alertly turned around, inducing a rundown, which ultimately allowed both him and Kid to get back to second and third safely and put Ray on first with a fielder's choice to load the bases.

The Red Sox messing up that rundown was a huge break for us and would set up a big inning.

Our next batter, Heep, acting as our designated hitter that night, made them pay, ripping a single to center-field to drive home Keith and Gary to give us a 4–0 lead before our starter, Bobby O., had even stepped on the mound.

And that was the best gift we could've given him.

Ojeda told me before the game that he "wanted this one badly."

Bobby wasn't one to ever complain, but he may have been a little sore about falling out of favor in Boston and how they just kind of let him go in the trade with us. I think he wanted to prove something to them, which is perfectly normal. Most players who come back and play against their former team want to do especially well against them. I think in Bobby's case, it was self-motivating. Not that he needed a lot of that pitching in a World Series game, but he had that little extra revenge factor at play that night.

Ojeda was outstanding, giving up just one run and five hits in seven innings against the potent Red Sox lineup, before McDowell pitched a flawless eighth and ninth inning to close it out for a convincing 7–1 victory.

The momentum was back on our side now. We were down just a game with the Game 4 matchup clearly in our favor. Ronnie would go up against right-hander Al Nipper, who had struggled mightily during the regular season with a losing record and an ERA north of five.

A win here would guarantee that the series would return to Shea. There was some talk among the media prior to the game on why I didn't start Sid Fernandez in place of Darling, who would be pitching on short rest. But I loved the idea of having Sid available in long relief, as the Red Sox hitters were struggling a bit against him and his high-rising fastball. Plus, he would be a great help to McDowell, who had thrown a lot of innings already in the postseason.

As it turned out, I made the right decision.

Darling would overcome bouts of wildness—walking six—but would still deliver seven shutout innings, while Lenny went deep again and Carter hit two over the Green Monster. We cruised to a 6–2 victory to even the series at two games apiece.

Just as I had done with Ronnie, I rolled the dice a little bit by bringing Doc back on short rest for Game 5. The result, unfortunately, was very different.

Gooden gave up four runs on nine hits in just four-plus innings to put us in an early 4–0 hole. Like in Game 2, he looked like a shell of the outstanding pitcher he had always been for us. And I don't believe it had anything to do with the short rest, which may limit your pitch count but rarely your command. I can't be sure what was going on with Doc again that night, but he looked very out of sync.

On the Red Sox's side, Hurst held us in check just as he had in Game 1 with a good fastball and tricky screwball, pitching another complete game gem to put Boston one win away from its first world championship since 1918.

While we were obviously disappointed in Doc's outing and being down 3–2 in the series, we had accomplished our ultimate goal in Boston, which was to take 2 of 3 and return the series to New York.

We knew we had our work cut out for us, but still believed we had a good chance to win it all in front of our home fans.

Sometimes all you need is a day off.

twenty-three

October 25, 1986:
The Art of the Comeback

I NEVER LOST HOPE.

I'll admit, things were looking bleak for us.

But I never lost hope. Not for a minute.

In Game 6, in the bottom of the 10th inning, we were down 5–3 with two outs and nobody on base. I looked across the field and the whole Boston bench was on the top step of their dugout, ready to storm the pitcher's mound to celebrate a World Series championship.

This was real hairy, but I knew what our ballclub was capable of. We had come back from behind all season long—in more than 40 games, in fact. So I had the utmost faith in our guys. And the one thing about baseball—you can never take anything for granted. I've seen teams down eight runs come back and win games.

Plus, for as talented a pitcher as Schiraldi was—he had an explosive fastball—he was still young and was still learning to locate his pitches. I mean, his first major league save was just that *August*. He was certainly beatable.

So I kept on managing.

As Carter approached the plate, I was already anticipating that he would get on base, already working on my next move. I knew I needed a pinch-hitter for Aguilera, who was due up next. I looked over on the bench for Mitchell, but he was nowhere to be found.

I saw Mookie behind me by the bat rack.

"Mookie," I said, "Quick, go find Mitchell. I need him to pinch hit."

I guess Mitchell didn't think I would use him against Boston's right-handed closer Schiraldi, as he was on the clubhouse phone making airplane reservations back home to San Diego. He wasn't alone in the clubhouse at that point, as some of the other players were there as well—guys who probably couldn't stomach the sight of watching the Red Sox celebrate on our field from our dugout. I know that Mex and a few others were watching the game on the television in my office.

Mitchell dropped the phone, sprinted up the clubhouse tunnel, grabbed a bat, and started loosening up in the on-deck circle.

In the meantime, Carter worked the count to 2–1. Schiraldi then fired a high fastball that Kid lined into left field in front of Jim Rice for a single.

I happened to glance over at the Boston dugout at that very moment and noticed a couple of their guys moving back down from the top step. Maybe they were thinking, *Not so fast.*

Normally, this would have been Strawberry's turn at bat, and would have given us a chance to tie the game with the long ball, but when I brought in Aggie to start the top of the ninth, I double-switched Mazzilli, who had pinch hit for Orosco in the eighth, into the game in right field to replace Darryl. At the time I made the move, I thought the game would be decided before Straw would come to bat again.

Even still, Mitchell was a great hitter and Straw had really struggled throughout the postseason—so I felt good about having Kevin at the plate in that situation.

And Mitch would come through, hitting an 0–1 Schiraldi slider, again up in the zone, for a single into center-field to put the tying runs on base for Knight.

In the dugout, just like in Houston during the NLCS, I had Stotts by my side. Only this time, there was silence. I wasn't saying how it didn't get any better than this or anything like that. We had a little rally going and I wasn't going to say anything to jinx it.

Schiraldi would get two quick strikes on Ray and we were now down to our final strike of the game, the series, and our season. Everything we had accomplished—the 108 regular season wins and the thrilling NLCS victory over the Astros—was on the line.

Schiraldi threw the next pitch right down the middle and Knight blooped one into center field for a single to score Carter and cut the Sox's lead to 5–4. Mitchell alertly judged that the ball would drop in right between center fielder Dave Henderson and right fielder Dwight Evans and hustled all the way to third base, a largely overlooked play at the time, which would prove critical.

The crowd was alive again!

That would bring up Mookie, but would also bring out McNamara from the Boston dugout to pull Schiraldi and bring in Bob Stanley.

Stanley, a onetime very effective pitcher, had struggled in '86 and lost his closer role to Schiraldi late that summer. But he certainly had a golden opportunity to redeem himself by getting just one out.

Wilson loved swinging at anything that was remotely near the strike zone. If he could reach it, he was swinging at it. Usually, it was two or three pitches and he was either on base or sitting back in the dugout. But in this particular at-bat, he was completely locked in. The at-bat seemed like it lasted an hour. There is no question in my mind it was Mookie's longest at-bat I had ever seen.

After four pitches, the count was 2–2 and we were again down to our final strike.

The drama and the tension mounted some more as Mookie fouled off the next two pitches.

But then on the seventh pitch, as far as I'm concerned, we

won the game *and* the World Series. With Red Sox catcher Rich Gedman set up outside, Stanley threw one way *inside*—just missing hitting Mookie—for a wild pitch to bring home Mitch with the tying run and move Knight to second base.

The crowd noise was deafening and you could feel the vibrations under your feet—just pure pandemonium.

The momentum had completely shifted to our side with that wild pitch. When you're down two runs with two outs and two strikes and you come back to tie the game, in the dugout we knew we were going to win that game and nothing would stop us from winning Game 7, too. I didn't know if we would finish them off on the next pitch or the next inning—it didn't matter. We were going to win the game and the series. And that's the truth.

The Red Sox were completely frazzled at this point. Two pitches later, Knight was leading way too far off second base and Marty Barrett cut across to the bag waiting for a pickoff throw from Stanley. But there was just one problem—Stanley missed the sign given by Gedman to throw over there.

Had Stanley picked up the sign, it likely would have ended the inning right there.

Knight always took an overaggressive lead. He wasn't fast, but he was an excellent base runner who liked jumping off the base. In all the excitement, he was probably thinking one thing: *Anywhere this ball's hit, I'm going! I'm going to score the winning run by any means possible.*

After the wild pitch, Mookie had fouled off the next two pitches. But then, finally, on pitch 10, he put the ball in play and solidified his place in Mets lore.

Wilson hit a slow roller up along the first-base line. First baseman Bill Buckner was playing with badly sprained ankles and, to make matters even worse, was shifted away from the line for two reasons: one, Mookie hardly ever hit balls down there and, two, Buck needed to cover some of Barrett's ground as Marty tried to keep Knight close at second. With Mookie's speed and with his body already going toward first base as he pulled the ball, it was a recipe for disaster for the Red Sox.

I thought Wilson had a great chance to beat it out.

But we'll never know for sure because when Buckner went down to field the ball, it skidded under his glove and rolled into right field. Knight came around to score and we won the game—completing the greatest comeback in World Series history!

But a split second before I ran out toward home plate to join the other guys to mob Knight, I took a quick glance into the Red Sox's dugout at McNamara, and thought to myself, *Payback! I got him back! Now we're even!*

I'm not kidding, the beauty of it all for me wasn't the Buckner error, but how after more than 23 years since that awful day in Binghamton when McNamara, the opposing catcher, had called for a fastball up- and -in that hit me in the coconut and smashed my nose and front teeth, I had finally gotten my revenge by managing a team that beat him in such an agonizing way in a World Series.

And McNamara has never lived down not putting in late-inning defensive replacement Dave Stapleton for the gimpy Buckner like he had throughout that entire postseason.

Karma's a bitch, isn't it?

But for all the joy I felt in winning that game, I did feel bad for Buckner—and still do. When we played together with the Cubs, he was a good first baseman, a great hitter, and an excellent teammate. Of course, by this point in 1986, although he was still a good hitter, it was near the end of his career and he was playing so badly hurt. But here was a guy with 2,715 career hits and, for many, he is remembered mostly for that one error. It's really sad. The reality is that in Game 6, it was all the late hits we got and the wild pitch that caused their loss, not Buckner's error. And I've heard how he's gone through some hell over it. It's just not fair—he's too good a guy for all that.

Besides, there was still a Game 7 to be played.

But after staging a comeback for the ages, nothing was going to stop us from winning the final game.

******

The Red Sox had caught what would seem like a major break. A rainout between the sixth and seventh games enabled them to skip over Oil Can and pitch Hurst in Game 7.

But so devastating to the Red Sox was the Game 6 loss, we could see during batting practice that they didn't have the look of a team that could bounce back and win that night.

Even after Evans and Gedman hit back-to-back homers and Boggs ripped an RBI single to complete a three-run second-inning outburst, we were unfazed.

Down 3–0? No problem. We still knew we were going to win that ballgame.

Darling wouldn't have it that night, and I went to Sid in the top of the fourth inning to stop the damage. And Fernandez was nothing short of outstanding, not allowing a hit over 2⅓ innings of relief while striking out four. Sid held the Sox at bay until our lineup got a third look at Hurst. As good as Bruce had been against us in that Series and to that point in Game 7, we knew it was just a matter of time before our bats woke up and we got to him.

In the bottom of the sixth, with Boston still leading 3–0, we went to work.

Mazzilli, pinch hitting for Sid, started a rally for us with a one-out single. Mookie then followed with a line-drive single to left to put two on for Teufel, who would then walk to load the bases.

That brought up Hernandez, who was "Mr. Clutch" for us all year long and the best hitter on the club—*by far*. And he absolutely loved situations like this one with men on base, because he knew the opposing pitcher was going to pitch him down and away to try to get him to pull the ball and ground into a double play.

Instead, Keith would hit that pitch that would run away from him over the shortstop's head to drive in runs. He would do that again and again. Mex would tell me before going to the plate in so many of those situations, "This is what I'm going to do." And when you tell yourself and others you're going to do something, your subconscious is like, *This is what's going to happen.*

And Keith did it again—driving a Hurst pitch up and away into the left-center-field gap to easily score Maz and the speedy Mookie, and move Teufel to third, to cut the lead to 3–2.

Carter then tied the game at three apiece by blooping the first pitch he saw into right field, where Evans dived for and trapped the ball, then threw to second to force out Keith, while pinch runner Backman came in to score from third.

We had again come all the way back against the Red Sox.

After retiring Straw on a fly ball to left that Rice made a terrific sliding catch on to end the sixth, Hurst was done for the night. It was now their bullpen against ours—I loved our chances.

Schiraldi started the bottom of the seventh for the Sox and Knight immediately launched a long home run over the left-center wall to give us a 4–3 lead.

I have to hand it to Ray: from the time he came into my office prior to Game 3 pleading with me to play, he was passionate about wanting to be "the man," and he would end up winning MVP of the World Series. I felt a little bad about not getting HoJo more playing time, but Knight just would not be denied.

Then Dykstra, up to pinch hit for Mitch, followed by ripping a single to right and would advance to second on a wild pitch on a *pitch out.*

Schiraldi was clearly imploding.

Then Santana, simply trying to move Dykstra over to third, punched the next pitch past Buckner down the first-base line and into right field, bringing home Lenny to give us a 5–3 lead.

I left reliever McDowell in the game to bat because all I wanted next was to move Santana into scoring position—and Roger did just that, bunting him over to second.

Joe Sambito was brought in to relieve Schiraldi and intentionally walked Mookie to set up the double-play ball. But then he made the costly mistake of walking Wally, too, to load the bases.

That would bring up Hernandez again with the bases loaded, with a chance to really put this game away. Keith would swing at the first pitch he saw—a pitch right down the middle—and drive it to deep center, far enough for Santana to tag up and score—and to move Mookie to third—to make it 6–3.

Stanley was then brought in to face Carter, and Kid hit a chopper to short that Spike Owen charged hard, getting him by half a step at first or else we would have added another run. But as it was, we now had a sizable three-run lead and were feeling pretty good about ourselves.

But even though I felt the Red Sox were pretty demoralized at this point, I didn't think we had the game in the bag. That was because both Roger and Jesse hadn't had as much success against Boston as I thought they would have in the series.

And sure enough, the Red Sox made things interesting against McDowell in the top of the eighth. Buckner and Rice opened the frame with singles, and then scored when Evans doubled to right to quickly cut our lead to 6–5.

I would bring in Orosco, and he did a terrific job getting us out of that jam by retiring the next three hitters to leave Evans, the potential tying run, stranded at second base.

McNamara went to his bullpen again to start the bottom of the eighth, this time bringing in Nipper to face Straw. Darryl's struggles had continued to that point in the game, as he was 0-for-3 and batting just .174 in the series. And he was a little angry and disappointed that I had pulled him late in Game 6 as part of a double switch.

He now had something to prove.

And he did so in dramatic fashion.

Straw would connect on Nipper's third pitch and hit a majestic shot—high and deep over the right-field fence—that landed at the base of the scoreboard for a home run to give us a 7–5 edge. Darryl would take forever to circle the bases, apparently to make a statement that he shouldn't ever be pulled out of a game, no matter what the situation. Well, if I would have known that about him before, and that he could hit moon shots like the one he did that night to express his feelings, I would have double switched him out more often during the season!

We would tack on one more run a few hitters later from the unlikeliest of sources—Orosco. With runners on first and second, we put the sacrifice bunt on the first couple of pitches. But after the count went to 1–1, I looked at the Red Sox's defensive alignment and noticed on the previous pitch how their shortstop, Eddie Romero, had held his ground near second base instead of racing to third to cover for a charging Boggs, opening up a huge hole on the left side of the infield. So on the next pitch, we had Jesse fake the bunt and swing—the "butcher-boy" play—and he bounced one into center field to bring home Knight to make it 8–5.

We were a little lucky because, on that third pitch, Romero *did* break toward third with Boggs charging home. Had Eddie held his ground at second like on the previous pitch, it may have been a double-play ball.

Anyway, we now had our three-run lead back with Jesse out on the mound in the top of the ninth to try to close things out. Orosco would make quick work out of Romero and Boggs, and then, after striking out Barrett to end the game, he flung his glove high in the air, dropped to his knees, and raised his arms straight to the heavens—a *great* reaction.

Our guys jubilantly rushed the mound and knocked Jesse clear off his feet, onto the ground, and under a pile of his teammates. I was a little late to the party out there because I hardly even wanted to go on the field—I felt it was *their* show. Besides, it was more fun for me to watch them overjoyed because they had just come out on top in two heavily contested battles. It was just a such big sigh of relief for all of us. Just unbelievable. In all the baseball Octobers that I either witnessed or was a part of, nothing ever came close to '86.

And the fans that year were incredible. It was like a love affair with them. We had such characters at every position and had so much diversity on our club that there was something for everyone. And because of our close bond with the fans, we didn't want to disappoint them. We knew a championship would be great for the city, and it was.

For me, it was the most fun I ever had in my career.

And the ticker tape parade up the "Canyon of Heroes" in lower Manhattan was off the charts. More than two million fans came to honor our club, the largest crowd ever for a parade in New York City history, and I wanted to reach out and hug every last one of them.

And all the confetti! It felt like we were driving up through a blizzard. I didn't know where it was all coming from.

At the City Hall ceremony following the parade, after accepting one of the keys to the city that everyone on our club received, I got up to speak to the crowd.

"I want to thank you for the wonderful parade," I told them. "This was so much fun, I think we ought to try to do it again next year!"

And with the tremendous team we had, I truly felt we would be right back there at City Hall again the next October.

| twenty-four |
April 1, 1987: The Hangover

"UMM, SKIP, I'VE GOT a problem," a visibly embarrassed Doc Gooden quietly told me in my St. Petersburg manager's office near the end of spring training.

"I've got to go to drug rehab."

I leaned back in my chair—positively *floored*.

A rush of thoughts quickly entered my mind.

How could this be?

Nobody's happier coming to the ballpark than Doc.

I've had him since he was 17 at Kingsport.

Great parents.

Great high school coach.

Great arm.

Gifted athlete.

And…so smart.

Absolutely nothing could have prepared me for this. I never saw one sign. I was crying inside. He was like a son to me. I simply couldn't believe it.

"Doc," I replied with heartbreak and great disappointment in my voice. "You've *got* to be kidding me."

But he wasn't kidding. It may have been April 1, but this was no April Fools' joke. Gooden had failed a drug test for cocaine use.

I accepted what he told me, that he would likely be at the Smithers Alcohol Treatment and Training Center in Manhattan doing some sort of rehabilitation for two months. And then he left my office, leaving me to try and make sense of it all.

Doc's issue was never knowing how to say no to some of his homeboys. They would tell him stuff like, "Oh, you're not a homie anymore? You're too big for us now?"

And while Gooden should have just said, "No, I'm not too big for you, but I'm not doing drugs," he just couldn't do it. He may have wanted to, but he didn't know how to express it.

I tried to be positive, thinking, *Well, maybe it's just a start of a problem and rehab is the way to nip it in the bud.*

But it didn't help.

Having Doc come into my office and tell me what he did was the most devastating thing that ever happened to me in my managing career.

But as it would turn out, it was just a harbinger of things to come.

******

My relationship with Frank Cashen had begun to sour.

Prior to the '86 season, acting on my own behalf since I didn't have an agent, I negotiated a contract extension through the '88 season. One of the provisions I insisted on was that if new Yankees manager Lou Piniella ever received a contract that paid him more than me, then we would have to renegotiate mine. I didn't think it would be fair for Lou to get a higher salary than me for not having done anything in the Yankees' organization yet.

Frank agreed, and we wrote it into the contract. We referred to the provision as the "Piniella Clause."

About three-quarters of the way through the '86 season, Piniella got a big raise. Of course, by that point in the season, we were running away with the NL East title. So I didn't hesitate. I went right into Frank's office to talk about it.

"I don't have a contract," I told him.

But there was silence. He didn't say a word to me.

So I left, thinking, *It's fine. After the season's over, Frank will work that out.*

Well, he didn't. And as general manager, he had all the power, so he must have figured he could do whatever he wanted to.

About a month after the World Series, I was out playing golf at the Interlachen Country Club near my home in Winter Park. There were reporters there, and one of them asked about the upcoming winter meetings.

"Oh, I'm not going," I told him. "I don't have a contract. I have to renegotiate that because of the Piniella Clause."

When the news got back to Frank, he got really mad at me, but it was *his* fault, not mine. The clause was in the contract, but I guess he had decided not to go along with it.

But now Cashen's reputation was on the line. I had forced his hand publicly to honor our agreement, and I would get a major raise from $225,000 to $325,000 a year for the final two years of my contract.

There is no question this caused a rift in our relationship because he hadn't been truthful—and then got caught. Yet, he probably believed it was my fault because I was being, in his mind, insubordinate.

The simple reality was I wanted what I had coming to me. It was a matter of principle more than the money.

Another issue I had with Frank following the '86 season was his decision to begin grooming his front office lieutenants, Joe McIlvaine and Al Harazin, for the general manager's post. McIlvaine would become more involved in deals and Harazin would handle contracts. So now not only did I have to deal with

Frank, but also Joe and Al. I had absolutely nothing against those two guys personally—it was McIlvaine, after all, who had brought me into the organization—but it felt like I was working for three bosses now.

Cashen had either forgotten or ignored my insistence way back when he hired me that I wanted to report to him and only him. And he originally honored my demand, allowing his assistant GM Lou Gorman to leave the Mets and accept the Red Sox's offer to become their VP of Baseball Operations.

But not now.

And worst of all, I wasn't being consulted as much as I should have been in trade talks.

Just six weeks after winning the World Series, the three quasi GMs began dismantling our championship team. And it began with an eight-player deal I was adamantly opposed to—the trade that sent Kevin Mitchell to San Diego for Kevin McReynolds. This one really upset me, and I fought Cashen hard against making it.

"Mitch is going to be my left fielder," I told Frank. "He's got one of the best strokes I've ever seen—short and straight to the ball—with power. He's been awesome for us and can hit certain opposing pitchers nobody else in our lineup can touch."

"I'm concerned Mitchell is going to be a bad influence on Strawberry and Doc." Cashen countered.

"Frank, Mitch is not going to be a bad influence on anybody," I told him. "In fact, he's going to be a *good* influence. He grew up in the roughest neighborhood in San Diego and never did drugs or drank. He was a tough guy. He stood his ground. If anybody gave him a hard time, he could whoop them."

"No, Davey, he's going to drag Darryl and Doc down," Cashen insisted. "We've got to get rid of him."

So we traded Mitchell to San Diego and then the Padres made the same mistake we did by dealing him halfway through the '87 season to San Francisco, where he never touched drugs and soon would win the NL MVP Award in leading the Giants to a pennant in '89. Mitch became a superstar out west. I had wanted him to become one for us in New York.

Later that off-season, I watched as Ray Knight didn't accept what he perceived as a lowball Mets contract offer and instead signed on as a free agent with Baltimore. Although I had nothing to say in those negotiations, this deal was a little different from the Mitchell one. I felt Howard Johnson needed more playing time at third that Ray would have taken away from him by staying with the club. Make no mistake, I greatly admired the contributions Knight had made to the ballclub—he was the MVP of the World Series, after all! And he led by example by playing hard on the field. But I thought Howard had learned a lot in '86 and could turn out to be a 30-homer, 30-stolen-base guy—plus switch-hit. And I turned out to be right about that.

So I didn't fight the quasi GMs' decision not to aggressively try to re-sign him.

One free agent I did badly want us to sign was Expos outfielder Andre Dawson. We needed a right-handed bat and the future Hall of Famer would have perfectly fit the bill. Dawson was an elite player—a Gold Glove outfielder with a rifle arm and thunder in his bat. I was also looking ahead, realizing that Carter and Hernandez were getting near the end of the road.

And for 1987, at least, we could have gotten Dawson relatively cheap.

I pleaded with Cashen on that one.

"*Sign* the guy!" I exclaimed to Frank. "He's a great middle-of-the-lineup bat. We *need* him!"

But Cashen wouldn't sign him or *any* free agents back then. He actually made staying out of the free agent market a club policy.

So I probably got on his "shit list" for being so vocal about it.

But if we had kept the versatile Mitchell, moving him around the outfield as well as at third and shortstop, and plugged a guy like Dawson into left field, we would have had the best lineup in baseball.

Sure enough, Dawson ended up signing with the Cubs, hitting 49 home runs with 137 RBI, and being awarded the National League MVP Award—and a Gold Glove—in '87.

Getting Dawson and keeping Mitchell would have kept our lineup potent well into the next decade.

But it wasn't to be.

******

Thankfully, we did pull the trigger on a deal late in spring training that would bolster our fortunes in the pitching department for years to come—but it almost didn't happen.

The Kansas City Royals needed a catcher and offered us a relatively unknown, hard-throwing right-hander named David Cone for Carter's backup, Ed Hearn.

Initially, McIlvaine turned the deal down, telling the Royals he had to think about it.

When I heard that, I went nuts. I thought, *What is he thinking?!*

"Mac! *Holy moly!*" I exclaimed when I saw him. "Cone hasn't established himself yet and has had some control problems, but he's got a *great* arm. And Eddie's a backup catcher. A *backup* catcher."

"But Davey, Hearn had a phenomenal year," McIlvaine said.

"That's true, but he's still a *backup*." I replied. "With Cone, you're talking about a potential frontline pitcher with his kind of arm. You should call the Royals back and make that deal."

Thankfully, McIlvaine listened to me, and it turned out to be one of the best trades I've ever seen—at least on a par with the Mazzilli for Darling and Terrell deal we made several years earlier. Cone would eventually become our best pitcher and have a remarkable career, while Eddie, sadly, would battle one injury after another and would play his last game just two years later.

Still, in what should have been a joyous time as we broke camp and headed north as defending champs, we had Doc in the drug tank and our best right-handed reliever, McDowell, on the disabled list after having an operation for appendicitis.

We would face challenges right away that the '86 club never had to deal with.

******

"What are you doing? What's going on here?" I asked Frank as we boarded a plane for our first road trip of the '87 season. "Why are Al and Mac making the trip?"

"As you know, Davey," Cashen said dryly, "I'm training them to be GMs, teaching them everything they need to know. So they need to travel with the team."

"Well, don't put them on me," I said. "I'm dealing with you, Mr. Cashen, and I don't want to have to argue with Mac and Al, too. I don't need the "triumvirate" [the new name I'd given them] teaming up three-against-one on me all the time and traveling with the team. Let's just let Al be the business guy and Mac be a scouting guru and you and I alone will deal with the day-to-day aspects of the ballclub."

Not surprisingly, Frank didn't respond and just walked away.

I was *very* upset about the triumvirate traveling with us. It was becoming more and more apparent to me that Mac would become a middleman between Frank and me. And it makes it very difficult on a manager if he doesn't have a straight shot to the general manager on player personnel decisions. When it came to putting players on the disabled list and taking others off, they weren't communicating with me as much as they should have been and, when they did, it was Mac who spoke with me the most. It was hard enough to figure out what Frank was thinking. Now I had more guys to figure out.

But Cashen apparently knew what he was doing. Both Mac and Al would get opportunities later on to become general managers with the Mets. So I guess Frank was right and I was wrong. But it certainly wasn't helping me in '87. I was getting beaten down on about everything you can think of by the triumvirate. It was like they had somehow lost confidence in my abilities, like my opinion was no longer valued. And I had just managed the team to a *world championship*!

******

We didn't get off to a quick start like we had the year before, but were still in first place by a game near the end of April. But right away, the press was looking for a reason—*any reason*—why we weren't dominating like we had the year before.

Had they forgotten about our losing Mitchell in a trade? Or Doc to rehab? Or McDowell to the DL?

Instead, the focus in the tabloids was on how some of the players, especially the pitchers, were spending a lot of time in the clubhouse and not on the bench during games. But to be honest, it wasn't important to me. I didn't try to tell them how they needed to act when they weren't in the lineup or weren't pitching. I didn't have strict rules. As I've often said, I wanted the clubhouse to be like a second home to them.

A couple of times I might have said to them something like, "How about coming down and cheering?" But as long as they were ready to pinch hit, enter the game as a defensive replacement, or ready take the mound, nothing else mattered. In fact, sometimes it's actually better for a pitcher to watch the game on the clubhouse television to see how opposing hitters are reacting to certain pitches if you have to come in to face them later.

These guys were professionals. I never felt anyone would do anything detrimental to hurt any of their teammates, or not support them, or not be prepared when they were going to be on the field. And when they did get in, they all played at a high level.

The one thing I did cut back on was the card playing. It's not like they were playing cards during the game—that I wouldn't allow. But as with anything, sometimes things can start to get a little out of hand. There were times when money was exchanged during those card games and my biggest concern was over how some guys were losing more cash than they had a right to lose. I wanted to protect the younger players who were making the league minimum, especially the ones who were married. So I was more concerned about some guys getting hurt financially than I was about how long and when they were playing.

Still, that May, after we fell out of first place, I held a closed-door meeting in which I announced a new rule that all card playing had to stop 15 minutes before infield practice. I let the players chew on that and basically that was the end of the problem. They got the message and cut back on the gambling.

At the same meeting, I made another announcement. The front office thought it would be a good idea for me to officially name Keith the team captain in case something was bothering a player and he didn't feel like coming to me. So Mex was now officially the captain, but the reality was he had been the de facto one since the day he arrived from St. Louis. Everybody always gravitated toward Keith and nobody led by example on our club better than him.

******

It became apparent early in the season that we would be battling the Cardinals to the end, much like we had two seasons before. They swept us in our first three-game set of the year with them and then took 2-of-3 in the next series. After a brutal slide in '86, they were back and stronger than ever.

By early July, they had opened a 10½-game lead on us.

By that point, we had lost Bobby O.—our biggest weapon against the Cardinals—for the season following elbow surgery. Bobby recorded a 3–0 record with a 1.50 ERA against them in '86 by keeping them off balance with his change of speeds.

Whitey Herzog had assembled a speedy corps of players in '87 and encouraged them to pound balls down into the turf and run hard—that was his strategy. And it worked. The Cards were averaging nearly six runs a game, over a run a game more than our long-ball-hitting lineup, which would amass 192 home runs that season.

And against us, if one of his fine starting pitchers faltered, he could bring in a left-hander such as Ricky Horton to neutralize the heart of our lineup—Hernandez, Strawberry, and even HoJo, since Howard wasn't as productive from the right side.

I had tremendous admiration for Whitey as both a manager and as a human being. We may have been rivals on the field, but were great friends off it. In fact, along with a few of my coaches, Whitey and I were business partners in the Celebrity Fish Camp on Orange Lake near Ocala, Florida. It was kind of like one of those fantasy baseball camps for adults, only for fishing.

We even did a fishing show together. One morning, while we were out on the lake with the cameras rolling, we were talking baseball while a rocket was shooting up into the sky over Cape Canaveral. Whitey turned to me and, alluding to the pressure of pennant race baseball we endured, goes, "Davey, come July in St. Louis or in New York, I think we're probably going to wish we were on that thing."

The remark drew a few laughs from the crew—but was *completely* true!

Privately, we'd talk about a big bass we may have caught, our respective front offices, or baseball in general—but never about the strengths and weaknesses of our own players. It would have been taboo to discuss those things with another manager outside of your own organization. Even with a guy I trusted like Herzog.

As a baseball man, I loved the way Whitey managed a ballgame—especially how he handled his bullpen. I learned a lot from him. By closely observing his managerial style, I picked up plenty of things I liked. Conversely, the things he did that I didn't like, I discarded. But with Whitey, there was hardly anything I could find him doing wrong. And that made managing *against* him really exciting.

In Herzog, I was up against a Hall of Fame manager who had

outmaneuvered me in the past, which only made me want to return the favor all the more. It was always a challenge—like a chess match—and I never wanted to give him any good options. My level of concentration in those games against Whitey was off the charts. I didn't miss a thing. If he wiggled a finger in his dugout, I was watching it. And when one of my players did something good, like drive in a run or hit a home run, I couldn't wait to check out his reaction and see what his next move would be.

We had all kinds of battles. Herzog once took HoJo's bat out of a game so it could be checked for cork. The umpire placed it behind the screen. But I walked back there and retrieved it for HoJo. I didn't know if the bat was corked or not, but I wouldn't allow Whitey to embarrass one of my players like that. I thought that was going over the edge. But there were no hard feelings over it. It was just a show of gamesmanship on Whitey's part. And I couldn't fault him for trying.

******

Despite losing each of our five primary starting pitchers at different points in the season, we had a new arsenal of young arms I plugged into the staff that helped lead us back into the pennant race in the second half.

Terry Leach was arguably our best pitcher, going 11–1 with an ERA of 3.22—just a hair above Doc's team-best for our starters.

Cone began showing signs of the brilliant pitcher he would become for us by winning some key games down the stretch.

And out of the bullpen, Randy Myers could be dominant, striking out better than a hitter an inning, giving me a strong alternative from the left side to Orosco, who struggled a bit that season.

On the offensive front, we were raking.

HoJo caught fire to have the outstanding season I knew he was always capable of, with 36 home runs and 32 stolen bases.

McReynolds was more than solid with his 29 homers and 95 ribbies.

But this would go down as the year that Straw really broke out and became the superstar we always knew he had the potential to be. Darryl would lead the team with 39 home runs, 104 RBIs, and 36 stolen bases—just the complete package.

Straw had become "the guy" in New York. He had the legs, the arm, the power, the strength, the good looks, the athleticism, and limitless talent. I'm sure his phone probably never stopped ringing. But there is a pressure that goes along with all that fame and, for some, it can be a very difficult thing to handle—especially in New York.

And Darryl was no exception.

For as great a season as Straw had, something just wasn't right about him. He seemed agitated and even combative at times, accusing me of treating some players differently from others, while threatening teammates he thought were blaming him for some of the team's problems that year. He would be great for a while and then would just go off the deep end a little bit. I continued to try to be the father figure he never had, so I had to sometimes chastise him for loafing or fine him for being late to the ballpark. I tried to keep him on the straight and narrow, first, because I loved the guy, and, second, because the sky was the limit for the Hall of Fame potential he brought to the game. But it was a constant battle with Straw that year.

By the last week of August, we were surging, enjoying our best month of the year. On August 26, we were just 4½ games behind the Cardinals. I should have been enjoying our success. Instead, more turmoil was just around the corner.

Dave Anderson, the Pulitzer Prize–winning *New York Times* sportswriter, said to me, "You're doing so great, Davey. Have you talked to Cashen about an extension?"

All I said back to him was, "I have no comment. You need to ask Frank."

So Anderson and another prominent sports columnist, Mike Lupica of the *Daily News*, went to Frank. But Cashen just grinned at them and turned away, without saying a word, so his silence made the writers assume that I had asked for an extension, which was exactly the opposite of the truth. But they wrote it that way anyway, without getting any confirmation from me.

Lupica took it a step further, blasting me in his column that it was inappropriate for me to ask for an extension. Both articles were total baloney, but Mike's was the worst.

The truth was that Frank had come out of the blue earlier in the season and volunteered to me, without my asking about it, that he wasn't going to extend me.

So the next day, after the articles came out, I was steamed. It was just another headache I didn't need.

I sent word to Lupica that, from that point forward, he didn't need to talk to me. Instead, he could talk to the other writers and get from them anything I had to say moving forward.

The reason I hadn't initially said something to Anderson or Lupica like "Yeah, Frank volunteered to me that he wasn't going to extend me" was because I didn't want to embarrass Cashen. Despite everything that was going on between Frank and me, I still respected the chain of command.

And, in fairness, Frank should have been up front and honest to the columnists and simply said something like, "No, I'm not extending Davey."

So after about a year's sabbatical from Lupica, Marty Noble, a writer from *Newsday*, came to me and said, "I think you're being too hard on Mike."

"Yeah, I probably am," I said. "But if he didn't go and check that story out with me, then he didn't need to talk to me any longer. He could just talk to the other writers."

Then, after a short pause, I told Marty, "Okay, I'll talk to him."

I actually always really liked Lupica, one of the most widely read sports columnists in the world. I just thought he made a huge mistake on that particular article he wrote about me—which was based on fiction. But we buried the hatchet and, actually, from that point on, I almost felt embarrassed by how I thought he was being *too nice* to me in his columns.

******

We managed to pull to within just a game and a half of St. Louis in September, but could never overtake the Cards. Still, we were able to win 92 games and finish second in a season in which we lost all five starters and McDowell for lengthy periods.

And if we hadn't lost Darling, our hottest pitcher in the second half, to a freak jammed thumb injury in an early-September game against the Cardinals while he was pitching a one-hitter in the seventh (a game in which we blew a three-run lead after he left), we still may have pulled off a division title.

By comparison, the '85 Cubs also lost all of their starting pitchers at various points that season after winning the division the year before, but all they could muster was 77 wins and a fourth place finish. A total collapse.

So while I was disappointed that we didn't get a chance to repeat as world champions, our club *never* quit. We remained competitive until the very end.

And while I never really paid much attention to my own personal achievements, I had more wins in my first four years with the Mets than any manager in National League history had ever won in their first four years on the job.

And, yet, by his actions, Cashen clearly didn't see the value I was bringing to the organization from the dugout. After we talked about my future with the club following our elimination, Frank announced to the media before the second-to-last game of the season in St. Louis that I would manage in '88, but then move upstairs to become a "special assistant," which meant I would serve as an adviser and scout.

My players were shocked by the news.

But I decided to take the high road and not bad-mouth anyone in the front office.

My entire focus now was bringing the Mets back to the World Series, whether it would truly be my final year managing the club or not. And if we stayed healthy, I believed we had the talent to get there.

But not long after his announcement to the press, Frank made a speech before some group and told them *he* could have managed the Mets in '86 to a world championship. And then he added he probably could have done better than me in '87.

If I didn't love my job so much, that probably would have been the final straw. In retrospect, I shouldn't have taken that shit from a former newspaperman like Frank who probably never picked up a baseball in his life.

But here's what happens with general managers. They sit upstairs in their box looking down on the field and have all these scouts talking to them, giving them their two cents. When you're that high up above the field you feel like you're smarter than everybody down below. Trust me, I've never seen it *not* happen.

For example, somebody gets an idea like if we shorten Gooden's delivery or shorten his leg kick, it'll save his arm.

What the hell do they know about it?

I just know one thing. When you start messing with mechanics, whether it's a pitcher or a hitter, and the player has been successful, you're playing with fire. Bob Gibson had the biggest rotation in his motion of anybody I ever saw. Nobody was going to mess with him. But Doc was younger and more susceptible to change. And after the geniuses upstairs got through with him, he was never quite the same dominant pitcher he had been before.

This is what I had to deal with.

So with a year left on my contract, I was suddenly a lame-duck manager.

twenty-five

October 9, 1988:
Bit by a Bulldog

DOC WAS NEARLY UNHITTABLE. And the Dodgers' season was on the brink.

We had a 4–2 lead in the ninth inning of Game 4 of the NLCS—seemingly on our way to a commanding three-games-to-one lead. We would be just one victory away from our second World Series appearance in three seasons.

Entering the series, the odds were overwhelmingly stacked in our favor.

We had thoroughly dominated Los Angeles during the regular season, winning 10 of 11 while outscoring them 49–18. Everyone's expectations were that we would brush them aside in the playoffs, that they would be a mere stepping stone for us on our way to the Fall Classic. And nothing that had happened up to this point in the series would make us think otherwise.

The Dodgers would start the inning by bringing up left-handed hitters John Shelby and Mike Scioscia against the right-handed-throwing Gooden.

Bring in my lefty closer Randy Myers?

No shot. I didn't even have him warming up.

The fans were so boisterous and into the game—chanting, "Beat L.A.! Beat L.A.!"

Doc was just breezing along—and his 18 strikeouts in his two games pitched to that point were just one shy of the championship series record. Dwight had always dominated the Dodgers, boasting an 8–1 record and 1.24 ERA against them lifetime. His pitch count in this game was reasonable and he had only given up three singles—two of them way back in the first inning.

Gooden's rhythm and confidence were as good as they had been at any point that night.

He quickly got ahead of Shelby—an earlier strikeout victim—with a fastball and then a curve, leaving him to swing defensively and just looking to make contact for the rest of the at-bat.

Dwight would then throw a fastball up and inside to set up the next pitch—a breaking ball—beautifully, but Shelby was able to chop it foul. Doc then came back with another breaking ball—similar to the one he had struck out John with earlier—but missed just low. Now 2–2, Shelby was fooled badly on an inside curveball, just barely able to put wood on it to stay alive.

Shelby was battling and, on the next pitch, Doc couldn't get him to chase a fastball up and away to run the count full.

But then the key pitch of the inning—and perhaps our season—was when Shelby appeared to go around with a swing that would have struck him out, but third-base umpire Harry Wendelstedt said he checked it and awarded him first base. I really thought we had him. Obviously if we had, it would have changed the entire complexion of the inning.

Still, with Scioscia coming up representing the tying run, I didn't believe pulling Doc there in favor of Myers was the right call. In fact, I still didn't have Randy or anybody else up in the bullpen. After all, Scioscia, despite being a strong guy, was a mere contact hitter at the plate, having hit only 35 home runs over the course of an eight-and-a-half-year career. And Gooden had not given up many home runs in '88 anyway—just 10 in 260-plus innings in both the regular season and this series combined. So I certainly didn't see Scioscia as a threat to hit one out of the ballpark.

Besides, I had watched Doc close out more games than anybody. His pitch count was now at 115, which was about right for him come the ninth inning. I didn't care if it was Mike Scioscia or Lou Gehrig up in that situation, I was sticking with Doc.

Of course, my decision didn't work out too well, as Scioscia lined the first pitch by Gooden—a fastball right down the middle—over Straw's head and into the right-field bullpen for a game-tying home run. After the walk to Shelby, Doc wanted to get ahead in the count and paid the price. Of course, everyone was shocked and the Shea crowd that had been so loud just moments before now sat in stunned silence. I could hear the Dodgers celebrating in the dugout across the field.

But I still believe Doc was my best choice there. And even though it didn't turn out to be, I never second-guessed myself because I always had more information on the teams I managed than anybody on the planet. I knew what my options were in that situation, weighed them, balanced them out, and stayed with Gooden.

I would do it again.

I left Doc out there for two more hitters—a strikeout of Jeff Hamilton and a single by Alfredo Griffin—before bringing in Myers to close out the frame with the score tied at four apiece. Some in the press questioned me after the game for leaving Gooden out there for as long as I did.

"It was never my intent to 'Lasorda' Doc," I told them.

I was alluding to how Tommy would have Fernando Valenzuela out there for 160 pitches some nights.

The next day, the phone rang in my office.

"What the fuck do you mean by 'Lasorda'd'?!" an angry and upset Lasorda asked me.

"Relax, Tommy," I told him. "I think you're a great manager."

Lasorda, after a pause, hung up the phone, apparently pacified by my reply.

We had several opportunities to win the game in extra innings—the first time in the 10th inning.

Mookie led off with a walk on four straight pitches from Dodgers reliever Alejandro Pena. That brought up Gregg Jefferies, the two-time Minor League Player of the Year, to attempt to put down a bunt to move Wilson into scoring position with the heart of the order to follow. But Jefferies, who had batted in the three-hole all the way up through the minor league system, was never asked to bunt, and popped one up to Scioscia in front of the plate for the first out. Mex would then strike out and Mookie got caught stealing to end the inning.

Our second chance came in the 11th, when we put two runners on base with two outs for HoJo, but he popped out on the third-base side to end that threat.

The game remained tied until the top of the 12th when, with two outs, Kirk Gibson—the only true home run threat in a weak, but resilient, Dodgers lineup—came to the plate. Gibson had had a terrible night to that point, going 0-for-5 without hitting a ball out of the infield, and was just 1-for-16 in the series. McDowell, by contrast, was cruising along, having retired all three batters he faced. Plus, Roger had been terrific for us all year, and had given up just one home run.

But in what would be a prelude to the dramatic home run Gibson would go on to hit in the World Series later that month, Kirk connected on Roger's second pitch—a misplaced sinker down the middle—with a towering drive over the right-center-field fence to give the Dodgers a 5–4 lead.

But I knew we weren't dead yet and our third opportunity to win in extra innings was in play. The Dodgers' bullpen was depleted by the absence of Jay Howell, ejected from Game 3 and subsequently suspended after I had alerted the umpires that he had pine tar on his glove, and they had to use one of their starting pitchers, Tim

Leary, to begin the bottom of the inning.

Leary didn't look comfortable at all in the role of relief pitcher.

After leadoff batter Mackey Sasser, now in the game at catcher, worked the count full, he ripped a single to right to get us going. Then, Mazzilli, whom I sent up to pinch hit for McDowell, was in an obvious sacrifice bunting role. But Maz hadn't laid one down in three years, so after not moving the runner over after the first two pitches, I gave him the green light to swing away with a 1–1 count. He swung and missed the third pitch, but then drove a single into left-center field on the next one to give us runners on first and second with nobody out.

That brought Jefferies up again in a critical sacrifice bunting situation to move the tying and winning runs into scoring position. But after he jabbed at the first pitch and fouling it straight back, I took the bunt sign off, letting him swing away. Gregg lofted the next pitch to Gibson in left for the first out—another missed opportunity for sure.

With Mex and Straw up next in the order, Lasorda brought in a familiar face, southpaw Jesse Orosco, to face them. We had traded Jesse to the Dodgers in the off-season as a part of a three-team deal.

And while Orosco faced Mex, the "Bulldog," Orel Hershiser, who had just pitched seven innings in Game 3 the day before and, eight-plus innings in Game 1, was warming up in the Dodgers bullpen. I could hardly believe Lasorda would even consider using his best starter in back-to-back games, much less in three of the first four of this series. But without his best right-handed reliever, Howell, in the ballpark, I guess he figured he didn't have much of a choice.

While Hershiser got ready, Keith came all the way back from being down 1–2 in the count to work out a walk to load the bases. Now all we needed was a fly ball from Strawberry to tie up the game.

But Straw would pop up to Steve Sax for the second out.

Now, with McReynolds coming up as a hitter who had owned

Jesse throughout his career and with the pennant on the line for the Dodgers, Lasorda did indeed bring in Hershiser to get one out.

Still, despite Hershiser's greatness, K-Mac had been terrific all season long in bases-loaded situations, batting over .500. And it appeared like he might pad that stat and win the ballgame for us after hitting a broken-bat looper into short center field. Shelby was playing deep, but read the trajectory of the ball immediately, racing in hard for what seemed like a marathon to make a terrific catch to end the game.

It was a crushing defeat.

The NLCS was now tied at two games each. We had the Dodgers on the hook and let them off it. Even though we were the better team, the momentum had turned, and it was suddenly anybody's series.

******

After losing Game 5 a matter of hours later in an early-afternoon game at Shea 7–4, we returned to Dodger Stadium facing elimination. But David Cone, who was remarkable during the regular season with a 20–3 record and a 2.22 ERA, helped force a Game 7 with a brilliant five-hit complete game effort.

Now I had a choice to make. Would I start Darling on full rest or Doc on short rest?

I went with Ronnie.

And this is where the hypocrisy of the media was at play. Some questioned my pitch counts with Doc or when I pitched him on short rest. But now some of those same reporters thought I should pitch Gooden over Darling in the decisive game.

But I didn't care. I knew how each of my guys was feeling. I knew what they were doing in the training room. And I knew what they were doing in the exercise room. With all of my young pitchers, I was always right there with the trainer checking their pulse every day.

It was just unfortunate that Ronnie picked the wrong day to have a bad start. Darling lasted just five Dodgers hitters into the second inning. Our relievers—Doc, Terry Leach, and Rick Aguilera—wouldn't give up another run the rest of the way. But it didn't matter. The Dodgers led 6–0 after two and it might as well have been 60–0 with Hershiser on the mound.

The "Bulldog" went the distance, pitching a five-hit shutout.

In the series, Hershiser appeared in four games, tossing 24 innings with a microscopic 1.09 ERA.

We couldn't touch him.

But we weren't the only ones to fall victim to Orel.

The Dodgers would again be heavy underdogs in the World Series, but would shock a far superior A's team in just five games. Hershiser would pitch two complete game victories—with an ERA of 1.00. The Bulldog had "willed" his club to a world championship.

It may have been the greatest postseason pitching performance I had ever seen.

******

While not making it back to the World Series was a tremendous disappointment, I was very proud of the regular season we had. We won 100 games, took the NL East by 15 games, and finished the season strong—winning our final 14 of 17 games.

For me personally, it was quite a turnaround season. I had entered it in April with my job on the line, and by the end of October was rewarded with a new three, year contract at $500,000 a year—with an option for a fourth. I felt that I wanted to stay with the Mets the rest of my career, just like Earl had with the Orioles.

And just as important to me was the conciliatory tone of some of Frank's comments during the conference call with the media, like taking the blame for some "misunderstandings" that had come between us and saying that "Davey's record speaks for itself."

It was like we were hitting a reset button.

I think what I learned the most that year was to not let the job of managing in New York destroy me. If it was going to be my last year managing the Mets, I wanted to enjoy it more. I didn't let things bother me as much. I started thinking about how what I could do better, how to be a better person, and how to handle certain things differently.

I had gone through an awful lot in '87, losing more of my input with the triumvirate than I would have liked.

But all of a sudden, I woke up, and thought, *Why fight it? I can't win that battle. I'll just take care of myself and not let anything knock me down and go from there.*

And so then rather than letting it really affect me and taking it personally, I just let things go more.

Ultimately, if I feel like I'm not making things better, it upsets me. I can get depressed when I'm not helping any organization I work for grow and prosper. But with the season we had in '88, I felt good about the results and the future of the ballclub.

And part of that future was going to be the difficult task of replacing Carter and Hernandez. I knew even then that the club wasn't going to renew their contracts following the '89 season, so I was already planning ahead for that. And because I wasn't comfortable with Dave Magadan—who was more of an on-base guy than a run producer—taking over at first nor Barry Lyons assuming the full-time catching duties, I was working guys such as Jefferies, a very gifted switch-hitter, into the lineup to help fill the offensive void we would soon have.

Of course, I got grief for that.

Here was a 20-year-old kid who came up late in the season and hit .321 with a slugging percentage of almost .600 for us, but wasn't well-received by his teammates—to say the least. That was mostly because Gregg was very cocky, was self-centered, and had kind of a shitty personality. And because he was a natural third baseman, he wasn't as good defensively as Backman or Teufel, so some of the guys would get on me for starting him at second. But since there was no way I was going to take HoJo's bat out of the lineup, I wanted to get Gregg as much playing time at second as I could.

I even got shit from the front office for it.

But I defended the move to Cashen.

"I've got to establish this kid because we can use his bat when Carter and Mex retire," I told him.

Of course, Cashen traded him a few years later for a bucket of balls, and Jefferies went on to become a .300 hitter and All-Star with the Cardinals.

Of our younger players, everybody liked another second baseman, Keith Miller, the most. But Miller wasn't close to being the hitter Jefferies was—batting just .214 in '88.

So on this issue, I stuck to my guns and made Jefferies the everyday second baseman the following season.

I was looking forward to our prospects for '89. I loved challenges and I didn't think there was any bigger than managing the New York Mets during that period.

| twenty-six |

October 24, 1989:
The Last Straw

"FIRE *ME*, DON'T FIRE *them*!" I shouted at Cashen over the phone from my home in Florida.

"No, I can't do that," he said. "You work for me and I pay those guys. I can fire them if I want to."

"They may work for you, Frank, but I hired them!"

But in his mind, Cashen needed someone to take the fall for an 87-win season in which we fell to second place.

So who better for him to ax in order to agitate me the most than two of my best coaches, whom I also happened to be close friends with—Bill Robinson and Sam Perlozzo?

In Bill and Sam, I couldn't have asked for more high-class, talented, and hardworking coaches. I had Robinson as my first-base/hitting coach my entire first six years as manager and Perlozzo as my third-base coach the last three.

Cashen could not possibly have picked two worse choices to dismiss.

And you know what?

A lot of times I *still* look back at that day and believe I should have resigned right then and there. When I allowed Frank to fire them, I should have taken responsibility. I was upset with myself for a long time afterward that I let it happen and that I didn't go with them. Trust me.

So why didn't I quit?

At the time, I thought maybe that's what the triumvirate wanted me to do. And I never had quit anything in my life.

Plus, despite the struggles and dismantling of the ballclub that season—and my loss of some authority—I still loved my job.

It's a regret that I've had to live with for a long time.

I let a lot of things slide, but this one hurt both the organization and me badly.

It was astonishing.

******

That '89 season was a strange and tumultuous one from the very beginning of spring training.

In an ominous sign of things to come, Darryl and Keith were seated next to one another during the team photo session. Straw was in the midst of a contract dispute and had threatened to leave camp if it wasn't renegotiated and I guess Keith had made some derogatory comment about Darryl's agent, Eric Goldsmith.

So then Straw turned to Mex and Kid and said, "Why should I want to take a team picture with you two overpaid guys who do nothing?"

And it was on! The two of them started going at it with fisticuffs, with Straw yelling at Keith, "I have been tired of you for years!"

The two were restrained by teammates who jumped into the fray, but Mex wanted more, shouting, "Don't hold him back!"

But Hernandez couldn't break free from Carter's grip on him—which was probably a good thing.

Then Kid brought some levity to the situation by saying, "Hey, let's take another picture!"

Personally, I defended Straw's right to hold out. Sometimes it's necessary in order to get a better contract. So when he walked out of camp the next day, I fined him $750, but when he returned the following day, it was business as usual.

Hey, I held out when I was a player, too, so it was all good with me.

But what wasn't good was Darryl's aggressive attitude. I think there were more issues going on with Straw during that period that had him high-strung and a little on edge. And those issues were clearly affecting the way he was handling his relationships on the club.

Here were two guys—Mex and Straw—who always respected each other and got along great. They were longtime teammates. They were always ready to fight the other team—but never each other.

And now they're fighting on team photo day!

If some of the things that were going on outside the baseball world were affecting Darryl's attitude towards the team, Keith was within his bounds to address it. He was the leader of that ballclub and he showed it that day. And Straw was wrong to bring that attitude into camp.

So after that drama was over with, a week later I had to deal with the triumvirate looking to deal some of my players—most notably HoJo and Sid—in an effort to land pitcher Mark Langston.

Not only would that have been a bad trade for us, but the worst part was how the rumor had gotten out and the negative effect it was having on Johnson and Fernandez. It was a major distraction for the club.

I let the front office know my feelings about the potential trade, and maybe this time, they actually listened, especially with the additional authority I may have gained after signing the new three-year contract. But I think they ultimately didn't make the deal because Langston was earning a lot of money.

Whatever the reason, I was relieved.

I had really hoped this would be more of an uneventful spring training—without any controversies—and one in which the entire focus would be on getting the guys ready for another 100-win season.

I was a little more at peace with the organization, communicating better with the front office, and choosing my words more wisely.

And I started having a better relationship with the press, too. Not that I ever thought it was that bad, but I no longer cared if they ripped me. You just come to the point of thinking, *I've had it. I'm not letting Lupica or Anderson or anybody get under my skin again for no reason.*

So after five years of taking a beating from some writers and the front office, I decided I wasn't going to let any negative thoughts come into my head or allow anyone to upset me any longer. I was going to be more content, which I hoped the club wouldn't confuse with complacency.

******

It became fairly apparent throughout the first half of the season that there would be no running away with the division like in '88. We spent those initial three months of the season in a tight race—never in first by more than a game and a half or out of it by more than five.

All things considered, we were fortunate to even be in the race.

To begin with, we lost our top two catchers—Carter and Lyons—and our perennial Gold Glove first baseman Hernandez for lengthy periods of time. We had Jefferies learning a new position at second base. We had to bring up two starting pitchers—David West and Kevin Tapani—from the minors and make them relievers. We lost Doc, who had been pitching great, on July 1, with a poor prognosis for the rest of the year. Straw broke his toe. Magadan strained a ligament in his lower back. And Teufel had a badly bruised lower back.

So we were dealing with a lot of fundamental breakdowns in the field, which was to be expected with the kids we had to bring up and having others play out of position.

But while things weren't going as smoothly as I would have liked, at no time was I writing off the season. And that's what made some of our in-season trades so reckless and ill-advised.

On June 18, with more than three months left in the season, and with the club just two games out of first, the triumvirate thought it would be a good idea to deal Dykstra and McDowell to the Phillies for Juan Samuel.

"I'm against our doing it for a lot of reasons," I told the three of them. "Look, we've got to give Lenny a chance to play every day. But we'll need some patience. The first year, he may struggle a bit, and probably hit .220 because he's been mostly facing right-handed pitching his whole career. But, remember, I had him as a kid back in the minors when he played against everybody. He'll take pitches, he'll walk a lot, and his on-base percentage will still be over .330.

"Then in his second year as a regular, his numbers are going to go up." I continued. "He's liable to hit .300 and be the best leadoff hitter in baseball. He's going to be a star."

But my argument fell on deaf ears.

"We can't take a drop down," Cashen said. "We can't have a guy hit .220 out in center."

"But Frank, this is for the long haul. It's not going to hurt us doing that."

A pregnant pause allowed me to bring up McDowell.

"And Roger, too?" I asked rhetorically. "He's still an effective long and short man from the right side. We need to keep him."

I was adamant that I didn't want to make this trade. I fought it tooth and nail. And I actually liked Samuel. I thought he was an explosive player as a second baseman. But I already had Jefferies and Teufel over there. And I would never have wanted to put him in center field—it wasn't his natural position.

And besides Lenny, we still had Mookie, too.

It all made zero sense.

After the public outcry from the media and Mets fans after the trade was made, the triumvirate said *I* was the one that wanted to make it. It simply wasn't true.

Does anyone honestly think I would've wanted to trade Lenny and Roger?

So Dykstra goes to Philly and plays every day. He hits .222 with an on-base percentage of .297 the last 90 games of the season. Then the next season, he leads the league in hits, bats .325, and has a league-best on-base percentage of *.418*.

And McDowell?

He immediately became the Phillies' closer, saved 19 games, and sported a *1.11 ERA!*

You can't make this stuff up!

And Samuel?

He hit .228 with just three home runs for us the rest of the season. And he was gone by the end of the year—traded to L.A.

So much for building for the future.

By the trading deadline on July 31, we were in fourth place, but still just seven games out of first. And with no team in our division having better than just a decent season—the very catchable Expos were in first—I still believed we had a good chance to make a run. The walking wounded would soon return.

With Mookie miserable from not playing center field and batting just .205 at the deadline, he was dealt to the Toronto Blue Jays for reliever Jeff Musselman. Wilson would become a regular for the Jays, hit .298 for them down the stretch, and help lead them to a division title in the AL East.

Mookie was a victim of the trade for Samuel. After we dealt McDowell and Dykstra to get him, I had no choice but to find a spot for Juan. And with the club not reupping Keith and Gary, I had to try to establish Jefferies in the lineup and play him at second base.

I hated to see Mookie go, but there was no longer a place for him—so I didn't fight that deal.

But the trade at the deadline that *did* upset me was the one that sent Rick Aguilera and four other promising pitching prospects to the Twins for Frank Viola.

First of all, we already had five outstanding starting pitchers in Gooden, Ojeda, Fernandez, Darling, and Cone.

Why in the world would I need a sixth one?

If Doc didn't stay on the DL for the rest of the season, I would have to move Ojeda to the bullpen—something I didn't want to do to a quality starter.

And then, to deal Aggie, whom I had just turned into a closer that year and watched him thrive in that role—plus my three best pitching prospects in West, Tapani, and Drummond—was just beyond belief. Of those three prospects, Tapani would become a big winner, enjoying a long, terrific career with the Twins and the Cubs.

And Aguilera?

Rick would become a perennial All-Star closer for the Twins, help them win a World Series, and save more than 300 games in his career.

And worse yet, Viola was gone two years later, signing as a free agent with the Red Sox. Like with the Samuel deal, the front office had once again mortgaged the Mets' future for a guy who wasn't around very long.

But never once did I consider going to the owners, Nelson Doubleday and Fred Wilpon, for help or to inform them how the triumvirate wasn't considering my input. Even though I may have had the right to do so, I never wanted to embarrass my boss by going over Frank's head. It was the "Army brat" code that had been instilled in me as a youth—whatever the commanding officer said or did, you never went around him.

I just had to just accept what was going on.

******

Primarily on the strength of our starting pitching, we had our best month of the season in August, going 19–10, and pulled to within just two games of the first-place Cubs. The Expos and Cardinals were still very much in the hunt, as well, and it looked like it would be a four-team race right to the finish of the season.

But after losing the first four games of September, and seven of the first ten, we started fracturing a little bit from within.

Carter, whom I had made co-captain the year before because I wanted to show him more respect than maybe he was being shown by the rest of the club, took shots at me in the press, like saying how he rushed back from knee surgery and I wasn't giving him a chance to play.

But Kid was hitting under .200 and his power was gone.

And it wasn't just an off season because of the surgery—Gary's power numbers the previous year were less than half of what they once were with more than 500 at-bats.

Carter was such a great player, but he was having problems— like most stars near the end of their careers—that he was having a hard time accepting.

Keith was going through the same thing, as his average dropped to just .233 in limited action in '89, but he just came to grips with the reality of aging better than Gary did.

And Kid didn't know what I knew—that the club had no plans to re-sign him. So that meant I had to develop Lyons and Sasser and get them more playing time. The end result was that Carter had to sit more than he would have liked. He accused me of not communicating with him better, but my hands were tied—I couldn't tell him then the Mets weren't reupping him.

I knew how competitive Gary was, so his comments didn't upset me too much.

But what did upset me was how, with two weeks left in the season and us five and a half games out, Straw and McReynolds were in our Wrigley Field clubhouse—already out of uniform—while we were rallying in the ninth inning in an effort to come back in a game against the first-place Cubs. After we had sent seven men to the plate, both Kevin and Darryl had to get dressed and rush back to the dugout. Straw quickly got ready to hit and struck out to end the game—and, realistically, our last hope to catch Chicago.

I fined each of them $500.

McReynolds paid his fine right away. Straw did not.

So when I posted the lineup before the next day's afternoon game, still steamed, I decided to bench them both. I then held a team meeting in which Kevin apologized to the club. But Straw stood up and questioned why they were being benched and accused me of leaking what happened to the press.

I was *incensed*—it was the most upset I had ever been at a player since becoming the Mets' manager. I got right in Straw's face and came extremely close to coming to blows with him. It got pretty hot. Had Darling not stepped between us, I think we would have.

And to make matters worse, the triumvirate had traveled with the club to Chicago, so this incident was only going to give them an opportunity to take more authority away from me if they thought I was losing the clubhouse.

But at that point, I didn't care what they thought.

With all the trades, injuries, and turmoil, it's hard to believe we won 87 games and were in the race until the end of September. For most clubs, that would have been a good season. But I didn't think in those terms. If you don't win the pennant and go to the World Series—no matter what happens—then it's not a good year.

But I also knew it was a growing year—a year in transition. We were moving away from some superstars and trying to get the younger guys in there. Some things I had control over, others I didn't. And when the front office traded away Dykstra, McDowell, Aguilera, and Wilson, and we had long-term injuries to Mex, Kid, and Doc, there was just too great a void to fill.

But none of that mattered to the triumvirate.

My days were likely numbered.

| twenty-seven |

April 7, 1990:
Buddy's Bow Tie

I KNEW I WAS in trouble when I went to the Mets' Welcome Home Dinner and saw Buddy Harrelson wearing a bow tie.

Of course, wearing bow ties was a Cashen trademark going back to his days in the newspaper business. He wouldn't wear long ties for fear of getting ink on them.

So there was Buddy and Frank, sitting together at the same table, with their bow ties.

I thought, *Oh boy, this is going to be a short year.*

Frank and I had been through some awfully tough times to get to this point. And despite the poor trades that I had nothing to do with, I knew it was going to all come down on me. It was like my future was right there in front of me—Buddy would probably be taking over soon.

This was a difficult time in my life—both on the field and off.

After 26 years of marriage, I was separated from my wife Mary Nan and would soon be divorced. We were opposite types of people—she was an English teacher and I was a ballplayer-turned-manager. We had married when we were both so young—on my

21st birthday so I wouldn't forget our anniversary.

The baseball life is hard on marriages. Mary Nan raised our three children while I was on the road much of the time. So it's easy to grow apart.

But that didn't make separating any less difficult—especially when you have children involved.

******

I was right. It didn't take long.

After a sluggish start to the season—a 20–22 record—I bumped into Harazin in the lobby of our Cincinnati hotel.

"Davey, go up to your room. Frank's there."

I looked at Al with a look of resignation and knew what was coming.

"Oh no," I said. "I guess he's come here to fire me."

So I went up to my room and sat down with Frank. Considering our long history together going back to our days in Baltimore, it wasn't an especially long conversation.

"Davey, we've got to let you go."

"Well, Frank, it's been great. I've really enjoyed the run. And I appreciate the opportunity you gave me all those years ago. What do you want me to do to make it easy on you?"

"We'd like you to leave out the back door of the hotel. We've got a car ready to take you to the airport. We would appreciate it if you didn't say anything to the players, the coaches, or the press."

"I can't say goodbye to my players?" I asked.

"It would be easier for the team with Buddy taking over if you just take off," Cashen said.

I was crushed. I had been with a lot of these guys not just the six-plus years at the major league level, but, in some cases, 10 years going back to the minor leagues and all the way through. I wanted to wish them well and tell them not to worry about me.

I did agree with Frank on one thing—not speaking with the

press. There would have been a bit too much media if I hung around, which would only have served as a distraction to the team. And that's the last thing I wanted to put them through.

With that in mind, I told Frank curtly, "Sure, I'll just slide out of here. Sneak out of here. Go home."

So he won. I was leaving town.

It was awful. To this day, I still regret not being able to say goodbye to my team.

So I walked down the back stairwell of the hotel and out the door at street level. While walking toward the car service, with my luggage in hand, I bumped into longtime Mets announcer Bob Murphy.

"Where are you going?" he asked.

I thought for a moment and simply said, "I'm just going to be happy."

******

The media was, in large part, pretty critical of my firing. Lupica, of all people, wrote that it was a "cowardly" move by Cashen.

So Frank went into face-saving mode, saying how the club was underachieving, it lacked fire in its belly, and I had become too soft and easygoing.

But none of that nonsense mattered to me. I knew the problems better than he or anybody else did. We were trying to get younger players who could do some of the things that Carter and Hernandez did. But it was going to take more time.

Obviously, you have to have a reason for firing somebody. So those reasons he gave were as good as any. Just bring them all out.

But I knew better. Right after he fired me, I could have stayed at the hotel and bad-mouthed the triumvirate to the press—told them everything. But I took the high road and just left.

As time went by, more negative untruths were leaked to the press about me.

It was reported how, on a West Coast trip prior to my getting fired, I asked Frank how much time I had to turn the club around.

But that never happened. I would never ask that. It was *always* my job to turn the club around. I didn't need a schedule for it. Every day, I always did what I thought was best for the club. And as long as I did that, I didn't care about whether they were going to fire me or not. It was of no significance to me. My goal was to do everything in my power to increase the assets of the ballclub and help the organization succeed.

And I know in my heart I did everything I could.

But that's where it ends. I didn't have control over what the triumvirate was doing.

They blamed their bad trades on me to the press, but the fact is I never made a trade in my entire life. It was Frank who traded away Mitchell, Dykstra, McDowell, Backman, Jesse, Aggie, Tapani, and Mookie—not me. I wish we had email back then so there would be some sort of paper trail to prove which trades I was not in favor of their making. But the technology wasn't there yet, so the triumvirate was shaping the facts however it wanted them to appear in the press. And everything just deteriorated from there.

All I could do was give the triumvirate recommendations that I felt would make the club better. But when they ignored them, and things didn't work out, they held me accountable.

But what gets lost in all of this are all the positives.

In my time with the club, we turned around a perennial loser into a World Series champion, won another division title, packed the stands every night, got sky-high television ratings, and made lots of money for the organization.

As manager, I averaged 96 wins over six seasons and had more victories than anyone else during that period.

But most important to me was, from the time I arrived, everybody on that team knew their role and went about their business to do the best they could to help the club. We had chemistry. We had gamers. And we had 50,000 fans—screaming and hollering—every night whom our guys fed off and reveled in, whether they were cheering or booing us.

But all of that wasn't fully appreciated by the front office, and the subtle bashing continued well after I was gone. I came to understand that the reason I couldn't get another job in baseball for nearly three years after leaving the Mets was, in part, due to unfounded rumors circulating around the game about me.

It was being said I had a drinking problem and was a womanizer.

Well, I might have two or three drinks after a game—maybe that was more than I should have had. But I never got a DUI, a traffic ticket, or into a fight because of it. And it never affected the way I did my job, contrary to what Lenny wrote in his book. But he can call me a drunk if he wants—he needs the money.

And a *womanizer?*

Please. I started seeing someone when I was separated and was completely up front about that with everyone concerned.

But the onset of the rumors was simple to figure out.

Everything that was being said about me in the papers and behind the scenes was done to disguise how the front office had blown up a championship team—piece by piece—in a few short years.

And just two full seasons after I left, the Mets franchise, which couldn't have been assembled (or disassembled) worse if they tried, was in a state of devastation with a record of 59–103.

I spent a big part of my life building that organization up and I took no pleasure in seeing it go down the tubes.

It was hard to watch.

******

In retrospect, if I could have changed one thing about my time managing the Mets, it would have been to keep Doc and Darryl on the straight and narrow and off drugs. The sky was the limit for both of them. If I would have been better at my job, they would both be in the Hall of Fame right now. As their manager, because I couldn't completely help them reach the top of their potential, I blame myself for that.

I tried to give Darryl advice all the time, but maybe there were other things I could have done that would have completely committed him to being a superstar.

With Doc, it was a little different.

I sometimes think, *Maybe I asked too much of him.*

Or, *What did I do wrong that made him less than great?*

That's because with Gooden, I never think about what *he* might have done wrong—because to me he was always perfect. From the day I met him as a 17-year-old at Kingsport, I couldn't say enough about him. He never did anything but what you would expect a great athlete to do—which is what made his addiction so confounding to me.

Today, I feel the worst about Gooden because, unlike Straw, who has straightened out his life, Doc *still* has some problems he's dealing with.

I truly wish things would have turned out differently for both of them.

As for myself, I wanted to be the Mets' manager forever.

But once it was over, like the Army brat I've always been, I was ready to move on to the next challenge.

twenty-eight

May 24, 1993:
The Red Menace

"I'M GOING TO FIRE Tony Perez," Reds general manager Jim Bowden told me by phone as I was getting ready to go to a golf tournament in Tahoe. "Come to Cincinnati and you can manage for us."

I had done a little scouting work for Jim during spring training. I always thought he was a very intelligent baseball man and a good judge of talent, but he put a Reds team together with the wrong balance. He had *three* closers—Jeff Reardon, Rob Dibble, and Bobby Ayala—in the bullpen. And while the starting position players were strong, he had a bench of mostly Triple A guys who couldn't make a Triple A club.

"Don't fire him," I told Bowden. "You've got eight All-Stars on the field, but a manager needs a good bench and bullpen. You've got it all arranged wrong."

I tried to talk Bowden out of it, but his mind was made up. He was dismissing Perez just 44 games into the season—the fourth-quickest firing of a rookie manager in baseball history. So I accepted the job and made my way out to Cincinnati.

Tony, of course, was an icon in Cincinnati and very popular with the players, so Bowden's attempt at a clubhouse meeting my first day with the Reds to explain the dismissal pretty much fell on deaf ears. After Jim left the silent clubhouse, I basically told the guys, "That's enough talk, let's turn the page."

I then went back to the manager's office and tried to make a phone call. But there was just one problem—the phone was cut off. Evidently, it had been taken out of service by owner Marge Schott since it was discovered that Pete Rose was using it to call in his sports bets. And it would never be turned back on through my stint there.

So one of my first worries was whether the dugout-to-bullpen phone would work. I was afraid that even if it did work, it could get shut off at any time.

I thought, *Will I have to use a telegraph?*

I was more worried about that situation than I was about anything else.

But if that wasn't odd enough, once the game started, our batboy handed me a note. I told him I wasn't taking any during the game. But he said it was from Marge, though it wasn't *really* from Marge. It was from her St. Bernard, Schottzie, whom Marge frequently walked on the field during batting practice.

It read, GOOD LUCK. WE NEED A WIN. WOOFS AND LICKS. And it was signed by what looked like a dog's footprint.

I thought, *Oh boy.*

It would be the start of many notes I would receive from Schottzie during my tenure with the Reds. Another, making reference to my fiancée, read, IF YOU DON'T WIN THE GAME, SUSIE'S NOT GOING HOME WITH YOU TONIGHT.

Marge was in love with that dog. One night, after a ballgame, she invited Susan and me up to her suite. While we're sitting with her over dinner, Schottzie starts licking the mayonnaise bowl!

"Boy, look at that," I said to her. "We need to get—"

But before I could finish my sentence, Marge took a spoon and just started stirring and stirring the mayonnaise around the bowl!

"Now it's fine," Schott said, to Susan's and my amazement. "Oh, he didn't have any of that mayonnaise!"

It's hard to make this crap up!

So then the wine comes. Now, at that time I wasn't really drinking, but usually when I did the bottle had a cork in it. But Marge brings out this bottle of Mogen David with a screw-off top—it couldn't have cost more than five bucks. Maybe not even that much. But she was proud to pour me a drink of wine.

After dinner, I just couldn't resist.

"Marge, if you want me back, you can at least get a bottle of wine that has a *cork* in it," I told her.

For a woman whose personal wealth came from inheriting her husband's auto dealership business—the largest in the state of Ohio—she was *extremely* frugal.

Despite the unusual dining experience with Marge, Susan was thrilled by my getting hired in Cincinnati. She was originally from there and her parents were big Reds fans. In fact, it was always her mother's dream that she would grow up and one day marry a Reds player. So when we went there, it was like meeting family.

Susan had two sons, Jake and Jeremiah, and a daughter, Ellie, from a previous marriage. Since baseball life had kind of led to my divorce with Mary Nan, I decided right then and there that I wanted Susan to experience it firsthand to see if she could deal with it.

"You just come with me," I told her. "We'll have this rule that we don't stay apart for more than a week and see if you like the life of a baseball manager."

So for the next four months, we adhered to that rule—road trips and all.

As for the team, the '93 Reds would be decimated by injuries. Two-thirds of our starting outfield, most of our starting pitchers, the entire infield, and our No. 1 closer—Dibble—were all out for extended periods of time.

But again, the biggest problem with that club was all the holes in the bench and bullpen. You can't have holes if you want to win. The club finished near the bottom of the division, which was typical of the teams I inherited throughout my managing career.

In the off-season, a lot of important personnel decisions needed to be made. Bowden was a really great asset, and we worked well together to get the pieces we needed for the next season. Specifically, we addressed what I called "crunch time"—the personnel that you have as a manager from the fifth inning on, when you truly manage against the other team. I now had better options on the bench and in the bullpen than the ones Perez had. When we were done with our moves, he actually complimented me on helping him know exactly how a team should be put together.

It's only been the last 10 years in baseball that general managers have truly realized how critical the bullpen and bench are. I knew this from the first year I managed more than 30 years ago.

Anyway, with the moves we made, I was very optimistic about the Reds' future.

******

"If you don't marry Susan and make an honest woman out of her," Schott told me following the season, "then you can't come back and manage the team."

Marge had been banned from the day-to-day operations of the Reds for the entire '93 season by Major League Baseball for making an abundance of racial slurs against various ethnic and religious groups.

But now she was back—and on a mission for fidelity.

Marge was a different kind of woman. Since her father never sired a son, he treated Marge like one—even nicknaming her Butch. She smoked an occasional cigar and was more comfortable with men than women. Schott wasn't big on remembering people's names, often just calling them "honey" in her raspy voice.

Her late husband, Charles Schott—who came from a wealthy

society family in Cincinnati—gambled, caroused, drank heavily, and was rumored to have died from a heart attack while either in the bed or bathtub of his mistress, Lois Kenning. Marge was a widow at 39.

So it was no doubt her distrust in men that drove her to wanting her ballplayers—and *manager*—to be faithful and committed to their women. She was also a self-proclaimed old-school Catholic who believed that living with a woman outside of marriage was a sin.

Now, I've never been one to judge, but if Marge was going to play the holier-than-thou card, should she have been sharing a bed with another woman—a delightful person by the way—while owner of the Reds? And did she really need to make Susan feel like a floozy while she had two kids in bible school and another who was severely handicapped?

Anyway, by the end of the '93 season, Susan had had enough of a taste of big-league life to determine that she could handle it—and we married on January 15, 1994.

So, in a way, that ended that issue.

Or so I thought.

Marge had become enamored with one of the coaches I brought in when I was hired—Ray Knight.

I love Ray. Knight was a guy who helped me in New York and was always a gamer. He loves baseball and putting on the uniform. Although he was good at his analyst job at ESPN before joining my staff, being on television was probably the least of his desires. He's an outdoorsman, has a bunch of acres in Georgia, feeds wildlife, and hunts. But he loves being on a ballfield most of all.

So high on Ray was Schott that she had me name him my assistant manager for the '94 season, which was something I'd never heard of before in baseball.

I knew Ray wanted my job and somehow he made a positive enough impression on Marge to put him on such a track. Maybe he picked the weeds from her front yard. Maybe he led her to believe he was Catholic—which he was not. Maybe he convinced her that he was a saint—which, while I liked and respected Ray, he was not.

I really didn't know for sure.

But that was fine with me. I always wanted the best coaches possible under me in case I ever missed something, and I would tell them stuff like, "If you can take over my job, you can have it. More power to you."

A lot of managers don't do that. They hire people who won't be a threat to them. I always felt that if you're smart, you get the brightest coaches in the world to work with you.

Aside from Ray, I also brought Bobby Valentine on to my staff when I went over to the Reds. I had known Bobby a long time— he was one of my coaches with the Mets—and admired him as a player.

But I went through some tough times with Valentine as my third-base coach.

First of all, a couple of times I thought he was overly aggressive with no outs trying to score a runner. But the bigger issue was when Bobby didn't always communicate with the players things I wanted accomplished—like not putting the signs I wanted on. We were at odds over that.

He claimed innocence, saying he missed them. So I had a little discussion with Ray.

"You know my signs," I said to Knight. "Watch what I give and see what Bobby gives to the guys."

Sure enough, Knight confirmed Bobby wasn't always giving the right signs.

So Bobby and I had a chat.

"This can't happen," I told him. "I can't have a coach overrule my signs."

So I moved Bobby out of the third-base coaching box and put Ray over there.

Valentine was trying to get a big-league job at any expense—it didn't matter to him. He was always out for himself. Bobby left the club after the season, eventually working his way up to the Mets' manager post a few years later. I was glad for him.

And I didn't mind that Bobby may not have agreed with all of my strategies and decisions. In fact, I would never want one of my coaches agreeing with me 100 percent of the time. If he did, I would think he's a smart son of a gun for agreeing with me, but I never had a problem with someone trying to show me another way. But you can't have a coach break the chain of command like he did.

I also had some run-ins with Ray because he, too, would do some things I didn't want him to do while coaching third. We would go head-to-head—Knight had a *big* temper. In fact, one time I thought he was going to hit me when I got on him about it.

"Go ahead!" I yelled at him. "*Hit me!*"

I know he wanted to—the veins in his neck were bulging as he shouted back at me.

But we cleared the air and it was over. We've always been close friends—Ray would tell you I'm his *best* friend. And it's true. Sometimes love and hate can kind of go together at times. Stuff just happens along the way. But it doesn't detract from your affection for one another. I care immensely about the success and lives of every teammate or every player who ever played for me—both on and off the field.

It was the same with Kevin Mitchell, whom I was managing again on that Reds team. One time he missed a game—an unexcused absence—and I docked him a day's pay—$20,000. I told him about the fine when he arrived at the ballpark and thought we were over it, but then later I heard him still barking about it in this little room behind the training room. I opened the door and he was all hacked off. I tried to talk to him, but he just pushed me—two hands hard into my chest. So I immediately swung at him, hitting him in the chest as hard as I possibly could. But the next thing I saw was him cock back his big right arm, so I put my head down and he pounded me on top of the head. It felt like I was hit by a bowling ball.

Then Knight busted through the door and subdued Mitch.

But that was the end of it. Everybody was fine. I still loved Mitch. Still loved Ray. Shit happens.

******

We were having a terrific season in '94—first place in the NL Central and 18 games over .500—when the strike ended it all in mid-August. Still, it was a big, quick turnaround from the season before. I felt that the moves I had made with Bowden to improve the club were some of my best work. And the chemistry on the team was very good.

But despite it all, that October, Marge announced I would manage in '95 with no raise in salary and then Knight would take over the following season—essentially making me a lame-duck manager even if we won the World Series.

My pride was saying, "No way," but my loyalty and consideration for the players came into play as well. We had some unfinished business.

Still, later in the off-season, Marge gave the Orioles permission to talk to me about their open managerial position. For me, having grown up in the Baltimore organization, it felt like that would be a dream position. So I went to talk with them.

But at the time, it was a similar arrangement to the headache I had left with the Mets. The Orioles had their own triumvirate—a general manager, Roland Hemond, and two GMs-in-waiting, Doug Melvin and Frank Robinson.

So even though I would have ultimately reported to Hemond if hired, I interviewed with the three of them together.

I remember Frank saying, "If I was your general manager and came down and told you to play so-and-so for no other reason than to play him, what would you say?"

While I was thinking I would say, *Go fuck yourself*, my answer in the meeting was more diplomatic.

"Hey, Frank," I said, "I would hope the general manager and

the manager communicate on a daily basis so there are never any surprises. You come down and manage and let me be general manager and then see what kind of respect the players give you."

I'm not sure if that was the answer they were looking for, but I didn't care. You can't ever let the general manager make decisions on personnel. If that got out, you would have no control over the team. Zero!

The players wouldn't respect you. If you're not making decisions, then why are you even on the bench? That's why I said what I said to Frank.

So they went ahead and hired someone else. But to be honest, I really didn't care. If they're that stupid, why work for them? That's how I've felt my whole life. I know what I bring to the table and I know how good I can be for an organization. If they couldn't see that, then I didn't want to work for them anyway. All I try to do is make an organization successful and establish its assets in making them more valuable. If people don't appreciate it, I could care less about them. Do I want to work for them? Absolutely not.

Besides, I was looking forward to the next challenge—trying to bring a world championship to Cincinnati.

******

I was shocked and really taken aback.

Prior to boarding a bus at the Reds' spring training site in Plant City, Florida, I was with my bullpen coach, Grant Jackson, and third-base/hitting coach, Hal McRae—both African American— as the players walked by.

"Why do you have so many black players on your roster?" McRae asked me. "You have like, 15 or 16 guys when you're only allowed four!"

Jackson shook his head in agreement.

I thought, *Where the hell did that come from? This is 1995!*

"How do you guys even think about that stuff?" I said.

It may have been a subtle jab at Schott. There had been testimony given by a former Reds controller alleging Marge had put out an unwritten rule against hiring blacks, which I didn't realize at the time. My focus was on the team.

As a baseball man, I *never* looked at color. You just take your best guys. Period. It was all about talent, not race.

After they said it, I thought, maybe I've got to make sure Bret Boone and Hal Morris get into the lineup because, if I don't, people might think I'm racist against white people! I hate to say it, but that's what I thought. I was scared to death that both of them would come down sick one day and I wouldn't have Caucasians represented in the lineup!

But anyway, I had 100 percent authority over who made my teams coming out of spring training and couldn't give a rat's ass if there was some unwritten quota going on with the Reds. Still, it stunned me to even hear something like that from two of my coaches. That was an unbelievable statement.

******

Even for Marge, this time she had truly outdone herself.

We started the season off slumping at 1–8. So she walked on to the field during batting practice with a small plastic bag in her hand. Inside the bag were clumps of hair from the deceased St. Bernard she had during the Reds' last world championship in 1990.

As she neared the batting cage, she took some of the hair and started rubbing it on some of my players' chests and legs for good luck. Then she put some clumps in my pocket.

I'm thinking, *She can't be serious.*

But sure enough, that night we came back from a late 11–4 deficit to pull off an improbable 13–11 win over the Mets. We then won our next five games.

Hair of the dog, indeed.

Of course, the reality was that our winning streak and what

would turn out to be an outstanding season had *everything* to do with our depth and experience as a ballclub. So when injuries hit us hard in the first half of the season, I had plenty of flexibility to get creative. By the end of the summer, I had used eight guys in the cleanup spot and had just as many start at first base.

We rolled to an 84–60 record in the strike-abbreviated season and won the NL Central division by nine games over second-place Houston.

Then we swept the Dodgers in the NL Division Series, outscoring them 22–7 over the three games.

We were now just one step away from the World Series.

But next up was a Braves team in the NLCS that would go onto win the World Series later that month. They would sweep us in four straight, though we played them tight, losing both of the first two games at home in extra innings.

We just couldn't stop their leadoff hitter, Marquis Grissom, from wreaking havoc on the bases, nor could we get the middle of their lineup out. Both Chipper Jones and Fred McGriff hit .438 and Javy Lopez batted .357 in the series. Those guys just wore us out.

And, of course, they had phenomenal starting pitching, which featured their three future Hall of Famers—Greg Maddox, John Smoltz, and Tom Glavine. We had a terrific offensive ballclub, but could only score five runs in 39 innings in the series.

It was no sin losing to Atlanta—they were as good a club as I've ever seen.

We had a great team and the organization was moving in the right direction—making significant strides in each of my two-plus seasons with the club.

But despite all that, Marge stuck to her plan. She let me go in favor of Knight despite his never having managed before on any professional level. But it was all fine with me. With such stupidity, I didn't want to work for Schott anymore.

I would just wait for the next challenge to come along.

| twenty-nine |

October 23, 1995: The Dream Job

BALTIMORE CAME CALLING AGAIN.

This time, however, their triumvirate was gone.

GM Roland Hemond had resigned to become senior VP of the Diamondbacks, Doug Melvin left to take a job as general manager of the Rangers, and the Orioles didn't renew Frank Robinson's contract.

So without a general manager in Baltimore, I met directly with team owner Peter Angelos over lunch. It was the first time I had ever met him. I really enjoyed our time and we had a great talk about the ballclub. He wanted me to manage the Orioles—my dream job—and I ultimately negotiated a three-year deal at $2.25 million plus perks.

The opportunity itself was a perfect fit for me. But while I had no way of knowing it then, my relationship with Angelos would pretty much go downhill from that day forward.

Still, it was an exciting time. I went right out and bought a big house in Phoenix, Maryland, in Baltimore County, with a pond in the back that I put 48 "brownie" trouts in. I *loved* that place. It was a fair distance from the ballpark, but an easy 30-minute ride down the interstate.

I was home again and had everything I wanted.

However, there was some baseball business to be worked out. We still needed a general manager. Angelos was talking to Kevin Malone about the position, but I told Angelos he wouldn't be a good choice. The best available guy out there was *clearly* Pat Gillick.

I first met Pat when we were minor league teammates in Elmira, New York, back in 1963, and we hit it off right away. The fact is, I used to date girls and then turn them over to him! We were tight.

As a southpaw, he had the best pickoff move I've *ever* seen in my life. No kidding, I think he sometimes walked guys just so he could pick them off.

It was a shame when arm troubles put an early end to his career. But he would later find new life as an outstanding baseball executive and was the chief architect in transforming the expansion Toronto Blue Jays into back-to-back world champions in 1992 and 1993. So good a general manager was Gillick that he would get inducted into the Baseball Hall of Fame in 2011.

Gillick had been out of baseball for a year when Angelos hired me, enjoying a well-deserved break after 17 seasons with Toronto, so I had a little selling to do.

"Pat, this is a *great* job," I told him over the phone. "You *need* to come here to Baltimore. Let's get back together!"

I persuaded him to meet with Angelos in Baltimore.

"I'll be your general manager," he told Peter. "But I want the same contract Davey got."

Angelos agreed.

I thought we made a perfect team that would be together for a long time.

Prior to Gillick getting the GM job, Malone, in addition to speaking with Peter, had called me numerous times about the opening. Kevin had held the same post with the Expos the two previous years before resigning. No team in baseball was more profoundly hurt by the baseball strike of '94–95 than Montreal, so Kevin was forced to rid the club of most of its biggest stars to drastically slash payroll.

So when Pat asked me if I would recommend anyone for the assistant general manager's opening, I mentioned Malone.

"Kevin Malone's looking for a job," I told him. "Maybe you should hire him."

"Why?" Gillick asked me.

"He's a good man," I said.

So Pat, after some consideration, hired him.

The fact was, I didn't really know Malone that well at the time. But he seemed like a nice enough guy. And like any young baseball executive out there, he was looking to get a better job and succeed at a higher level. I tipped my hat to him for his ambition.

Besides, the role of assistant GM is really designed to be a gofer for his boss—just a lot of legwork and stuff like that. So when he would eventually go from that job to the high-profile Dodgers general manager position, it was a miracle.

Our management team was set.

Now it was time for me to turn another sub-.500 club around—*again*!

* * * * * *

There was no question in my mind that the Orioles team I inherited was a potential championship-caliber club. Anytime you have hitters as great as Roberto Alomar, Rafael Palmeiro, Cal Ripken Jr., Brady Anderson, Chris Hoiles, B.J. Surhoff, and Bobby Bonilla; starting pitching like Mike Mussina, David Wells, and Scott Erickson; and a bullpen that included Randy Myers, Roger McDowell, and Jesse Orosco (who had all been with me on the Mets); you had an excellent chance to compete.

Like I had in New York and Cincinnati, it would be my job to create chemistry—so that everyone would know exactly what his role was going to be on the team and would be used in the proper way. I would let the players play and make decisions based on their talent.

And I would make sure the players would enjoy coming to the ballpark by making a happy clubhouse for them. My philosophy to them was always, *Come early, get your work in, no stress, and then go out and play.*

A lot of general managers didn't agree, but that's the way I wanted to be treated as a player and I wanted to treat my guys the same way.

Creating chemistry and a happy clubhouse applied to any kind of team I ever managed.

It's funny; when I managed the Mets, everybody remarked how great I was with young players. Then, when I moved on to the Reds and Orioles, it was always how great I was with older guys. It was never just, *Boy, he's great with players*—period.

Nobody ever seemed to understand that about me. It comes down to this: If I'm playing a 35-year-old ahead of a 25-year-old and everybody knows the older player is more talented, we've got great chemistry on the club.

I've been consistent with my values and my thought process my whole life. The main obligation I had was to make my players play up to their potential, show them that I cared and wanted them to be successful—all while establishing my authority at the same time.

I don't care who the hell you're managing. Managing in the big leagues is like managing in the minors. There are a whole lot of things you have to take into consideration to be successful and for the people around you to be successful.

Another thing I needed to do right away with that Orioles team was to make clear who the boss was from jump street. This is especially vital when you manage a veteran team like the one we had.

And nobody needed to hear that message more than our resident legend—Cal Ripken.

I loved Cal. His father had once coached me, so I had known the Ripken family for many years. But after we signed Alomar as a free agent to play second base, Manny Alexander was a man without a position. Thus, I was thinking seriously about moving Ripken to third and inserting Alexander at short.

Manny wasn't a great choice to play short, but at that time, he was a young player the organization was high on and it wanted to give him a shot.

So I thought, *Where else am I going to put him?*

Well, I basically played him everywhere—shortstop (late in some games), third, second, left field, designated hitter—but, to be truthful, he was kind of horseshit, batting just .103 with no extra-base hits in 73 plate appearances that season.

Ripken's basic message to me was, "Don't move me off of short for *Manny Alexander*."

And he was right. So I didn't.

But we talked about it around the batting cage and off the field. We even butted heads over the subject. I wanted him to understand that I had the total right to do what I wanted to do—that I could move him to third even though he was going to the Hall of Fame.

He once shot back with, "I'm still the best shortstop in the league."

To which I replied, "But *I'm* the manager of this club."

Even though he was a great player—the baseball icon who never missed a game—I was trying to show him that he needed to keep a straight line to me.

And that went for his consecutive games streak, too. I never did sit him in my two years in Baltimore, but I would have taken him out in a heartbeat if I felt he really needed the rest. Ripken knew that and we fought about that too. But I had a lot of respect for him and allowed him to keep it going.

However, I got my point across.

I never showed any kind of favoritism to any degree with any player I ever managed. None.

Brady Anderson would hit 50 home runs for us that year. Did I start treating him any differently?

Absolutely not.

Alomar?

Nope.

Palmeiro?

Never.

You can lose control of a club really quickly if you do.

Another issue I needed to address early on concerned the talented Mike Mussina.

After getting bombed in a couple of April games against Boston and Cleveland, I talked pitch selection with him.

"You're readable," I told him. "You're always using your fastball to go after guys and they're hitting you hard. You need to be able to go both ways. You should set up your breaking ball and change-up more than the fastball."

Once he started doing that, he won a bunch of games—finishing the season 19–8 to lead the league in wins and shutouts.

******

Entering that '96 season, the Indians were widely considered the team to beat. They were the defending American League champions coming off a historic season in which they had a winning percentage of nearly .700.

But I wasn't really overly concerned about them. I always looked at how my clubs matched up against opponents and I liked how we stacked up against Cleveland.

I was actually most concerned with Boston and New York. They were both in our division, came from big markets, and, for me personally, were longtime rivals.

And of the two, the Yankees were the team *my* Orioles had replaced as the No. 1 team in baseball in the '60s. So it was always a point of pride with me when it came to the Bombers.

New York also had more money than any other organization and could pick up a missing piece down the stretch run of the season if needed. So they were always a team on my radar.

We ended up having a very good season, finishing second to the Yankees in the AL East, but good enough to win the wild-card on the second-to-last game of the season in Toronto after Alomar hit a game-winning home run in the top of the 10th inning.

Going into that game, Roberto was catching major heat for spitting in home-plate umpire John Hirschbeck's face the night before after a called third strike in the first inning.

I've never fully addressed this before, so here's what I'll say. Alomar was a *great* all-around player—a good hitter, an excellent fielder, and a second baseman *par excellence*. I loved him.

He also had a great eye at the plate.

My recollection, which is pretty damn good, was that there were a couple of pitches that were off the plate inside. Roberto questioned Hirschbeck on them.

Alomar said something like, "Those are balls."

Then Hirschbeck said something back to him—but I couldn't hear what it was. Alomar would later say John cursed at him and said something insulting about his mother.

The next thing I know, Roberto spits at him and gets thrown out of the game—and rightfully so. Nothing that Hirschbeck may have said could have validated what happened at home plate—and I told John that prior to the next game.

So I smoothed everything over with Hirschbeck and we were all ready to move on.

But just when I thought it was over, Angelos summoned me to an office after the game where two attorneys he brought in were there waiting with him. They wanted me to sign an affidavit that said I had heard Hirschbeck call Alomar a son of a bitch and that's why Roberto spit on him. It was an obvious attempt to beef up an appeal of a five-game suspension the league office had levied on Alomar that would take place the following April.

"I can't do that," I told them. "No. 1—it will kill Baltimore. And No. 2—I didn't hear it."

So one of the attorneys tells me, "You're not much of a manager. You're not much of a leader of men."

Now I was pissed and could hardly believe what I was hearing.

"I *can't* sign to it," I told Angelos. "Tell them to get a lip reader. I was 30 feet away. I couldn't hear the conversation at home plate."

Their premise was that because Roberto was a good Catholic boy and was defending his mother's honor, he felt he *had* to spit on Hirschbeck.

Give me a break!

We might not have been able to get umpires to come to Baltimore if we put that out there. But most important, it just wasn't true—I hadn't heard a thing and wasn't going to lie and say I had.

Angelos, who had no proven baseball competence, was continuing a pattern of meddling in the affairs of our team that had begun at the start of the season.

It would only get worse from there.

******

As it turned out, after winning the wild-card, we would end up playing the Indians in the AL Division Series. It was the Orioles' first trip back to the postseason in 13 years.

So how did it feel to guide Baltimore back to serious October baseball?

It felt normal—that's all. It's where I felt the Orioles always belonged.

So when we took the Indians three games to one, I expected it. We won the first two games of the series decisively and then clinched in Game 4 when Alomar, despite being ferociously booed by Cleveland fans, hit the game-winning home run in the 12th inning.

We had a good team, one that I felt had a chance to do some big things.

With the Yankees winning their own division series over the Rangers, we would now face off against them in the ALCS. And really, it seemed only fitting that it would come down to Orioles-Yankees. Plus, to be back in New York for a postseason series just seemed like it was meant to be.

It fit.

But most important of all, we were now just four wins away from the World Series.

The turning point of that entire ALCS would occur right from jump street in Game 1 at Yankee Stadium. We were leading 4–3 in the bottom of the eighth when Derek Jeter came to the plate with no one on base and one out. My hard-throwing reliever, Armando Benitez, was dealing, having struck out the last two batters he faced.

I had my bullpen set up perfectly with closer Randy Myers ready—should we hold on to the lead—to come in and close out the game in the ninth.

But that's when Jeter hit a fly ball to relatively deep right field, toward the short porch in Yankee Stadium. Tony Tarasco, whom I had just put in the game as a defensive replacement for Bonilla to start the frame, had a beat on it, but when he reached up to attempt to make the catch, some kid leaned over and pulled the ball over the fence for what was ruled by right-field umpire Richie Garcia a home run to tie the game.

I couldn't believe the call.

I still remember seeing the interference clearly from the third-base dugout—*400 feet away!*

So I ran out to Garcia in right field to argue.

"How in the hell can I see this from 400 feet away and you can't see it standing right under it?! Are you blind?! Are you blind?!" I yelled at him.

There was nothing he could say. I mean, you blow a call—what can you say?

But I still wanted to get my point across—get my two cents in—and kept arguing.

"If you can't see *that*," I shouted, "*what* can you see?!"

"I'm throwing you out of the game," he tells me, before giving the heave-ho signal.

"That's *wonderful! You* blow a call and throw *me* out!" I said.

It was one of the craziest noncalls I've ever seen. Garcia was looking straight up at where the kid leaned over and still called it a home run. And then had the audacity to throw me out of the game.

My whole career was the same way. I get thrown out because another guy makes a mistake. What's the problem with this deal?

The Yankees would win it in the bottom of the 11th inning when Bernie Williams took Myers deep. But it was Garcia's noncall that cost us the game.

We would win the second game to even the series, but I couldn't help but think of what should have been—returning to Camden Yards with a 2–0 lead and a major psychological advantage. If we had, I believe we would have finished off the Yankees in Baltimore and gone on to the World Series.

As it turned out, New York would win all three games in Baltimore, in large part due to my old buddy Strawberry hitting two home runs in Game 4 and a tape-measure shot beyond our bullpen in the finale.

But it all goes back to Game 1. When strange things happen that are out of your control, like that errant home run call, and the momentum shifts against you, it's a feeling that's hard to describe.

It helped the Yankees, and hurt us.

They won and we lost.

Shortly after the series, Angelos ordered me to fire my pitching coach, Pat Dobson, and hire Ray Miller. He wanted this done despite the great work Pat had done with the staff all season long and my long association with Dobson going back to the Orioles' halcyon days.

I fought it tooth and nail, just like any other time an owner or general manager wanted to fire one of my coaches.

"Fire *me*, not him," I told Angelos.

But he forced the issue, and basically said the same thing you usually hear from any front office person in these situations: "We hire them, we fire them."

"No," I said. "*I* hired him. And you shouldn't be able to fire him unless you fire me, too."

Despite all the success the Orioles had in '96, this was just one more thing that ate at me.

Another was how my wife, Susan, had helped the club raise more than $150,000 toward the Boys and Girls Clubs of Metropolitan Baltimore after the Orioles' previous year's effort had only yielded around $25,000. For some reason, this upset Peter, and he bad mouthed her to the press.

Why?

I had no idea.

After all, he had encouraged Susan and me to do charitable work in the Baltimore area.

But that told me all I needed to know about the man.

I thought, *I don't think I want to work for Angelos much longer.*

| thirty |

November 5, 1997: Thanks for the Manager of the Year Award—Now I Quit

ON PAPER, OUR REGULAR season was as good as it gets.

Not only did the Orioles capture the AL East crown for the first time in 14 years, but we did it in wire-to-wire fashion—keeping a stranglehold on first place the entire 162-game season.

But not one bit of our success was by accident. You don't win 98 games playing in the toughest division in baseball without a formula for success and taking into account the psyche of every player on the roster—which I did.

Plus, we improved our pitching—the cornerstone of any team— by signing free agent Jimmy Key away from the Yankees, which helped us times two. And our bullpen, behind Myers' 45 saves and microscopic 1.51 ERA; the maturation of Benitez; and the turning-back-the-clock performance of 40-year-old Orosco; was now the most effective in baseball.

It was also the season I decided to move Ripken to third after we picked up free agent Mike Bordick—an outstanding defensive shortstop. So good was Bordick that Cal even volunteered to change positions to make room for him at short.

As a team, we could always hit, but now we had better pitching and defense than the year before.

We rolled into the Division Series with a date against one of the greatest offensive teams of that generation—the Seattle Mariners.

The Mariners had no holes in a lineup that featured a young Alex Rodriguez and an in-his-prime Ken Griffey Jr., as well as Edgar Martinez and Jay Buhner.

But in a short, best-of-five series like the one we were about to play them in, they would pitch the remarkable and intimidating 6'10" southpaw Randy Johnson twice. Because of this, despite our having the league's best record, the oddsmakers favored Seattle.

But I knew better.

I had a plan for beating Johnson. I was going to sit my two best hitters—Palmeiro and Alomar—and replace them with a couple of right-handed hitters off my bench—Jerome Walton at first base and Jeff Reboulet at second. It wasn't an easy decision to make, but I thought they would have more success against Johnson.

The media called it a monumental risk on my part.

They called me a riverboat gambler.

But I didn't look at it that way. The way I saw it, I was putting out a lineup with what I felt had the best chance to beat Johnson. I didn't give a rat's ass what anyone else thought. It was my decision and I would take full responsibility for it.

The result was that we beat Johnson—he of the 20–4 record and 2.28 ERA during the regular season—*twice*, taking Game 1 9–3 and the Game 4 clincher 3–1.

And it was Roboulet who got us off to a fast start in the finale, hitting a 96 mph Johnson fastball for a home run in the bottom of the first. So there was certainly some vindication with starting him over Alomar.

Unfortunately, we would lose to the Indians four games to two in a hard-fought ALCS, one in which we lost twice in extra innings. But I thought we did a good job getting to that point. Sometimes, it's just not in the cards. And when it isn't, I expect to take the blame for it.

Still, with the season we had and the moves I made in the Seattle series, I should have had as much support from ownership as any manager in baseball.

But it just wasn't so.

******

Angelos had seriously crossed the line.

Back in July of that '97 season, he had undermined me by calling down to the trainer's room and telling Alomar not to pay a $10,500 fine for missing an Opening Day team luncheon in April and a midseason exhibition game with our affiliate in Rochester without getting my permission. I had been too preoccupied with getting the Orioles to the World Series to address it at that time.

But now, with the season over, I felt the strong need to confront him. Not only had he undermined me with one of my players, but he'd brought my wife into it as well.

That year, Susan worked a couple of days a week as a consultaant/executive director for the Carson Scholars Fund. She didn't raise money for it—Dr. Ben Carson did most of that himself—but instead, her primary duty was to provide communication among him, the scholars, and the board.

Like I used to do with Strawberry when I fined him, I requested that Alomar pay his to a charity so he could write it off on his taxes as a deduction. I recommended that the fine go to the Carson Scholars Fund. I thought I was doing Roberto a favor by allowing him to make a charitable contribution.

The one thing I wouldn't allow, however, was for Alomar to decide where it should go.

I thought, *What kind of punishment would that be? A guy breaks a rule and has the option of choosing where the fine should go? I don't think so.*

I was aboveboard on everything. I had Gillick first approve and then prepare a letter with the details for Alomar.

And that should have been the end of it.

But it seemed apparent that Angelos was looking for a reason, *any* reason, to remove me as manager—and this was it. He went to the press and said I was engaging in "gross misconduct" in the handling of Alomar's fine because I suggested that the money go to a charity where my wife worked.

I thought, *Does Angelos think I typed the letter up? Doesn't he know it was typed by Gillick?*

The truth was, it didn't matter to me which charity was chosen. The team could have picked one out of a hat for all I cared.

I was quickly losing all hope of continuing to manage the Orioles because of how Angelos had infringed upon my authority with Alomar.

But to bring Susan's name into all of this infuriated me, and it was the last straw.

This was a woman who had founded a school for the deaf and blind. A woman who helped save the lives of 13 orphans who were on a 10-day die list in war-torn El Salvador because there weren't enough antibiotics for them (she found them foster parents in Florida). A woman who again went to El Salvador after a big earthquake and saved a six-week-old baby left for dead by a mother who thought she was blind (it was actually a bad eye infection) and found a home for her while the woman was arrested. A woman who helped raise $60,000 for a children's hospital. And a woman who formed Women in Major League Baseball, in which she organized the wives of ballplayers to serve the poorest children in their respective cities.

These were just some of the reasons I admired and loved her like I did.

So when Angelos brought her into this, it was *over* for me.

On November 5, I got Peter on the phone and called him every name in the book.

"I'm not firing you," he said.

Angelos knew that if he did, he would still have to pay me the last year of my contract—around $800,000.

I then got a call from Gillick, who pleaded with me not to resign.

But the deal was, Angelos wasn't going to fire me and I didn't want to work for him anymore. And Gillick wouldn't really protect me, so I had to resign.

So I called Angelos back.

"Well, since you're not going to fire me, I'll just resign."

"Put it on paper and fax it to me," he said. "I need to have it in writing."

"All right," I said.

Shortly after I sent off the fax, Angelos called me back.

"I accept your resignation," he said.

And that was the end of it. That was the whole story. I couldn't work for him and he didn't want me working for him. Resignation? Fired? Call it anything you want. I was hoping it wouldn't come down to that, but it did.

There was a lot written afterward about how I wanted to renegotiate my contract or that my fax to Angelos was anything more than just my resignation. But it was all fake news. I had the best record in the American League, so it doesn't take a rocket scientist to figure out what was going on—Angelos had to leak every kind of thing conceivable to justify why he wanted me replaced.

The Mets did the same thing—calling me a drunkard and a womanizer after I left. It's what some teams do when a manager's successful and the owner or general manager wants you out.

They basically have to cover their ass. They *need* to have an excuse.

Well, the reality is that *every* club I worked for through my time with Baltimore went right down the shitter immediately after I left. You can look it up.

Still, it makes me mad—*very* mad—when the truth doesn't

come out and I hear lies and inaccuracies through a third party. That's part of the reason I never gave a shit about the newspapers. I never read even one word of what was written after I resigned or was fired from any team I managed.

Part of what I hope this book accomplishes, aside from helping people deal with their lives and challenges while learning from my successes and mistakes, is to set the record straight on a few things. I can prove facts, but newspaper people often don't care about them. They just write what they want to write. So it's really frustrating for me to hear sometimes how screwed up "the record" is.

I'm a realist and love life. I want everybody to be successful. But when I see and hear some of the false things that have been written, it bothers me.

******

That same day I was resigning from the Orioles, I was informed by Jack O'Connell, the secretary/treasurer of the Baseball Writers Association of America, that I had been voted the American League Manager of the Year.

I had to do a television interview later that afternoon after the announcement was made public, and I informed the interviewer that I had resigned.

People right away assumed I resigned because I had another job lined up. But I didn't. I left $800,000 on the table based purely on principle. I was never one to hold my tongue. I spoke my mind freely where other managers might have kept their mouths shut more than I did.

In this case, I thought, *If I'm not wanted, I don't want to take that man's money. Life's too short. I'll survive.*

What happened in Baltimore came down to this. With someone like Angelos, a nonbaseball man, he felt threatened when his manager was successful in putting a team together and started getting a little bit of positive publicity for it. He never liked the fact that somebody was getting more credit for the Orioles making the playoffs two years in a row than he was. So he arbitrarily wanted to get rid of me.

A similar thing happened with Cashen—another nonbaseball man.

I don't understand why it has to be like that, but it's a fact of life in baseball.

I have no ax to grind—I'm just telling the truth.

thirty-one

October 23, 1998:
La La Land

I WAS PERFECTLY HAPPY at home in Winter Park.

I had a thriving commercial real estate business, was playing a lot of golf, and enjoyed the benefits of being with my family year-round.

But when Rupert Murdoch reached out to me about the Los Angeles Dodgers' managerial opening, it really intrigued me.

I thought, *How many people get to sit down and deal with such a powerful person?*

Murdoch was the owner of media empire the Fox Entertainment Group, which bought the Dodgers in 1998 for an astounding $311 million—an unheard-of sum of money for a sports team at that time. And he was friendly with Bob Daly, co-chairman of Warner Brothers, who would leave that role a year later to take a 10 percent stake in the Dodgers and become managing partner—enjoying full control over the organization.

But at that time, Daly, a lifelong Dodgers fan who grew up in Brooklyn attending games at Ebbets Field, was regularly just offering his advice to Rupert about the ballclub. I like smart, successful people, and those two certainly fell into that category in a big way.

The three of us met at Daly's house by the sixth hole of the famous and very exclusive Riviera Country Club west of Bel Air. Rupert was with a very attractive Asian woman, Wendi Deng, whom he introduced to me as one of his financial executives at his Star TV network in Hong Kong. Though Murdoch was 37 years her senior, they would marry the next year, less than three weeks after his divorce to his second wife, Anna, was finalized. Years later, when Murdoch suspected that Deng was having an affair with former British Prime Minister Tony Blair, he filed for divorce, citing irreconcilable differences. Murdoch is now married for a fourth time to former model Jerry Hall—who has four children with Mick Jagger.

I'll tell you—Rupert's crazy! I can't keep up!

But he is a great businessman and was smart enough to hire me that day, October 23, 1998, to manage the Dodgers.

The month before, Kevin Malone was brought on as general manager, though he was not a part of my negotiations with the ballclub. The fact was, he didn't want me in L.A.—only Rupert and Bob did. Malone's first choice for manager—Felipe Alou—was from his old club he GM'd in Montreal. But Alou turned Kevin down, opting to remain the pilot of the Expos.

Against my wishes, Malone brought over another buddy of his from Montreal, Felipe's bench coach Jim Tracy, and would give him that same role on my staff. I would have preferred Mike Scioscia for that spot, but Kevin was adamant about giving it to Tracy.

So there were problems with Kevin from the start. We just weren't on the same page.

But, at least initially, I was still happy to be a Dodger.

More than the money—$4.5 million for three years—this was like another dream job, not unlike what I had in the beginning with the Orioles. As a kid, I was a big Dodgers fan. They were the only team I could listen to regularly on the radio. I grew up rooting for players like Pee Wee Reese, Carl Furillo, and Duke Snider—and *idolizing* Jackie Robinson.

So becoming the manager of this iconic team was undoubtedly one of the greatest moments in my baseball life.

But then reality kind of set in a little bit. There was a lot of work to be done.

This was a club that needed a serious mental change after having not been very good the previous decade.

And although the Dodgers had one of the biggest payrolls in baseball at $85 million, there were a lot of question marks and an overabundance of right-handed hitters and pitchers. And Malone's trades and signings that off-season did nothing to help that situation.

His biggest splash was going out and signing free agent right-handed pitcher Kevin Brown—making him baseball's first $100 million player with a seven-year, $105 million contract. And while Brown was a very good pitcher, I would have much preferred we signed left-hander Randy Johnson instead. That's because I knew our division and knew what kind of hitters we were up against.

Plus, a seven-year contract for any pitcher is a long deal.

We could have had the "Big Unit," a more dominant pitcher, for less money and fewer years. Arizona, a division rival, ended up signing him for $52 million over four seasons. Over that time, Johnson would incredibly win *four straight* Cy Young Awards. He was damn near unhittable.

I have made some pretty good calls and decisions throughout my career, but not everybody—particularly Malone—took advantage of them. Kevin put this Dodgers team together without my input.

So despite the fact that we had some talented players such as Gary Sheffield, Raul Mondesi, and Eric Karros in the middle of the lineup—all right-handed hitters by the way—the bullpen was shallow and the infield defense was questionable. And worst of all, the farm system was in terrible shape. I think Lasorda had depleted it to acquire some quality players in his final years as manager and his brief tenure as interim general manager. The Dodgers historically had one of the best systems in baseball, but during this period, there just weren't many good prospects at all.

Our starting pitching, aside from Brown, would underachieve badly. Chan Ho Park and Darren Dreifort both pitched to ERAs of around 5, while my only left-hander, Carlos Perez, was 2–10 with an ERA of 7.43!

So it was a tough situation that first season and we finished a distant third in the NL West.

But with some time, I felt confident I could rebuild the club into a winner.

First and foremost, we needed more balance.

******

A month following the '99 season, I finally got Malone to trade for a big left-handed bat when we acquired power-hitting outfielder Shawn Green from the Toronto Blue Jays in exchange for Mondesi and reliever Pedro Borbon.

Green was coming off a huge, MVP-type season, belting 42 home runs with 123 RBIs while earning a Gold Glove in right field.

He was *exactly* what we needed.

As a result, our offensive attack greatly improved with him in the middle of the lineup. Opposing pitchers could no longer give us a steady diet of right-handed pitching. They had to respect a hitter from the left side like Green.

Sheffield would put together his best season in 2000 with 43 home runs; young third baseman Adrian Beltre would break out for the first of many seasons in what would develop into a terrific career; and Karros would put up big power numbers once again.

The addition of Green gave us one of the most potent lineups in baseball.

Our pitching also improved, with Park winning 18 games to lead the staff.

We also had a 24-year-old pitcher, Eric Gagne, who had great stuff—threw hard and had a good breaking ball and a nice slider. But the thing I liked most about him was he was from Canada. He was a real *gutsy* son of a bitch.

The problem with Gagne was that when I started him, opposing teams began hitting him hard after four or five innings.

Late in the 2000 season, I remember telling Tracy, "Next year, I'm going to put him in the 'pen."

Two seasons later, he became the premier closer in all of baseball—setting a record by converting 84 *consecutive* save opportunities—and would win a Cy Young Award in 2003.

He just went off the charts.

But despite our nine-game improvement over the previous season—from 77 wins in 1999 to 86 victories in 2000—I couldn't work with Malone anymore. We weren't aligned on player personnel decisions and I couldn't deal with his publicly questioning the club's character and intensity.

I thought, *Either he's got to go or I will.*

Derrick Hall, who was then the Dodgers' senior vice president of communications (he's now president of the Diamondbacks) and the smartest guy we had in the front office—a *great* baseball man— pleaded with me to stay.

"Don't go, Davey," he told me. "We *need* you here. Just manage and don't worry about what anyone else does."

"They want me out," I told him. "So enough."

"But look at how much the club has improved," he said.

"Well, we've got a long way to go," I told him, even though I knew we were not far off from competing for a title. "Besides, it's either me or Malone. I can't work for the guy."

I also knew that Malone wanted Tracy to take over as manager.

Anyway, one of us had to go—and everybody knew it.

So I went to see Daly.

"It's Malone or me," I told Daly. "I can't work for him. We're not in sync. Fire one of us. Fire *me* if you want to. Since Kevin signed most of the players we have on the roster, it should probably be me to go. I'm easy—just can me."

Daly reflected on what I told him, before saying, "Well, it's his team he put together, so okay."

And just like that, I was fired.

But there was another dynamic at work—a tragedy in my life—going on at that time.

My youngest daughter, Andrea, was very sick, and I needed to get home to Florida to be with her. It was a stressful time for my family, and it would take a toll on me physically when my heart would go into arrhythmia every once in a while.

If this reality hadn't existed, I might have asked Daly to fire Malone instead of me.

In a sense, a part of me welcomed leaving the Dodgers. I can look back at my tenure there knowing I did the best I could and left a team headed in the right direction. We were making real progress. The Dodgers would win 92 games a couple of years after I left, in large part due to the rebuilding process I was a part of.

There may have been some unfinished business, but I accomplished a lot in L.A. I enjoyed the challenges it presented and wouldn't have changed a thing.

I loved wearing the Dodgers uniform while I could and there were no hard feelings when it was over.

Now I had a daughter to care for.

thirty-two

June 8, 2005: My Little Surfer Girl

ANDREA LYN WAS THE love of my life.

My youngest child.

A sweet, beautiful girl filled with optimism and laughter.

An accomplished pianist.

And—her greatest passion—a great surfer.

When my three kids—Davey, Dawn, and Andrea—were really young, we went to New Smyrna Beach one afternoon. They were all good swimmers, but at one point while they played in the ocean, a strong tide pulled Davey and Dawn deep out to sea—bringing them both to an understandable state of panic. I swam as fast as I could and was able to grab them both—one in each arm—and paddle the three of us safely to shore on my back.

It was a hard moment—one of those moments you think about often.

I could have lost those two kids if I wasn't there. They needed me to save their lives.

But Andrea was always different. Even at a very young age, she was a gifted, fearless swimmer who loved the water.

So she took up surfing.

I never worried about her because she was simply pursuing her life's dream, like I did with baseball. She was actually a lot like me—a risk taker. I always admired her for that. I loved all my children the same, but because Andrea and I were so similar, she was the closest to me.

When she was old enough to drive, I bought her a Mustang with a fold-down back seat so she could put her surfboard in it when driving to the beach. Her favorite local spot to surf was at Cocoa Beach because it had the biggest waves in the area. It was normal for Andrea to wake up at our home in Winter Park at 6:00 AM to check the surf reports and head on over to the beach to hone her skills.

It was the joy of her life—she was happiest in the water and competing.

And compete she did, becoming a professional surfer in her late teens. She didn't want to go to college—the ocean was her classroom.

Andrea won numerous competitions—including four Eastern Surfing Association titles—and was ranked in the top five female surfers in the country. She was *really* good.

Like me, she wanted to travel the world to express her talent. She went to the best places—like flying all the way to Hawaii to surf the North Shore. Or competing off the coast of New Zealand in shark-infested waters. The potential danger never fazed her— she'd probably just kick those sharks out of the way if they came near her.

The sky was the limit for Andrea—seemingly nothing could stand in her way of continued success.

But then, at the top of her game, she began hearing voices.

******

The doctors' diagnosis would be a combination of a bipolar

disorder and schizophrenia—and Andrea would begin years of medication and hospitalization.

It was heartbreaking. And a part of me blames myself.

Andrea's illness began when she was in her early twenties—shortly after I separated from Mary Nan. I always felt like my kids thought I was separating from them, too—which, of course, couldn't have been further from the truth. Thus, I really believe that the separation had something to do with causing Andrea's problems—which makes me feel awful.

Shortly after the diagnosis, I found Andrea a home near Mary Nan where caretakers gave her the daily care she needed.

Over the next several years, I was traveling quite a bit—first as manager in Baltimore and then in Los Angeles—but went to see her every chance I got.

Those were difficult days.

As a loving parent, you just try to do what's best. There were some terrible episodes for Andrea—both emotionally and physically—that we were dealing with. Aside from the effects of the schizophrenia, she had put on a good deal of weight from the pills she was taking. But despite all of this, you never lose hope that everything's going to work out. You remain optimistic because you've had so much joy in raising a child like that. You recall how she was once in perfect health—a great athlete—and pray that she would be again.

Following the 2000 season with the Dodgers, I was really burned out. The fact was, I was ready to go and try to make things better at home. I needed to be with my sick daughter.

And that's what I did—for the next three years.

I had no intention of returning to managing. I had my commercial real estate business, was helping out at two nearby colleges, and worked as a consultant for a company representing golfers and baseball players.

But then one afternoon I got a call from my agent, Alan Nero.

Alan told me about the plight of Robert Eenhoorn, a former

Yankees shortstop, who was now the manager of the Dutch national team. Eenhoorn's six-year-old son, Ryan, was dying of Wilms' tumor, a cancer that originates in the kidney. Nero asked if I would be willing to fill in for Eenhoorn during the European championship and Olympic qualifying competitions in Haarlem, the Netherlands, during the summer of 2003.

I had never met Eenhoorn before, nor had I ever been to the Netherlands, but having a very sick child myself, I understood what he was going through—so I gladly accepted the assignment.

I thought, *You can't say no to somebody else's tragedy—especially when it's their child.*

So I was eager to help.

Tragically, on just my second day as manager, I would accompany the Dutch team to young Ryan's funeral. The boy had died just days earlier in his father's arms. Although I had just met Robert, we immediately formed a close bond because of our children.

With Eenhoorn tending to family matters, I managed the Dutch national team all the way to the Gold Medal Game of the European Championship. Robert returned to the dugout for that final game, and we defeating the Peter Angelos–backed Greek club to win it all.

And you know what?

A moment like that—winning the championship for Eenhoorn while he dealt with the grief of a dying child—was as important to me as winning the '86 World Series. No question about it.

And the next year, when Eenhoorn's Dutch club qualified for the 2004 Olympic Games in Athens, I stayed on the staff as a bench coach. I knew that even though it had been a year since Ryan's passing, and his wife had recently given birth to another son, he was still coping and might appreciate my support.

I was so glad to be there for him.

And being a part of that Olympics—in Athens—was a most memorable experience.

******

Not long after returning from the Olympics, I began having stomach pains. So I went to the hospital, where a doctor opened my stomach and told me I had an infection, possibly caused by a fish bone. I received the proper medical treatment, returned home, and felt fine.

But then, two months later, I had the same pain. I went back to the hospital and got a different doctor who opened me up the same way. But this experience would be far different from the first one. This doctor would take out the lower half of my stomach—a Billroth's operation II—without telling Susan, who was sitting out in the waiting room. He just went ahead and did this very serious and complex procedure.

The lower half of your stomach is where vitamin B-12 goes in and helps you digest protein. So with that removed, over the next two to three months, my weight dropped from 190 pounds down to just 146!

I remember sitting in the living room at my lowest weight, thinking, *I feel awful. I think I'm actually going to die.*

Susan came over to me and asked, "Do you want me to take you to the hospital?"

"No," I said. "Call 9-1-1. I think I'm *going.*"

The ambulance came—everything was just going south for me. But once at the hospital, they gave me an IV and I soon started feeling much better.

So after returning home, I thought maybe I would be fine.

But then the next day, after hearing what happened, a woman at the clothing store Susan owned said to her, "Davey's B-12 deficient. He needs to buy B-12."

Upon hearing this from Susan, I called my doctor to get B-12 to inject into my legs. I did it fairly regularly and, after three or four months, had my weight back up to 170.

The doctor who removed half my stomach never told me about

the importance of these shots—in fact, he didn't tell me about the need for B-12 at all.

I called the doctor's attorney and said, "Should I sue him for not telling me about this?"

And the lawyer said, "By the time you go to court, they'll see you're healthy and you won't have a case."

And then this was the topper.

"If you just died," he said, "*then* you'd have a case!"

I can't make this shit up!

So I know what I have to do to stay alive and, believe me, every two weeks I shoot myself in the leg with 1 cubic entimerer of B-12. I guess the one upside of having neuropathy in my legs is that it numbs them enough that I hardly feel the needle going in.

******

Andrea's overall condition was seemingly improving as summer approached in 2005. There was definitely reason to be optimistic. She had just moved into a new house, and the medication, despite the side effect of weight gain, was helping her to lead a more normal life.

She was also excited about a trip she planned to take with Mary Nan to see her maternal grandmother in Texas.

But early on the morning of June 8, the day they were to fly to Texas, our whole world would be turned upside down.

While staying at Mary Nan's house, Andrea went into septic shock during the night as a likely result of not taking a laxative—critical for the type of medication she was using—and was taken to the emergency room. Mary Nan called me and I rushed to the hospital. But by the time I arrived, many of Andrea's vital functions were already out. No brain. No kidney. No nothing.

She remained on life support for four hours until I was asked by the doctor on call what I wanted to do. With no chance of her survival without the machines, I solemnly uttered what no parent should ever have to say with respect to their own child.

"We have to pull the plug."

Andrea was gone five minutes later.

******

The death of my daughter was the most traumatic thing I've ever been through. You always think you're supposed to die before your kids do. So when it did happen to me, it was a horrible situation that I simply could't explain or make any sense of. You can't help but feel responsible or that there was something you could have done to protect your child.

You can't get over the fact that it happened or that the whole thing wasn't just a nightmare. There's remorse and regret and you question what you could have done differently.

It's not like when you manage a baseball team, and you're always thinking about how you can best make the assets better. When you fail as a family, you don't want to analyze it. You only want to remember the good.

That's why in my house today, I only display the beautiful pictures of Andrea when she was happy or out surfing. But the ones I have of her when she got a little heavy and was not herself—I don't look at those. It's still just too hard on me. Too painful.

When you lose a child, your life really becomes insignificant in comparison. You're still alive and whenever the Good Lord wants you He's going to take you—and I'm okay with all that. I feel like I've been a pretty good person all my life and whatever happens is fine. But when Andrea passed away, I thought, *How could that happen? My daughter before me?*

It's a reality that's very hard to live with.

I should have gone before her.

| thirty-three |
August 17, 2005: U-S-A!

IT'S ALWAYS FASCINATED ME how one great experience in life can lead to another.

After I came to the aid of the Dutch national team by filling in for its manager, Robert Eenhoorn, as he tended to family matters, it got the attention of USA Baseball's CEO, Paul Seiler.

"You really did a great job managing the Netherlands," Seiler called to tell me. "Eric Campbell [the general manager] and I were very impressed. Would you have interest in becoming manager of the USA team?"

The 2005 World Cup was coming up that September, so Seiler and Campbell needed to put together a team of minor leaguers—kids who were pursuing a career in baseball and wanted to represent their country.

I jumped at the opportunity.

It was another case of managing a team I felt I could help. I didn't need to do it. There was certainly no financial reward. But it didn't matter. I always enjoyed new challenges and experiences—and this certainly qualified.

I quickly formed a strong relationship with Seiler and Campbell as we went through the process of picking the team by sifting through player statistics and profiles we pulled off the Internet. My expertise is an ability to read numbers, so I knew right away who would be our first, second, and third picks—and so on. I knew where they would hit in the lineup and how the pitching would be set up without even seeing them. And then when I actually *would* see them in person, I was proved correct.

It was all like chemistry to me. And I loved doing it.

One of the players I chose for that 2005, USA team was a shortstop playing A ball at Salem, Virginia, in the Astros organization—Ben Zobrist.

Of course, Zobrist would later become a star in the big leagues.

But back then, still an unknown, he was one of my favorites—a guy you just gravitated to. He didn't have a lot of skills at short—a little lacking on range, arm strength, and other skills—but he was the best two-strike hitter I *ever* saw! And because of that, he was a master at reaching base. I knew very early on he was going to be a special player.

The next summer, Zobrist got traded to the Tampa Bay Devil Rays. Shortly thereafter, while in an airport, I bumped into Mike Cubbage, a special assignment scout for their club.

"Hey Mike," I said. "Damn, you got a great player in Zobrist."

"Nah, he's not much," Cubbage replied. "He's just kind of a bench player."

"Do you even know the guy you traded for Zobrist?" I asked rhetorically.

"*Aubrey Huff*," I continued. "And he's great!"

But Zobrist would become the more complete player in that deal and would go on to become an All-Star with Tampa Bay. They played him at every position except catcher. And this makes me happy as a clam. I *knew* he was a gamer—my kind of guy. And Cubbage evidently didn't even know what they had when Ben first went over there.

In a way, I was complimenting Mike and his organization on the trade. But I don't think they understood at all the player they were getting in Zobrist.

It was identifying the potential in kids such as Ben early on in their careers that made managing Team USA as important and rewarding to me as anything I had ever done in baseball.

Anyway, our team would make the 2005 World Cup playoffs, but would lose to powerhouse Cuba—the eventual champion—11–3.

But I was extremely proud of everything we accomplished and was looking forward to the next World Cup two years later in Taiwan.

And what a thrilling 2007 World Cup that would be for us.

The Cuba team came in looking to win a *10th* straight Cup in which it competed. It was favored, though I loved the team we had assembled, which included future major league star Evan Longoria.

We ended up going 9–1 to win the World Cup championship— the first time the USA ever won with Cuba participating in the event—and we capped it off by beating them in the gold medal game 6–3.

The pitching carried the way for us with an ERA of just 1.50 for the 10 games.

Winning the World Cup was as satisfying for me as winning a World Series. I was so proud to have the letters *U-S-A* embroidered across my jersey.

The next year it was on to the Olympics in Beijing.

Again, Seiler, Campbell, and I, along with general manager of baseball operations Bob Watson, would select the players for Team USA. The process began in spring training, but as late as the Futures Game at Yankee Stadium during the All-Star break, we were still evaluating a pool of 60 players for a 24-man roster with the Olympics just a month away.

But we got it done, and featured a team with future major league stars such as 19-year-old Stephen Strasburg out of San Diego State University; Jake Arrieta, then just a Single A pitcher in the Orioles organization; and Dexter Fowler, a Double A prospect with Colorado.

Again, it was so much fun evaluating young talent.

But it wasn't easy to put this team together, because we lost a bunch of players we liked who were called up to the majors.

I also loved my coaching staff, which included pitching coach Marcel Lachemann, hitting coach Reggie Smith, and third-base coach Rick Eckstein. We had worked together for three years by that point across several international tournaments.

We had a helluva team, and I planned on winning the gold. And there was added pressure on us to make a statement because Team USA hadn't even qualified for the 2004 Games. But that was fine with me—baseball's always a challenge and either you embrace it or you don't. But going into those 2008 Olympics, I figured we wouldn't be made the favorite. I thought it would be Japan, Cuba, and then us—in that order.

And that would be close to how it turned out.

While Cuba won the silver and we took the bronze, it was South Korea that stunned everybody by winning all seven of its games to take the gold.

But sadly for us all, baseball would be voted out of both the 2012 and 2016 Games.

Nobody seems to understand this, but the reason why baseball was shut out of the Olympics was because USA Baseball wouldn't let its major leaguers play in it. And on the world stage, fans really aren't interested in watching minor leaguers.

It will be interesting to see the level of interest when baseball returns to the Olympics in 2020 in Tokyo.

Anyway, from the 2008 Games, the next challenge for Team USA was the 2009 World Baseball Classic.

I'd had a taste of the WBC three years before as Buck Martinez's bench coach, but now was geared up to manage a team loaded with major league stars such as Derek Jeter, Chipper Jones, Ryan Braun, and Dustin Pedroia.

We had lofty expectations.

But the result of the tournament was disappointing. We would fall one game shy of the final game by losing to Japan and WBC MVP Daisuke Matsuzaka 9–4 in the semifinals at a frigid Dodger Stadium.

Japan would finish the job the next night with a win over South Kora to win the Cup.

At that time, I considered Olympic baseball—in a venue where the best athletes in the world compete—more prestigious than the World Baseball Classic. But today, the WBC has really come into its own in the international spotlight.

Not that the WBC is perfect.

The WBC still has a real problem, because guys aren't really ready just two weeks into spring training to perform at a high level.

But clearly I do think it has become a new Olympics for baseball.

And it's more talent-rich today than ever before.

In the 2017 WBC, I watched as Jim Leyland's USA team won it all with what was actually a very good club.

When I managed them, I could hardly have any major leaguers—they weren't allowed to go by their teams. But now, more and more players want in. They want to represent their country.

I feel very fortunate to have played a part in Team USA baseball. But it's kind of ironic that I may never have experienced it had I not helped a *Dutch* team to the European Championship.

thirty-four

May 5, 2011: King Jake

IT COULD BE SAID that a special, young teenager, Jake Allen, brought my wife, Susan, and me together.

I first met her late in 1990 at a Winter Park fund-raiser for the Jake Allen Center for Deaf-Blind Children.

Susan had no idea who I was. So when somebody told her she should be nice to me because I was a ballplayer, she thought that meant softball.

"I hear you play a little ball," she said to me.

I went along with it.

"Yeah, I've played a game or two," I said.

"Well, do you play on Wednesday nights or on the weekends?" she asked.

Amused, I just said, "No, I don't," and left it at that.

But we ended up spending the rest of the evening talking about other topics—including her son and the center named after him that she founded.

Jake was a rubella baby. When Susan unknowingly was just a couple weeks pregnant with him, she came down with a case of the

German measles. That can put an unborn child at risk for rubella. And the earlier a woman contracts the disease, the worse it could be for the baby.

In Jake's case, he would be born deaf and blind.

I also learned a little bit about what an amazing woman Susan was.

Once Jake was around four years old and could get out of his crib, Susan, even while pregnant, would sleep on pillows and blankets on the floor outside his bedroom door. She did this to protect Jake from injuring himself if he woke up and started walking around his room in the middle of the night. Jake couldn't differentiate night from day. And he didn't have any sense of a calendar or of chunks of time.

She couldn't just lock him in his bedroom—she had to see him all the time.

This went on for more than three years.

Susan also couldn't tell for a time when he was hungry or wanted to be bathed. To solve this problem, she developed a system of hanging pegs so Jake could grab on to things like a spoon or a bar of soap as a means of communicating his needs and wants.

Susan's mentality was, *I'm going to save this kid. I'm going to teach him.*

She explained that these were some of the primary reasons for starting the Jake Allen Center, because the school he went to wasn't teaching him a "language" to help with such issues.

The Jake Allen Center would have eight residential students and 20 staff members. The children who went there were all in the same situation as Jake, had all failed in traditional schools, and had all arrived without a language. So successful was the center in helping these kids that the Florida state government asked Susan to open a second school, the Jake Allen PreSchool, which it partially funded. The preschool was designed to capture young children before they might potentially become violent due to the frustrations caused by their condition.

Susan's passion for helping Jake and others in need—while remaining so upbeat—was the total focus of her life and I admired that tremendously about her right away. She was obsessed with trying to find all the answers so that Jake and other children could live somewhat normal lives.

And to a great extent, she had succeeded.

At the time I met her, Susan was winding down her work at the Jake Allen Center and had taken an office job in Winter Park. And because of how well Jake—then 14—had thrived with his communication skills at the Center, Susan had just transferred him to the Helen Keller Talladega School in Alabama—a deaf/blind facility.

So the day after the fund-raiser, I thought I would surprise her.

I drove to her office parking lot and called her office, but didn't tell the secretary who I was. So as soon as Susan picked up the phone, I started singing the Beatles song "Something in the Way She Moves."

She goes, "Who in the world is this?"

"Is your memory so short that you don't remember meeting me last night?" I said.

"Who *is* this?" she asked.

"It's David Johnson."

"Yes, of course," she said. "I remember meeting you."

"Well, get up and look out your window."

So Susan looked out and saw me.

"I'm in your parking lot and have lunch. Do you have lunch plans?"

Luckily, she didn't, so she came down and I drove her to the Winter Park Cemetery, where we had lunch on the back of my truck on a picture-perfect day. Now you might think that's an odd place to take someone on a first date, but it really is beautiful there.

A few weeks went by, and I picked up Susan at the airport after she visited Jake in Alabama. He was in big trouble there. He simply wasn't doing well with the transition.

For Susan, this was a major crisis.

I thought I would cheer her up by taking her out to a nice seafood place.

As the dinner went on, I started asking her a little bit about how Jake was doing. Things were going fine until, all of a sudden, Susan started sobbing hysterically.

"I don't know what I've done!" she exclaimed. "I've closed the center that was his lifeline! He's *failing!* I don't know what's going to happen to him! He's *miserable!* He's *violent!* He's never been..."

And she went on and on right there in the restaurant.

Now, I was sitting right across from the table from her, thinking, *How do I calm her down? What can I do to help her?*

So, very softly, I said, "You know what? I'm going to help you sort this out as your friend. Why don't we try to sort this out together?

I noticed Susan begin to relax a little bit.

So I continued, speaking straight from the heart.

"I think you have so much on your plate that I don't even know how you're getting up every day and walking around. You have a new job, two other children, and everything going on with Jake. I'm falling in love with you. I don't think you could ever know if you're falling in love with me because of everything that's happening to you. I mean, how could you ever even have time to think about that? The plan, I think, should be that I'll help you figure this out and, if at the end of figuring this out, you want to fly away—you're free as a butterfly. I just want to help you and love you and then set you free if that's what it takes."

By this point, Susan had completely calmed down—and was at a loss for words. So I kept on talking.

"You don't need to cry about this," I continued. "We're going to figure this out. Let's just worry about unpacking your bags tonight after dinner. Tomorrow, we'll start."

To be honest, I never thought helping Susan with Jake's special condition was that big of a deal.

The next week, Jake got kicked out of school, which, all things considered, was of little surprise to us. So I had a Plan B.

"I think we should move him to my fishing camp and hire a round-the-clock staff to help him out," I said. "Just have him relax and spend some time there."

So for the next few months, that's what we did.

And Jake loved it.

That Christmas, Susan and I went there with Jake's younger brother, Jeremy, and sister, Ellie, to celebrate the holiday with him. We all had a terrific time and I was amazed at how well Jake could convey his wants and needs.

We called him "King Jake" because Susan and her kids' lives revolved around his. And I was just so impressed with Jeremy and Ellie, whom, like Jake, I would come to love as my own children. They never complained a single day about the limitations and sacrifices Jake's special needs placed on their activities and everyday life. They all had to give up stuff so Jake could survive.

But it wasn't all smooth sailing from there.

About a year later, I took Susan, Jeremy, and Ellie out to the West Coast with me on a two-week golf vacation. Jake visited with his father in North Carolina. But a day before we were to pick up Jake and return him to the fishing camp, we found out his father had made the decision with the local school system to have him institutionalized.

It took two years in the courts to get Jake out, as he was deemed a danger to himself and others.

Thankfully, the Helen Keller National Center helped us and we moved him to the facility in Sands Point, Long Island.

He would spend the next two years there before moving back to North Carolina, where I bought him a house to live in. The state had funding for Jake and, besides, he *had* to live there—a judge had ruled that Jake needed to live within one hour of his father so he could afford to visit him.

But it turned out to be a positive experience. Jake had a full-time staff and a roommate named Tim, who had similar issues to Jake. The state of North Carolina had deinstitutionalized a bunch of people, so we took in this young man who had no family and was a ward of the state. We became his family.

Jake would live there contently and independently for the next 12 years. And practically every day of those dozen years, Susan sent them crafts to work on. Needless to say, they got to know the UPS driver very well.

But when Jake was 32, during one of Susan's visits to see him, he wasn't responding to her. Then, while walking inside his house, which he knew like the back of his hand, he bumped into his recliner and fell to the floor.

He got up and signed with his hand, "I'm sorry."

Susan said, "What's wrong, Jake?"

Jake put his hands on her hands and then cupped his eyes.

She understood that to mean he was not seeing a thing.

Although Jake had been classified as completely blind, he had at least been able to see light. And we could use sign language with him if done two inches from one of his eyes, which had much less than 1 percent vision.

But now even that was gone.

After a visit to a doctor at Duke, it was determined that he had a detached retina. The next six months were a nightmare. Jake had all kinds of surgeries and had to be sedated and kept in intensive care because he couldn't touch his eyes.

Upon finally returning to his home in North Carolina, and realizing that he had no sight, he was so upset that he refused to come out of the bathroom for hours at a time for several days.

He would remain deeply depressed.

Susan would visit him and return home to Winter Park every two days for several weeks.

I finally just said to her, "What do you think should happen?"

"I don't know," she said. "He doesn't even have a language now."

But on one of her visits to see him, it became clear what we needed to do. Jake would start calling the home Susan and I had "home," and his place "Jake's house."

So after she came home from that trip, I asked her, "What do you think he *really* wants?"

"I think we need to move him here," she said. "But how can we do that? There's no funding in Florida."

"We *have* to bring him here." I said.

Susan was concerned about the cost of having round-the-clock care for Jake. But I really wasn't.

"You know what?" I said. "We'll find a way to afford it. If it's the right thing for Jake, we'll figure it out."

So that's what we did. In June of 2010, Jake, now 33, was living with us. And it was absolutely the right thing to do.

After Susan created another language for Jake by signing in his hand, he started to thrive again. He was so happy being with us he actually would smile and beam.

The only significant challenge we faced was getting him to go to sleep. His total blindness still disturbed him to the point where he would go days and days without sleep. We had to hire a sleep specialist to help. His basic message was that Jake needed to be out in the sun by seven in the morning to get light on his optic nerves so his body would begin to produce melatonin 14 hours later. That got him back on schedule.

Then I had some security guys install an alarm underneath the rug in his bedroom so that when his feet touched the ground, it rang in our bedroom. And if the door opened or if he sat up, a different sound would go off. This allowed Susan to relax and get her sleep, knowing that she didn't need to be concerned unless one of the sounds went off in the house.

In a way, it was like she was starting some things all over again with him as an adult that she had undertaken when he was a child.

But for all the challenges that we had with Jake, we had far more precious moments—times that, when I look back, make me smile.

There was one time when Susan had Jake by the arm in a crowded roast beef place. They got to the table with their lunch, and Susan noticed that Jake already had a sandwich in his hand.

She said, "Holy mackerel, where did you get a sandwich?"

While Jake was feeling his way along, he hit somebody's sandwich, picked it up, kept on going, and just started eating it!

It was something like that with Jake every day—*every single day.* Some of the things he did made us laugh so hard. He was living in a different world from the rest of us.

And then there were other times when Jake would be a byproduct of humor, like when Marge Schott came over to our house for a Reds' wives' Sunday brunch Susan was hosting. Jeremy was greeting people at the door when Marge turned to Susan and said, "Man, for a profoundly disabled kid, he is doing amazing!"

Priceless.

After about a year with us, Jake was improving to such an extent with his new language that I bought him a house down the road from us. He would spend Tuesdays and Wednesdays there and the other five days of the week at our home. He quickly acclimated to his new surroundings. In time, we were planning on gradually extending his staying on his own to three days a week.

But in April of 2011, just before Easter, Jake came down with what we would later find out was adenovirus—typically a very treatable virus.

However, all he could communicate was, "I'm sick. I'm sick."

We would ask, "Where?"

But he couldn't really tell us.

So we took him to see a doctor who was in his Medicaid pool. We weren't impressed. Some of the staff in the office weren't even dressed in medical clothes, while others wore shoes with no shoelaces. It was just so unprofessional.

But the worst thing about it was how scared to death the doctor was of Jake. He didn't touch him or listen to his heart.

So when Jake got sicker and started urinating all the time, we took him to another doctor, who prescribed Cipro, a very powerful antibiotic commonly used for urinary tract infections.

But his condition continued to worsen over the next two weeks and he began suffering from terrible bowel problems.

This time, we took him to the emergency room, where they did some blood tests. But the doctor on call said he couldn't see anything because Jake had been on Cipro for 15 days. The drug was masking the problem. So he said to come back in 10 days, after the Cipro was out of his system.

But a few days later, Jake became enraged, yanking the shower curtains in the bathroom to the floor. Then he grabbed the back of the toilet off, slammed it down and pounded his hand to communicate, "I'm sick! I'm sick!"

So we rushed him back to the emergency room, but Jake refused to let the doctor touch him. His stomach had distended.

He had a terrible virus that had taken over his lungs, his kidneys, and his bladder. By the time everyone figured that out, he had lost consciousness.

Jake was now clinging to life support.

Later that same week, with the Cipro now out of his system, doctors were able to diagnose the adenovirus. But by this time, pneumonia had taken over his lungs.

Jake never did regain consciousness.

Again, I was faced with a doctor telling me that one of my children had lost all functions. So like with Andrea, we took Jake off of life support—on May 5, 2011—and he was soon gone.

There was absolutely no sense of relief when Jake died. And for the 34 years that Susan was his mother, I never heard of her ever asking, "Why me?"

Instead, it was more like, "Why not me?"

Susan was always madly in love with Jake. And I loved him like the son he was to me.

We were both, of course, heartbroken that he had to live without ever hearing music or his mother's voice. Or being able to see all the beauty in the world.

But never did we regret a single moment spent with King Jake.

Because of him and his fighting spirit, we became richer, deeper people with a truer understanding of what's most important in life.

thirty-five

June 24, 2011: A Capital Idea

SUSAN AND I HAD always dreamed of visiting Alaska.

For years and years, we talked about it and planned for it, but never did it because some job offer in baseball always forced us to put it off.

On June 24, 2011, we were finally going to book it. With Jake's passing the month before, we had been on an emotional roller coaster and thought the trip would do us some good. We had until around 8:00 PM that evening to call the agent in Alaska to finalize it.

And then my phone rang.

It was Washington Nationals general manager Mike Rizzo.

"As you know, Davey, Jim [Riggleman] resigned yesterday," Rizzo told me. "You're the perfect fit to take over and manage the club. You've got the track record and know the system, the players, the staff, and what's best for the organization. Think it over and call me back."

Rizzo was right—I did know the organization well. Shortly after I managed Team USA in the 2009 WBC, Mike hired me as his senior advisor, a position where I offered, among other things, my expertise in player evaluations and development, as well as help with amateur draft decisions. And three years prior to that, I had been a special consultant to then–Nationals GM Jim Bowden. So my roots with the Nationals ran deep. And again, I've always believed that knowing the entire system of any organization from the ground up is critical to the success of any manager.

I wasn't looking for the manager's job, but was open to doing anything I could to help the organization during a time of turmoil. In this case, Riggleman apparently had a problem communicating with his players and the clubhouse was in total disarray, with a good deal of infighting. So one of my jobs would be to straighten all that out and make baseball fun again for the Nationals.

I discussed Rizzo's offer with Susan and, ultimately, we believed the timing to be perfect.

The most important factor in our decision to accept the job was my health, which was better than it had been in years.

One of my biggest issues had been with my arrhythmia, which I had been getting on a pretty regular basis. But just that February, I had undergone a 10-hour procedure at the Mayo Clinic called an ablation. An ablation is where doctors insert a catheter through the groin area up into your heart tissue that delivers a high-frequency electrical pulse. In layman's terms, they shock the areas where your nerves are making the heart beat too fast or irregular. The surgery normally takes two hours, but with me being me, it took them 10.

When I woke up, I felt incredible. I was running up and down the halls of the hospital. It was an unbelievable feeling. And since that point in time, I don't think I've had another case of arrhythmia because of the ablation. They must have shocked the shit out of my heart!

I also got my weight back up to a healthy level. The B-12 shots were working their magic.

At 68 years old, I was slimmer, tanner, and more energetic than I'd been in years. I felt like a kid again.

And now, with the passing of Jake, who had always been the top priority for Susan and me, managing the Nationals would help fill a void left by his absence in our lives.

The Nats had never had a winning record in their history. The District of Columbia had not seen postseason baseball since the 1933 Senators. This would be an all-too-familiar challenge for me of turning around the fortunes of a struggling franchise.

I felt right at home.

Alaska would have to wait once more.

******

Although we actually were in wild-card contention until the very end of the 2011 season—a big step in the right direction for the organization—I spent much of the last three months of the campaign evaluating my young players and laying down the building blocks for future success.

And part of that success would be built around our two brightest young stars—23-year-old pitcher Stephen Strasburg and 19-year-old right fielder Bryce Harper—perhaps the best young duo to come along since, well, another pretty special pair I had in New York nearly three decades before.

The electrifying and talented Strasburg and Harper were like a reincarnation of Gooden and Strawberry with the Mets back in 1984.

In fact, both of those teams—the '84 Mets and the '12 Nationals—were similar in that they both broke out with big seasons after years of ineptitude.

With Strasburg, when I first laid eyes on him while managing Team USA gearing up for the Beijing Olympics, I thought he may have even been a little more advanced than Doc was at the same age. One of the greatest pitching prospects in the history of the amateur draft, the Nationals would use their No. 1 pick in the country on him in 2009.

And with Bryce, I knew how gifted he was going all the way back to when I first saw him hit as a 16-year-old at a tournament in St. Petersburg. I presented him with a trophy that day for hitting the longest home run—*more than 400 feet*—in a baseball skills tournament. I talked with young Bryce and his parents after giving a speech there and came away very impressed with how he conducted himself.

So when Bryce entered the 2010 amateur draft as a 17-year-old, I advised the Nationals to use their No. 1 on him. Thankfully, they listened.

Prior to the 2012 season during spring training, my advice to Bryce was simple.

"Just have fun," I told him again and again. "It's a great game. Just enjoy it."

Harper's ability was so great that nothing was going to keep him out of the big leagues. But I didn't want him to feel any pressure. And I certainly didn't want to push him.

I promoted Harper to our big-league club on April 28, to great fanfare. Plugging him into the lineup instantly made us a strong contender for the division title.

And now, with Strasburg back in the rotation following Tommy John surgery the previous year, we were ready to roll.

Despite injuries to our closer, Drew Storen; catcher, Wilson Ramos; left fielder Mike Morse; and right fielder Jayson Werth for extended periods of time, we grabbed a hold of first place on May 22 and never let go of it for the rest of the season.

We had a young ballclub and, like I had done with my other teams, my goal was to always put them into situations where they could be successful.

With my hitters, I encouraged them to be aggressive at the plate, not worry so much about working the count, and cut loose on inside fastballs instead of pushing the ball the other way.

And with my pitchers, I wanted them to have positive outings— and not get lit up late. If that meant turning the ball over to a reliever even though the starter might be better, that was fine with me. That's because my starters had four days between starts to think about their last outing, and I wanted them to feel good about themselves. And if the bullpen could hold and save the game for them, then that was the best of all worlds—something to build on for everybody.

By early September, we had the best record in baseball and our biggest lead of the year—8.5 games up in the NL East—on our way to the division crown. We even had the swagger of some of my clubs with the Mets. It was exciting, as Washington was a baseball town again for the first time in generations.

But it was around this time that Rizzo shut down Strasburg for the season—obviously a blow to the ballclub as we prepared for a postseason run.

Rizzo wanted to protect Strasburg long-term by placing an innings limit on him a year after his reconstructive elbow surgery. He had done the same thing the year before with Zimmermann after his own Tommy John surgery in 2010. The only difference now was that we were primed to make a run at the World Series in 2012—unlike in 2011.

Even though I adamantly disagreed with the decision, I defended it publicly, saying how I managed for today but with an eye on tomorrow. And I actually always adhered to that belief. In fact, even that season, none of my pitchers went more than 200 innings. I always protected young arms, going all the way back to Gooden.

But this decision by Rizzo and the team doctors was hard to swallow because of how great Strasburg was pitching. When we shut him down, he was our ace with a 15–6 record, 3.16 ERA, and 197 strikeouts in 159.1 innings.

I felt we would have gone to the World Series with Strasburg in the rotation during the playoffs. I really don't know how the team doctors came to the conclusion to keep Stephen under a given number of 160 innings. That was their deal, not mine. I had taken care of pitchers my whole life.

But I thought, *If that's what you want to do, fine.* I'm not going to come out and say I disagree with it, that it's totally wrong. But this was the best time of Strasburg's career and he should be pitching.

I always felt like ballplayers are used to routines and your throwing arm should be no different from your legs. If you don't constantly use your legs by doing a little running and jogging, they're not going to stay strong. I feel the same way with arms. I always had guys throw for 15 minutes before they did anything in their workouts.

I never had a problem with an arm—*ever.* Now they come up with this new technology, telling you that you can't throw more than 160 innings after throwing fewer than 100 or after surgery. I really don't know where it all comes from.

But I do know it weakened our Nationals team heading into the postseason without our ace.

******

I would be forced to use our fourth starter, Edwin Jackson, in place of Strasburg in our NL Division Series matchup against the Cardinals.

And it came back to bite us.

With the series tied at one apiece, Jackson started Game 3 and got hit hard. Before retiring a hitter in the top of the second, we were already down 4–0. On the other side, Chris Carpenter kept us in check and we lost this pivotal game 8–0 to put us down two games to one.

But the next day, we won in thrilling fashion when Werth hit a walk-off home run in the bottom of the ninth off of Lance Lynn to deadlock the series.

It really looked like we would maneuver around the loss of Strasburg and win this NLDS in Game 5.

We jumped out to a 6–0 lead after three innings, knocking Cardinals ace Adam Wainwright out of the game in the process.

But St. Louis pecked away at us, pulling to within 7–5 heading into the ninth.

Still, with Storen on the mound in the ninth with a two-run lead, I felt great about our chances to close it out and move on to the NLCS. And after getting two outs following a leadoff double by Carlos Beltran, Storen was twice just one strike away from finishing off the Cardinals before walking both Yadier Molina and David Freese to load the bases.

Then weak-hitting second baseman Daniel Descalso grounded the first pitch he saw for a two-run single to tie the game. Descalso then stole second to put runners on second and third.

With another weak hitter, shortstop Pete Kozma, up at the plate with a base open and their pitcher Jason Motte on deck, I decided to give Storen the opportunity to pitch Kozma tough. It backfired on me when he lined a single to right to give the Cardinals a 9–7 lead.

Of course, I got criticized for that after the game, but I didn't second-guess my decision. Storen had already walked two hitters that inning and by loading the bases it wouldn't have allowed him any room for error. Plus, I had confidence that he could get Kozma out.

We would go down quietly in the bottom of the ninth to finish off a heart-wrenching defeat.

In spite of how the season ended, I was proud of the tremendous strides the Nationals made in 2012. We had the best record in the major leagues with one of their youngest teams. We had a good farm system and were signing our top draft picks—a great way to feed the big-league club to ensure long-term success.

I was certainly looking forward to the next season.

But then something sort of bizarre happened.

In early November, just three days before I was named National League Manager of the Year, Rizzo and Mark Lerner, the Nationals' principal owner, presented me with a document they wanted me to sign stipulating that I would retire after the 2013 season. My contract was up after '13 anyway, so this was completely unnecessary. They could have simply not offered me a contract.

I thought, *Fine, I don't know why they want it in writing, but I'll do it if that's what they want.*

So I had to say in interviews every day, "This is my last year. I'm retiring following the season."

It was kind of a weird thing, but since that's what they wanted, I did it.

The only reason I could think of was that I was making around 4 million dollars a year and, had we won the World Series in '13, I would have been able to really cash in. They may not have wanted to pay me what I would have been worth.

What else could it be?

It was just the perfect culmination of my entire career in baseball.

The last time I won the Manager of the Year award, I basically got a pink slip in Baltimore.

And now this.

I thought, *How appropriate. It's been like this my whole life. It's really nothing new to me.*

******

I wasn't mad at Rizzo about having me sign that document. In fact, we're still friends today.

Actually, the only problem I had with him was how he handled some personnel decisions that off-season.

Just prior to my leaving for a trip to Africa, I had an organizational meeting with Rizzo.

I told him I was still comfortable with our right-handed relievers Tyler Clippard and Storen, but that we needed lefties.

"Sign some of our left-handed relievers," I told him. "We could lose three lefties to free agency—Mike Gonzalez, Tom Gorzelanny, and Sean Burnett."

"No," Rizzo said. "Our right-handers can get left-handed hitters out."

"Yeah, but they only get them out when they don't have to," I said. "At least sign Gorzelanny."

I left with hopes that he would heed my advice.

But when I came back from my trip, I found out Rizzo had signed Rafael Soriano, *another* right-hander. And no lefties.

I wasn't really happy about this, but figured there was pressure on him to sign a closer like Soriano, a premier reliever for the Yankees the year before who had compiled 42 saves.

I was, however, pleased that we re-signed our first baseman, Adam LaRoche, who had been granted free agency following the season. Adam was one of the few veterans on the team and led the club in home runs and RBIs, so it was critical to bring him back.

Although we were obviously expected to compete for the title again in 2013—"World Series or bust," as I told reporters— we were basically a .500 team through August before having a terrific September to make the division and wild-card races a little interesting near the end.

But it went back to our bullpen and not having the left-handers we had the year before. We didn't really have anyone to fill that void in '13.

And our bench was horrendous—especially the first half of the season. We had to use more of a set lineup, so I had some young guys on the bench who didn't see action for two and three weeks at a time. So when they had to perform, it was difficult for them.

At the end of the season, the Nationals gave me a nice ceremony with video tributes from guys I had played and worked with, as well as highlights from my career. It was very well done. But it kind of made me happy and sad at the same time—as well as uncomfortable.

I don't like living in the past like so many other baseball people.

Instead, I live for the moment and look forward to the next challenge in life.

That's the way I've always been.

About the Authors

Davey Johnson *(right)* was a four-time All-Star and two-time world champion second baseman with the Baltimore Orioles. As a manager, he retired with an astounding .588 winning percentage over 15-plus seasons, including a heralded Mets world championship in 1986.

Erik Sherman *(left)* is the co-author of three highly acclaimed baseball autobiographies: *Out at Home* (with Glenn Burke), *A Pirate for Life* (with Steve Blass), and the *New York Times* best seller *Mookie: Life, Baseball and the '86 Mets* (with Mookie Wilson). Sherman is also the author of the best seller *Kings of Queens: Life Beyond Baseball* with the '86 Mets.